THE
STRENGTHS APPROACH

sharing power • building hope • creating change

Wayne McCashen

Wayne McCashen is a social worker, author, trainer and consultant in the strengths approach. He is a pioneer and leader in the development and articulation of strengths-based practice and has written material and developed various frameworks that are used both nationally and internationally. His many years of experience in human services include youth work, family work, community development, staff supervision and management. He is the author of *Communities of Hope* and both editions of *The Strengths Approach*.

I acknowledge the original custodians of the land in which I live and pay respect to the elders past and present. I thank the families, young people, organisations, communities and colleagues I have been privileged to work alongside.

Dedication

This book is for Shae and Liam.

SECOND EDITION

THE
STRENGTHS APPROACH

sharing power • building hope • creating change

Wayne McCashen

First edition published in 2005. Reprinted in 2006, 2008,
2010 and 2014. This revised and expanded second edition
published in 2017 by:

Innovative
Resources

62 Collins Street Kangaroo Flat
Victoria 3555 Australia
p: + 61 3 5446 0500 f: +61 3 5447 2099
e: info@innovativeresources.org
w: innovativeresources.org

ABN: 97 397 067 466
Anglicare Victoria trading as St Luke's Innovative Resources.

National Library of Australia
Cataloguing-in-Publication entry

Creator: McCashen, Wayne, author.
Title: The strengths approach : sharing power,
building hope, creating change / Wayne McCashen.

Edition: Second edition.

ISBN: 9781925657005 (paperback)

Notes: Includes bibliographical references.

Subjects: Family social work--Victoria.
Autonomy (Psychology)
Community-based social services--Victoria.
Other Creators/Contributors: St Luke's Innovative
Resources, issuing body.

Edited by: Karen Bedford
Cover and page design by: Mat Jones
Front cover photograph 'The Twins' by: Billington Prideaux Partnership

CONTENTS:

DIAGRAMS AND TABLES

ACKNOWLEDGEMENTS

The articulation of the strengths approach in this book was influenced by years of experience and learning shared during the period 1988 to 1998 by various employees of a large social work agency known as St Luke's, based in Bendigo, Australia (St Luke's is now part of Anglicare Victoria). In particular, various frameworks and principles found in this book derive from material developed by me and my colleague at the time, Di O'Neil. Special recognition is also due to the team, led by Di O'Neil, which I was so fortunate to work with and who contributed so much to the early development of many of the ideas and practices articulated in this book. This material has now been widely adopted by trainers, consultants and organisations in Australia and internationally.

Russell Deal, who also contributed significantly to this work, instigated and led the development of innovative, strengths-based social work and therapeutic practice tools from the early 1990s. He founded Innovative Resources and for over twenty years he has authored, co-authored and overseen the production of more than sixty strengths-based resources with worldwide distribution.

Those who developed solution-focused and narrative therapies and various social work frameworks significantly informed our learning, particularly Michael Durrant, David Epston, Janice Fooks, Insoo Kim Berg, Bill O'Hanlon, Carl Rogers, Virginia Satir, Steve de Shazer, Michael White and pioneers of intensive family-based service models.

Many other professionals throughout Australia and New Zealand have shared their stories and experiences over the years, thus shoring up the efficacy of the strengths approach.

Thanks to Di Parker and Angie Lausell who contributed much to the development of the strengths approach to supervision, especially group supervision. Thanks also to Shannon Kerrigan for her feedback on chapters ten and eleven and Andrew Shirres for his feedback on various parts of the manuscript. Andrew also kindly contributed to the topics of 'clients as contributors' in chapter two, 'technology and client-owned recording' in chapter six, and 'practice stories' in chapter ten.

Linda Beilharz did much to bring the strengths approach to life in community development work captured in chapter eleven. Thanks to John Bonnice for his important contribution to material on social inclusion in chapter eleven. Thanks to Karen Bedford for her generosity in sharing the transcript of her interview on social inclusion with John in chapter eleven, and her contribution on 'visual and tactile resources' in chapter six.

Thanks to Rebecca Hall, Phil Watson, Carol Kelly, Nicole Ellerton and Karen Harris-Every for their generosity in sharing their inspiring practice stories, and to Alison Carson for her generosity in sharing her reflections on supervision. The remaining practice stories and examples derive from the author's experience.

Special thanks to Karen Bedford, managing editor at Innovative Resources, for her commitment to the first and second editions of this book, for her inspired reflection and feedback, and her diligence and integrity in the way she does her job! Thanks to Caitlyn Lehmann for assistance with proofreading.

Thanks to Mat Jones for his dedication and creative skill in book design, illustration and cover design. Thanks also to Barry Jubb for transcribing some of the video interviews used in the book.

PREFACE:
Introduction to the Second Edition

The Strengths Approach: A strengths-based resource for sharing power and creating change was first published in 2005 and has been reprinted four times since then. This revised and expanded second edition (2017) is re-titled *The Strengths Approach: sharing power • bringing hope • creating change*.

The second edition comes in response to widespread interest in the first. The principles, frameworks and processes described in this book have been widely acknowledged for their accessibility and for their important contribution to the strengths movement. In particular, they are acclaimed for underpinning ethical practice and contextualising strengths-based practice within a social justice framework; for placing the sharing of power and respect for human dignity at the centre of practice; and for naming and putting 'parallel practice' on the 'strengths agenda'.

Since first publication, this book has been used to develop certified courses in strengths-based practice and strengths-based supervision under the Australian Qualifications Framework, the national system of qualifications for schools, universities and vocational education and training. It is recommended or required reading for numerous university courses and is widely used for tutoring in human service organisations, many of which have adopted this practice framework. It is widely cited in social work practice stories and research literature, and is sourced by numerous consultants and trainers across Australia and internationally.

The second edition of *The Strengths Approach* includes:
- revised chapters throughout
- expanded discussions of core topics such as strengths, people as their own experts, power-over, power-with, reframing and externalising
- new discussions on links with narrative therapy and Appreciative Inquiry
- new commentary about the relevance of the strengths approach to social work and social inclusion
- new material on engagement and listening
- further explication of the strengths-based practice mind map and the column approach

- new sets of questions for strengths-based conversations
- new reflective and practice exercises that can be used in teams, in supervision, for professional development or for tutoring and mentoring
- some new practice examples
- a widely expanded chapter on parallel practice that explores strengths-based, power-with approaches to management and supervisory practices
- greatly expanded chapters on practical, empowering, supportive, strengths-based ways to provide for staff support and learning.

As with the first edition, the strongest influences on the strengths-based practices described in this book are principles of social justice and the solution-focused and narrative therapies that have gained worldwide prominence in human services over the past twenty-five years or so.

The strengths approach centres on the sharing of power. Clients and workers are colleagues who enter into partnerships as equals; sharing expertise, knowledge, ideas, skills and resources. We learn from each other. For this reason the term 'client' is used sparingly and with the deepest respect.

In summary, this book articulates:
- key characteristics of strengths-based, solution-focused and narrative approaches, social work values and principles, principles of social justice and the interaction between each of these
- ideas, conceptualisations and frameworks developed by the author
- principles of best practice in the field
- a holistic, generically-applicable approach to service delivery and management, recording, staff supervision, organisational practice and community building.

The Strengths Approach: sharing power. bringing hope. creating change describes attitudes and practices that enable empowerment and self-determination, and can be applied in any setting. It includes ideas, values, beliefs, and frameworks that arise from experience and best practice in the field coupled with the desire to find the most respectful and just ways of working with people. This book captures core principles of the strengths approach, which are, after all, simply principles of best practice. They are fundamentally ethical and just.

Chapter One

Foundations of The Strengths Approach

─────────────── FEATURED QUOTES FROM THIS CHAPTER ───────────────

'The connection between people's strengths represented through real stories of lived experience and their aspirations for something better, is the key to every successful action for change. It is crucial to hope and an essential characteristic of the strengths approach.'

~

'The strengths approach embraces socially-just practice which integrates principles of inclusion, collaboration, self-determination, transparency, respect, the sharing of resources and regard for human rights.'

~

'As with the strengths approach, the values and principles of social work emphasise human rights and social justice, respect for human dignity, self-determination, empowerment and finding and building on people's strengths.'

Every day, everywhere, human beings do amazing things! In a world that seems increasingly tense, dispirited, unjust and dangerous, many millions find ways, not only to overcome struggles, but to love, cooperate, share, learn, support, respect and value others, and even celebrate despite life's difficulties. Ordinary people everywhere do these things every day and they always have. The ability of human beings to adapt, change, grow, learn, and not only survive but even thrive in the face of adversity, is an utter inspiration!

Strengths, aspirations and hope

When people are asked about the sort of society they would like to live in they consistently talk about a world that is safe. In their own words they describe a peaceful society; one that is fair, just and respectful; a world where there is hope and purpose. When thinking about this, some people imagine a society very different to the one they have experienced. Others have been fortunate enough to have experienced life largely like this already. Somewhere, most people have had enough experience of goodness and humanity to be able to imagine what 'could be'.

The capacity to imagine what 'could be' is made richly possible by people's lived experience—their personal experience and observation of what happens when respect, justice and hope are present. In other words, people have aspirations that are made possible more by their positive experiences than their negative ones. These experiences are lived every day in communities, groups, neighbourhoods, families, workplaces, schools, clubs, other organisations and institutions, as well as in random encounters, lateral ties and informal links.

The connection between people's strengths represented through real stories of lived experience and their aspirations for something better, is the key to every successful action for change. It is crucial to hope and an essential characteristic of the strengths approach.

The word 'Hope' can be read as an acronym: H.O.P.E—standing for Helping Other Possibilities Emerge (thanks to Bernadette Glass, 1991). This leads people to think of hope as something they do rather than have. It is a deliberate and active process of creating new possibilities. These possibilities are built on what people already know and are more likely to become realities when people give continuity to those things in the past that have been experienced as positive, worthwhile and having potential.

This dynamic is evident in a story told by Carol Kelly (1997) in her role as a family support worker at the time.

Amanda had been my client for about six months and had made lots of progress to better parent her three sons. As a finishing off treat she attended a camp our service runs for women we work with. She returned from that camp saying it was the best time of her life. Within a week of returning she fell into what appeared to be a depression. I had not seen her that way before. She explained that going away on camp had showed her what life could be like and when she came home she realised it never would be.

A week later I visited another client who showed me lots of furniture that Amanda had given her. I left that house and visited Amanda. When I got there, I found two of the boys locked outside and the older boy told me that Mum had gone to give his brother away.

Following that weekend I was told that Amanda had given all three of her children away and she was leaving town. I went to visit that afternoon inviting her to coffee that evening to which she agreed. I was trying to work out why she would give away all her three children and all her possessions. Then I had a terrible thought that she was going to commit suicide. When I took Amanda out for coffee that evening I had a pack of Strengths Cards *in my bag [a set of 48 cards used to help people identify and discuss their strengths]. As she sat there telling me not to get on her back about giving her kids away, I wondered what I could say or do that wasn't 'shit' as she called all the other advice she had been given.*

I pulled out the Strengths Cards *and went through every one of the forty-eight cards and found something positive to say for all of them. By the time I had finished all those cards we were both in tears. She asked me if she could keep them and I said yes.*

I thought about her often over the next six months and then in my Christmas mail was a card from Amanda from Brisbane. She wrote, 'I am getting my life together. I have a job, two of the boys are with me and I'm doing fine. I still have the cards you gave me. I have coloured them in and have had them framed. They are hanging in my kitchen to remind me to be positive.'

the strengths approach

How simple yet profound it is to remind people of their strengths! Drawing on her past knowledge of Amanda, Carol reflects back to her the many stories of her strengths. These stories challenge Amanda's beliefs about herself, her life and what's possible. They become the foundation for Amanda to rebuild her life.

This focus or emphasis on people's strengths is one of the essential foundations of the strengths approach. There is a myriad of ways that people's strengths and the stories they reflect can be elicited and expressed to affect change, growth, learning and empowerment. Relationships of respect and the way human service workers listen to people can have a profound and abiding effect on people's lives.

The outcomes of Carol Kelly's response to Amanda's circumstances could not have come about without Amanda's respect for Carol and her view of her circumstances. Relationships of trust and respect are always essential for effective empowering practice. Nor was it possible without a particular way of listening to and interpreting experience. Carol, in reflecting on Amanda's strengths provides evidence from Amanda's life of her goodness and potential, borne of careful listening. In a fashion, Carol helped Amanda to 're-story' her life circumstances. She did this in a way that is respectful, genuine and evidence-based. And Amanda knew how true it all was!

Socially-just practice

The strengths approach does not simply involve an emphasis on strengths, however. It takes place with serious regard for socially-just practice. Socially-just practice, interchangeably referred to as 'just practice', integrates principles of social justice: inclusion, collaboration, self-determination, transparency, respect, the sharing of resources and regard for human rights.

Just practice respects the right to self-determination. People have the right to genuine ownership of, and participation in, the processes of change they engage in. Taking self-determination seriously means believing in people's capacity to drive these processes of change. It enables people to engage in action and reflection where they, not others, identify and define their strengths, capacities, aspirations and goals, and decide the steps and strategies for change.

Just practice also recognises and acts to address the structural and cultural dimensions of people's experiences that impinge on their ability to control their own lives.

Just practice is concerned with ways that dominant culture and the beliefs that underpin it can constrain growth, choice and change for individuals, groups, families, communities and organisations. Dominant culture and knowledge can define what is right and possible for people through socially-constructed ideas, labels and diagnoses. It can ignore or undermine the importance of diversity and, therefore, what can be gained from the richness of other ways of being and seeing the world. Workers need to be cautious about the potential of their own 'knowledge' and that of others (found in various professional disciplines) to harm and disempower people.

Principles of just practice lead us to address the structural, social, political and economic realities that marginalise and disempower people. They also lead us to explore and address the ideas and beliefs that define people and what is possible for them. Ideas that disempower, marginalise, oppress, discriminate against or exploit people need to be challenged. Just practice, therefore, always involves actions that address the impact that prevalent ways of thinking have on people's ability to learn, grow and take control of their lives.

All of these principles come together to be referred to as 'power-with' in the strengths approach. Power-with ensures that power imbalances between workers, agencies and those with whom they work, are acknowledged and action is taken to address them. Along with its emphasis on strengths, power-with is the other essential foundation of the strengths approach. It reflects belief in people and their potential.

The strengths approach enables us to bring the principles of social justice into our work regardless of the field of work or mode of practice we are engaged in, our job role or our status in organisations. It also enables us to address disempowering dynamics inherent in organisational practices by modelling and creating cultures of respect, collaboration, inclusion, and by building on strengths. The integrity of human service organisations is diminished if this does not happen. (Chapters eight, nine and ten explore the implications of the strengths approach for organisational practice.)

Where did the strengths approach come from?

The frameworks and practices put forward in this book had their beginnings in the late 1980s and early 1990s. The 1980s saw the emergence of strengths-based ideas in the fields of child and family welfare, mental health and disability in Australia and the United States in particular. Narrative Therapy, pioneered by social workers Michael White in Australia and David Epston in New Zealand, emerged alongside these developments from the 1980s to the 1990s, as did solution-focused therapy pioneered by social workers Steve De Shazer and Insoo Kim-Berg in the United States and therapist Bill O'Hanlon in New Zealand. Each is considered part of the 'strengths movement' and has strongly influenced social work and therapeutic practices worldwide.

During this period a small team of social workers at what was then St Luke's, a social work agency based in Bendigo, Australia (now merged with Anglicare Victoria) began its own work to develop strengths-based practice. This was driven by concerns about the challenges inherent in child and family welfare. Ways of responding to marginalised families, children and young people seemed to be adding to, rather than relieving difficulties faced by them. Social policy and social work practices often seemed to focus on deficits and tended to exclude clients from decision-making. This emphasis on problems only created an additional set of problems for everyone.

The Intensive Family Services movement pioneered the bringing together of clear structures of participatory, inclusive and strengths-based service delivery. This helped inform our practice. Newly emerging solution-focused ideas also informed our efforts to find ways of working that reflected what we knew intuitively: finding and building on strengths is an essential means to respectful and empowering practice.

While enthusiastic about these new practice developments, some of us were not entirely comfortable with certain aspects of these approaches. It seemed that they did not go far enough in addressing issues of justice and power. We were concerned with questions about how to address aspects of dominant culture and knowledge (including those of social welfare) that seemed, often, to have such a negative impact on people's lives. We were concerned whether or not we—as individual workers, as an agency and as a profession—were inadvertently acting in ways that ultimately kept people in their place or, worse still, contributed to further marginalisation and disempowerment. Simply focussing on people's strengths is not enough to liberate people from oppressive realities.

Most of the team at St Luke's who so intently and deliberately worked to develop the strengths approach came from a background in social action or were shaped by the social movements of their day; the women's movement, the peace movement, the black rights movement, the worker's rights movement, the gay rights movement, the environment movement, and the human rights movement generally. These movements had social justice imperatives in common but they were also optimistic about the future. It seems no coincidence that those who worked to develop strengths approaches were part of the same generation.

Feminist social work's exposure of the ways in which power, gender, class and race interact to oppress people gave us ways to make the connection between the personal and the political, and to address that connection. Radical and structural social work's concern with the socio-economic, political and structural contexts of people's lives also gave impetus to our efforts.

So the team at St Luke's revisited the principles and values on which we believed our work should be based: values of respect, self-determination, empowerment, social justice and the sharing of power. It meant defining and describing these principles in ways that are 'do-able'—that is, specifying, defining, practising and evaluating the skills and processes of change and empowerment. It meant finding ways to enter into partnerships with communities to overcome those aspects of casework and support services that get in the way of self-determination and empowerment, and challenging conventions in human service practice that do the same.

The third wave
Bill O'Hanlon (1994, pp. 22–23), New Zealand author, therapist and a pioneer of the 'solution-oriented' approach, identifies three waves of therapy that have been central in influencing the helping professions. The First Wave was pathology-focussed, psychodynamic psychiatry which diagnosed behaviour, personality and problems according to categories of illness based on history interpreted as absolute truths. The Second Wave (behavioural, cognitive and family therapies) tried to leave history and pathology behind to focus on the here-and-now (the immediate systems and circumstances surrounding clients) with a view to fixing them up so that they could get on with life, while the therapist was still seen as the expert. As put by O'Hanlon (1994, p. 23):

The First Wave's preoccupation with history acknowledged the reality of people's victimisation and yet seemed obsessed and defeated by it. The Second Wave's minimalist pragmatism helped people cope with day-to-day issues at the expense of acknowledging the depth of their pain and the richness of their lives. Both viewpoints are clearly incomplete, and this may explain some of the attraction of the Third Wave, which is arising in many different places in the world simultaneously.

The Third Wave, as described by O'Hanlon, includes strengths-based, solution-focused and narrative approaches as well as a range of other approaches referred to below. These approaches see people as the experts, and solutions as resting with them and their networks.

David Epston (2005, pp. vi–vii) reflects on the early work of St Luke's in the context of historical developments in what he refers to as 'constructive social practices'. These strongly advocate for community and social justice concerns and re-enliven social work practice as part of the 'third wave' that emphasises just, inclusive, strengths-based practices driven by people themselves, rather than professionals:

> When I consider what all those who have contributed to such a third wave have in common, I cannot overlook the fact that most have social work backgrounds or allegiances (for example, White, O'Hanlon, Saleeby, de Shazer, Kim Berg, etc), and that each of these streams came into being in the decade from 1985–1995.

> I have often wondered why this might be so. I tentatively conclude that it was against a social background of the reconstitution of the client as a faulty or defective person who needed repair. This occurred within the maelstrom of the state's relationship to social welfare in places such as the United States, United Kingdom, Australia and New Zealand where the state attempted to rationalise and 'scientise' increasing areas of social work activity.

> Other professions have made little protest in response to such a politic of problems ... Weick and Saleeby strongly argue for our realignment with other intellectual affiliations in 'ways that more powerfully capture the essential commitments underlying good social work practice. Their common assumptions reflect a strategy for consciously digging from the earthy roots of social work wisdom, a ground of understanding that evokes an essential realignment with our moral and civil covenants'.

Precursors and other developments

As with all new developments in social work and the helping professions generally there are precursors. The practices of strengths approaches that are widespread today can be traced to various influences as diverse as Eric Erikson, the Brief Therapy Institute, post-structuralist thinkers including Michel Foucault, the post-modernist philosophers, intensive family services and various family therapy models, to name but a few. The insights and practices of post-structuralist thinkers of the 1980s provided fertile ground for narrative and solution-focused ideas.

Other approaches can be referred to as strengths-based because they focus on strengths, positive potential, people as their own experts, empowerment, collaborative practices and hope. They can also, according to Chang and Nylund (2013 pp. 81, 82), accommodate solution-focused and narrative values. They include the mental health recovery model, positive psychology, and Saleebey's 'strengths perspective'. (American social worker, Dennis Saleebey, with colleagues Charles Rapp and Anne Weick from the University of Kansas, pioneers of strengths-based practice, formally developed what they referred to as 'the strengths perspective' in the United States in the 1980s.)

Asset-based community building, Appreciative Inquiry, resiliency theory and, in the author's view, motivational interviewing, are also strengths-based because they are based on self-agency, hope, strengths and collaborative effort, not pathology or 'expertness'.

The early work at St Luke's was both influenced by, and a part of, 'the third wave'. It was progressively articulated from the early 1990s by social workers Wayne McCashen (the author) and Di O'Neil who provided training and consultancy services to literally thousands of workers and hundreds of organisations throughout Australia and New Zealand during these and following years. This, in turn, generated a large cohort of leaders, consultants and trainers, and saw the proliferation of the strengths approach captured in the first and subsequent edition of this book (McCashen, 2005, 2017).

The strengths approach in its various iterations has become one of the most influential approaches to social work and human service practice in Australia and New Zealand. Its appeal has gone beyond social work to capture the imaginations and commitment of human service practitioners everywhere.

The strengths approach and social work

Power-with ways of working and the emphasis on people's strengths are at the heart of the strengths approach. It is worth highlighting the clear and unambivalent convergence of the strengths approach and social work values and principles. This is not surprising given the role of social workers in the development of strengths-based practices. The values and principles of social work emphasise human rights and social justice, respect for human dignity, self-determination, empowerment and finding and building on people's strengths. Notably, the International Federation of Social Workers (IFSW) *Statement of Ethical Principles Clause 2* states:

> The social work profession promotes social change, problem-solving in human relationships and the empowerment and liberation of people to enhance well-being. Utilising theories of human behaviour and social systems, social work intervenes at the points where people interact with their environments. Principles of human rights and social justice are fundamental to social work.

Clause 4.1 states:

> Social work is based on respect for the inherent worth and dignity of all people, and the rights that follow from this. Social workers should uphold and defend each person's physical, psychological, emotional and spiritual integrity and well being [sic]. This means:

1. Respecting the right to self-determination – Social workers should respect and promote people's right to make their own choices and decisions, irrespective of their values and life choices, provided this does not threaten the rights and legitimate interests of others.

2. Promoting the right to participation – Social workers should promote the full involvement and participation of people using their services in ways that enable them to be empowered in all aspects of decisions and actions affecting their lives.

3. Treating each person as a whole – Social workers should be concerned with the whole person, within the family, community, societal and natural environments, and should seek to recognise all aspects of a person's life.

4. Identifying and developing strengths – Social workers should focus on the strengths of all individuals, groups and communities and thus promote their empowerment.

Furthermore, the IFSW's *Statement of Ethical Principles Clause 4.2* states:

> Social workers have a responsibility to promote social justice, in relation to society generally, and in relation to the people with whom they work.

The British Association of Social Workers Code of Ethics (2012) captures the same principles (Clauses 1 and 2). The National Association of Social Work (2008) in the United States highlights service, social justice, dignity and worth of the person and the importance of human relationships.

The Australian Association of Social Workers Code of Ethics (2010, Clause 1.2) applies the same definition of social work as the International Federation of Social Workers and International Association of Schools of Social Work. Clause 3.1 specifies three core values of social work that include respect for human dignity, rights and autonomy, and commitment to social justice; fairness, human rights, and participation and change to systems and structures that are unjust. The Aotearoa New Zealand Association of Social Work (2007) again adopts the same definition and principles (see Clause 4 of the Code of Ethics).

It is evident that these ethics and principles are in essence the same as those of the strengths approach. Self-determination, empowerment, participation, respect for human dignity and worth of human beings, respect for human rights, social justice and focussing on and developing people's strengths. What a beautiful alignment of such important human values!

To quote Professor Jim Ife (2016, pp. 20—21) from Curtin University and the University of Queensland:

> Social work, unlike many other occupations, has always held a strong value base for its work, usually described in terms of social justice and human rights. It has refused to see itself as a value-free technical activity, despite the dominance of managerialism in our human service organisations. This has led social workers to be particularly strong when it comes to ethics. In my experience, social workers have a deep and consistent understanding of ethics matched by few other groups, and this is a concentration not just on constraining unethical conduct, but on positively acting ethically at all times, consistent with social work's value base. This has often led social workers to taking risky or unpopular stances in the name

of social justice, and is at the basis of a long tradition of social work activism going back to the founders of the profession such as Jane Addams, the great feminist, social activist, philosopher and Nobel Peace Prize winner... A profession that stands unequivocally for social justice and human rights, that takes ethical practice very seriously, and that focuses on the social rather than the individual, is surely the kind of profession we will need in the future.

THE STRENGTHS APPROACH: *a philosophy for practice*

The essence of the strengths approach is captured in the following set of core statements. These statements were presented as a 'manifesto' in the first edition of this book and are presented here again to underscore their importance:

- The strengths approach is a philosophy for working with people to bring about change.

- It is an approach to people that is primarily dependent upon positive attitudes about people's dignity, capacities, rights, uniqueness and commonalities.

- It emphasises people's ability to be their own agents of change by creating conditions that enable them to control and direct the processes of change they engage in.

- It creates conditions that enable people to identify, value and mobilise their strengths and capacities in the process of change.

- It provides and mobilises resources in a way that complements people's existing strengths and resources as opposed to compensating for perceived deficits.

- It acknowledges and addresses power imbalances between people working in human services and those they work with.

- It seeks to identify and address social, personal, cultural and structural constraints to people's growth and self-determination.

- It acknowledges and addresses power dynamics, cultures and structures in organisations that are incongruent with socially-just practice.

The strengths approach is an approach to practice based on a philosophy. It is not a model for practice. Therefore, it depends above all else on values and attitudes. It is values and attitudes (rather than skills and knowledge) that are the primary drivers of processes and outcomes. Skills and knowledge are mobilised as resources to serve principles that enable change. Doing otherwise can lead workers to act as experts and work against empowerment and self-determination. This relationship between values, skills and knowledge is illustrated in the following diagram.

Values, Skills and Knowledge Triangle

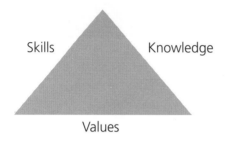

What we believe (our beliefs) and believe in (our values) are more influential in determining the ways in which we work with people (and the outcomes for them), than what we know or how skilled we are. As put by Madsen (1999, p. 15):

> The stance we take in relation to others reflects choice. We can position ourselves in relation to others. We can position ourselves in ways that invite respect, curiosity, and connection. We can also position ourselves in ways that invite judgement, disconnection, and disapproval. The stance we take has profound effects on relationship and is shaped by our values and conceptual assumptions.

The stance taken in the strengths approach is based on principles of just practice and an emphasis on strengths and aspirations as a means of working towards meaningful change. This stance challenges a great many assumptions about what it is to be helpful:

What we can't do:

- It is not possible to change or empower anyone.

- We are not, and don't need to be, experts on other people.

- We can't know the answers or solutions to people's problems.

- We can't compensate for deficits—perceived or real—and be respectful of people's potential at the same time.

What we can do:

- We can believe in people and stand by them.

- We can become facilitators of change.

- We can use frameworks and tools that help create conditions for change; conditions that enable strengths-based, self-determining plans and actions to mobilise and complement people's strengths and resources.

As a philosophy for practice the strengths approach draws us away from an emphasis on procedures, techniques and knowledge as the keys to change, and reminds us that each and every individual, family, group and community holds the keys to their own transformation. We use the term 'strengths approach' because it is a way of approaching or working *with* people, which is primarily dependent on positive attitudes *about* people.

Chapter Two

The Strengths Emphasis

'It's hard to imagine, in addition to stories of strengths, what could be more valuing and responsive than listening for, attending to, and honouring another person's values, hopes and dreams.'

~

'Stories about strengths give us a sense of how things might be and ideas about how to bring about the changes we want. They increase self-esteem and confidence, bringing hope and opening the way for change.'

~

'Approaching people as experts on their own lives and seeing ourselves as a possible resource rather than the expert, is the best starting point for a relationship that will enable self-determination and empowerment.'

The strengths approach has two critical interacting and inseparable foundations: an abiding emphasis on the strengths and potential of human beings (and all that this means) and socially-just, power-with principles. These are like two rocks where, if only one is removed, everything resting on both of them will fall. Both are absolutely necessary for practice that liberates and supports growth and empowerment through processes of participation and self-determination. This chapter explores one of these foundations: the strengths emphasis.

What is strengths-based practice?

Strengths-based practice is a way of working with individuals, families, groups, organisations and communities to bring hope and find solutions in the face of difficulties and to achieve fulfillment and learning in already positive circumstances. It embraces positive attitudes about people and their potential, focussing on their strengths, aspirations and resources as a means of bringing change. It honours people's potential and treats them as experts on their own lives and experience.

However, this emphasis on strengths does not mean ignoring problems or giving them a positive spin. It means framing problems and having conversations about them in ways that are respectful and that enable change and empowerment.

The term 'strengths approach' was originally adopted by the author and colleagues at a time when the term was not in common use. This was used to differentiate iterations of strengths-based practice that do not address power and social justice concerns. The strengths approach does not simply involve positive thinking and an emphasis on strengths. As noted earlier, the strengths approach is concerned with respect, inclusion, collaboration and empowerment. It is concerned about issues of power and self-determination. (This is explored at length in chapters three and four.)

What is a strength?

Whether or not we are aware of them or appreciate them, we all have strengths and capacities that enable us to live our lives. They can also help transform our lives. Strengths can be defined as anything people have that helps them to achieve, to overcome problems, to build on things that are already positive, to learn, grow and be fulfilled. Strengths can be understood in terms of personal qualities—positive characteristics and things that people are good at. Strengths include people's skills and capacities, their aspirations and values and the resources in their environment. These are defined as follows:

Skills and capacities as strengths

Strengths include people's intellectual, physical and interpersonal skills and capacities (Mallucio 1981). Hundreds of examples can be found in the living of any day. There are almost innumerable skills that people have, for example, with regard to intellectual skills: the ability to plan and prioritise, to count, to write a note, to reflect, to solve problems, to use a map, to imagine, to dream and hope, interpret, to make choices. With regard to physical skills: the ability to keep house, throw a ball, to make a piece of furniture, ride a bicycle, to plant flowers, to knit and sew, to go shopping, to wash, dress, cook, and so on. With regard to interpersonal skills: to show an interest in others, to listen, to ask questions, share one's ideas and feelings, to make a plan together, problem solve together, show compassion, to empathise, to be patient, to be respectful.

These categories of strengths are interconnected. They are rarely expressed in isolation from one another. In using interpersonal skills we also use physical and intellectual skills. In using physical skills we need to use intellectual skills and so on.

The ability to adapt, the ability to function in very difficult circumstances, the ability to rise above serious life difficulties, the ability to persist, to innovate, imagine, create, improve, learn ... all these are strengths. Every story a human being tells, every experience shared, no matter how simple or complex, how sad, how happy, is full to the brim with examples of skills people use.

Interests as strengths

Interests as strengths are important. They can seem irrelevant to the issues confronting people and yet they can be a significant means for growth and empowerment. Focussing on people's interests opens up ways of identifying numerous strengths and skills, provides a way of tapping aspirations, hopes and dreams and identifying resources. They can be a foundation on which change can be built.

Cameron at age fifteen spent most of his time on the streets. Homeless and out of school for two years he simply drifted and was constantly getting into trouble. The Child Protection Service had been involved in his life for four years and Juvenile Justice for two years. Narelle, Cameron's support worker, was going out to take photographs for a project she was involved in. She met Cameron and asked if he'd like to take some photographs. She was surprised when he said he was interested. A few days later she met Cameron and showed him the photos he'd taken and asked if he'd be interested in taking more. She was delighted when he said yes, because until now he'd not shown much interest in anything.

As the weeks went by his interest in photography grew with support and encouragement from Narelle. This led to an abiding interest and coincided with significant changes in Cameron's attitudes. Vandalism and aggressive behaviour ceased and Cameron began to engage in other interests, reconnected with his family and eventually took up education and job training options. His interest in photography became a catalyst for change. It opened the way for reflecting on his strengths, capacities and what he wanted for his life, allowing a new experience of himself.

Resources in people's environment as strengths

Resources in people's environment are strengths too. They include family, extended family, friends, neighbours, colleagues, and networks. They can include material resources, buildings, land, food sources, dwellings and other spaces. Information, knowledge, stories and experience that people hold can be considered as resources. Community, culture, customs, traditions and artifacts are resources as well. All of these resources are considered as strengths because they 'belong' to people and are part of the fabric of their lives.

Aspirations and values as strengths

Other strengths include people's dreams, aspirations and values. Aspirations drive change. Our strengths and capacities are the fuel we use to get where we want to go but without aspirations our direction can be unclear and our motivation diminished. When people are invited to share their aspirations they are being invited to share deeply-held values. Exposing and articulating our aspirations and the meaning they hold for us helps increase motivation, provides inspiration, and gives a meaningful context for the articulation of goals and action to reach them.

In the strengths approach we are passionately interested in people's aspirations! Most people who engage with human services come with diminished aspirations or, at worst, a deep sense of hopelessness. It's hard to imagine, in addition to stories of strengths, what could be more valuing and responsive than listening for, attending to, and honouring another person's values, hopes and dreams (or those of a family, group, team, community or organisation).

Aspirations may never be completely met but how can we move forward with at least some degree of purpose in life without them? What drives us to keep going? What gets us through life difficulties without our strengths, resources and dreams? Our aspirations reflect our hope and without hope how can we keep moving forward? We should never underestimate the power of exploring aspirations, hopes and dreams.

Human service workers often raise concerns about this aspect of the strengths approach because of a perceived risk of 'setting people up for failure'. That is, if we go too far in exploring hopes and dreams people may be left unable to reach them. This is a reasonable concern to have. But we can't presume to know whether or not people can achieve their hopes and aspirations. And how is it respectful to interfere with these or tell people they can never achieve them? We need to find ways to support them even if it is outside the artificial boundaries constructed around the services we provide.

The values that are interwoven in aspirations are, in the end, what help people stay focussed on, and persist with, their goals. Exploring aspirations opens up possibilities. It can inspire and motivate. A 'mechanical, clinical' process of goal setting constrained by service delivery structures or pragmatic practice limits people and their possibilities. (This crucial aspect of the strengths approach and the implications for practice are discussed at length in chapter five. The topic is also taken up in the context of social inclusion in chapter eleven.)

EXERCISE – *People's strengths*

- What are the strengths of the people you are working with?
- What are some examples of their physical, intellectual and interpersonal skills and capacities?
- What are their values and aspirations?
- What are some of the resources in their environments?
- What part do their interests, aspirations and dreams play in their lives?
- How do all of these play a part in enhancing their lives?

Contexts for considering strengths

A colleague (thank you, Di O'Neil 1990) recalled how she had worked with a family who had defrauded the social security system. She was curious about how they had done this and, while not condoning or making judgement about the behaviour, was able to identify various skills they had used. She was able to help them meet the various challenges in their lives by using many of these skills which included the ability to imagine possibilities, form goals, identify and use resources, develop plans, use various communication skills and so on.

Another worker might well have chosen to overlook the family's behaviour altogether. Smith (2006, pp. 25-28) contends that what a strength is depends on the context in which is used. This can be true. What is considered as a strength in one situation may be seen as a problem in another. However, what we consider as strengths is likely to depend more on our perspective and values. For example, do we consider someone struggling to make ends meet financially a failure or someone who is strong and persistent?

Another context for considering what a strength is relates to culture. Smith (2006 p. 25) notes that:

> Strengths are almost inevitably culturally expressed. Characteristics regarded as strengths in one culture may be viewed as weaknesses in another culture... For example, in cultures labeled as individualistic, autonomy is highly valued... Conversely, in cultures described as collectivist, relational skills may be emphasized more.

EXERCISE – *Finding strengths*

It's important that our exploration of strengths is not limited by narrow interpretation, value judgements, tools, compendiums or the like. But for the purposes of this exercise here is a list of just some of the strengths that people may have, to help prompt discussion and uncover even more strengths.

- Adventurous
- Organised
- Cheerful
- Courageous
- Respectful
- Considerate
- Caring
- Kind
- Loving
- Clear thinking
- Thrifty
- Easy going
- Spirited
- Laid back
- Relaxed
- Attentive
- Alert
- Sensible
- Determined
- Compassionate
- Happy
- Strong
- Assertive
- Motivated

- Goal-focussed
- Light-hearted
- Entertaining
- Humorous
- Reflective
- Analytical
- Spiritual
- Understanding
- Competent
- Successful
- Close
- Certain
- Open
- Flexible
- Careful
- Energetic
- Quiet
- Artistic
- Accepting
- Fair
- Wise
- Purposeful
- Friendly
- Warm

- Articulate
- Efficient
- Hardworking
- Enthusiastic
- Democratic
- Responsible
- Thoughtful
- Patient
- Tolerant
- Focussed
- Supportive
- Particular
- Creative
- Imaginative
- Sporting
- Empathetic
- Concerned
- Interested
- Skilled
- Watchful
- Comforting
- Optimistic
- Persistent
- Decisive

EXERCISE – *Finding strengths (Continued)*

In groups:

1. From the above list, choose a strength that you have.

2. Take turns to share an example or story of how you have used this strength.

3. Listen carefully to each other's stories and identify other strengths that you think are present in the story you just heard.

4. Provide feedback to each person about the strengths you identified and explain why you identified these strengths.

5. Reflect on your experience of doing the exercise using the following questions:

- How did you feel doing this exercise?

- How did you feel by the time you finished the exercise?

- What were the good things about it? Why were they good?

- What does this mean for your work with people?

- Was there anything you had discomfort with? If so, why?

- What does this mean for your work with people?

- How did you feel getting feedback about your strengths?

- How did you feel giving feedback to others about their strengths?

- What did you do that enabled you to identify the strengths?

Beliefs of the strengths approach

All learning and growth arises from existing strengths and capacities. Identifying and appreciating our strengths and capacities exposes stories that contradict negative and unhelpful beliefs. These 'strengths stories' give us a sense of how things might be and ideas about how to bring about the changes we want. They increase self-esteem and confidence—bringing hope and opening the way for change.

As noted in the opening to this chapter, strengths-based practice takes a positive view of people's potential focussing on their strengths, aspirations and resources and treating them as experts in their own lives. How we approach people, our relationships with them and how we work for change is determined more than anything else by our attitudes. Our beliefs are therefore the most critical aspect of our work.

The strengths emphasis is founded on the following beliefs:

- All people have strengths and capacities.
- People can change. Given the right conditions and resources people's capacity to learn and grow can be harnessed and mobilised.
- People change and grow through their strengths and capacities.
- People are the experts on their own situation.
- The problem is the problem; the person is not the problem.
- Problems can blind people from noticing and appreciating their strengths and capacity to find their own solutions.
- People have good intentions.
- People are doing the best they can.
- The power for change is within us.

The practical implications of these beliefs are explored throughout this book.

The deficit focus

By contrast with strengths-based practice there is a view in human services and society generally that if we understand a problem all we need to do is find an expert (or refer to expert knowledge) to analyse it and then find a prescription that will fix it. This way of thinking starts with a needs assessment. The belief is that if we know what's wrong and work out what the needs are we'll know what needs to be done. The analysis of a problem invariably includes an analysis of causes that are often perceived as residing in people. This can lead to simplistic solutions that rarely address the real issues in the long-term. Three decades after the first explicit assertions of strengths-based ways of working in human services, this view is still not uncommon; it is alive and well in many organisations!

In strengths-based work we refer to this as a 'deficit approach'. This emphasis on deficits—what people are believed to lack—leads to a cycle of focussing on what's wrong followed by reliance on experts. It does not provide the insights, learning and hopefulness that a focus on strengths and capacities does. When people act as experts on other people's problems and try to fix them, those who are facing the problem are denied the opportunity to participate, take control and learn. This focus lowers positive expectations and blocks opportunities for change. An inadvertent process of disempowerment takes place where people experience more of the same! This deficit focus is captured in the following diagram.

The Deficit Cycle

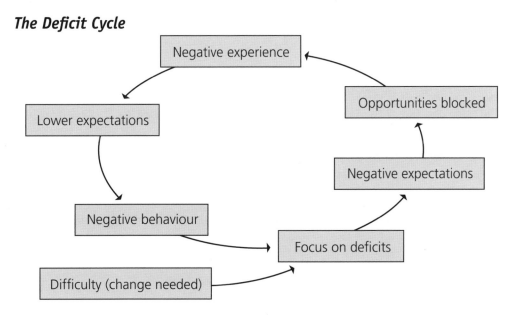

Examples of this deficit focus can be observed in families, schools, organisations and human service contexts. In the classroom or in parent-child relationships a deficit focus or cycle can be seen in the ways a parent or teacher might scold, label, or blame a child for unwanted behaviour. Being told what's wrong with you and what you are doing wrong can introduce or reinforce already existing and unhelpful notions that prevent change.

- What are some examples of the ways in which this deficit focus affects people?

- In what everyday situations do you observe this happening? (For example, in schools, families, communities, social institutions, etc.)

- How does it affect people?

- In what ways can organisations be affected through a deficit focus?

- In what ways can communities be affected through a deficit focus?

The strengths focus

By contrast, a focus on strengths sets a tone for practice that enables people to see themselves and their experiences differently. The strengths-based cycle, illustrated in the diagram below, captures this strengths emphasis. It begins with and emphasises people's strengths and resources in the process of change. Upon recognition of the need for change, problems and issues are acknowledged and validated, and strengths are identified and highlighted. This 'strengths exploration' changes the story about the problem. It creates positive expectations that open the way for the development of strengths.

The Strengths Cycle

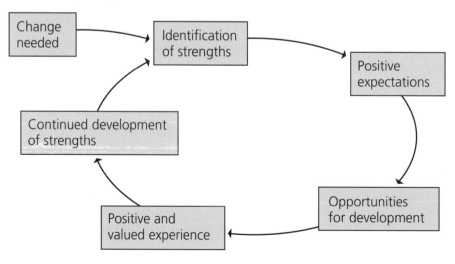

- What are some examples of the ways in which this focus on strengths can affect people; individuals, families and communities?

- In what everyday situations do you observe this happening?
  (For example, in schools, families, communities, social institutions, etc.)

- What do you see as the implications for working with people?

People are their own experts

In a strengths approach people are viewed as experts on their own lives and situations. While problems have a way of blinding us to our strengths, we are the ones who hold the knowledge of them. Furthermore:

- People make sense of their experience in their own way.

- People know themselves better than anyone else.

- People's knowledge of their strengths and capacities, aspirations, experiences and beliefs are within them.

- People know best what helps them change and what stops them.

- Nobody can really know how others feel.

- People know best why they do what they do.

These ideas about people lead us to seek and value what they have to offer. Treating people as their own experts leads to the exploration of strengths and capacities that can be mobilised to resolve problems. If workers assume the role of expert it is not likely to lead to people's empowerment. It is likely that they will end up trying to compensate for what they perceive as deficits and, in so doing, further disempower people. Approaching people as experts on their own lives and seeing ourselves as a possible resource rather than the expert is the best starting point for a relationship that will enable empowerment.

People as advisors, contributors, solution-finders and teachers

This critical strengths-based stance that sees people as their own experts is driven home by Andrew Shirres (2016). With regard to practices of social inclusion (see Chapter 11, pp. 258), he invites workers to consider people as advisors, contributors, solution-finders and teachers:

> ... if we see the people we work with as 'experts' we will appreciate their experience of the difficulties they face, their knowledge of what works best for them and their plan for making changes.

> If we see the people we work with as 'advisors' we will look for feedback on how we work, respect their unique understanding of service delivery, adopt their recommendations for improvements and see ourselves as beneficiaries of their ideas.

> If we see the people we work with as 'contributors' we will remove barriers to participation, rethink the purpose of our time with them and perhaps consider ourselves (workers) as recipients, rather than providers, of services.

> If we see the people we work with as 'solution-finders', we will follow rather than lead, be surprised rather than jaded, respond rather than provide advice.

> If those we work with are considered as 'teachers' we will see ourselves as learners and the 'tests' may be ours to 'pass' or 'fail'. Services will be more about curiosity and enquiry rather than dogma and setting goals for others to achieve.

The passive, deficit-laden, problem-focussed labels we ascribe to those attending our services can determine the service people receive. The power human service organisations wield can make it almost impossible for those they are supposed to support to avoid adopting the identities that can keep them dependent on those same services. While terminology like 'consumer', 'patient', 'customer', 'participant', 'service user' and 'client' remain the only way we think about those we work with, we will remain locked into an 'us' and 'them' paradigm that constrains rather than explores. Genuine, socially-inclusive practice can only exist by adopting labels that are, by necessity, complex rather than simplistic.

- In what ways are you your own expert?

- Think about the people you work with. In what ways are they their own experts?

- What is different in our relationships and our practice when we treat people as their own experts?

- What is different in human service work when people are viewed as contributors, advisors, solution-finders and teachers rather than service recipients?

The problem is the problem; the person is not the problem

The belief that 'the problem is the problem; the person is not the problem' is a highly significant one. This perceptive and profound view originated in the work of Michael White and David Epston (White and Epston 1990). Rather than framing the person (or family, group or community) as the problem, we approach people with the view that problems are something they 'have' or are affected by. Naming and externalising problems as separate from people can free them to take responsibility and influence their lives in ways not otherwise possible. (Externalising problems is discussed further in chapter five.)

In addition, structural, cultural, social, political and economic forces impinge on all of us. Consideration of these enables people to understand the factors that contribute to the problems they face and helps address debilitating blame. Naming and exploring the wider context in which experience takes place changes the way we see and define problems. It challenges disempowering beliefs about ourselves and others.

Mobilising resources to complement people's strengths

People need resources. Various resources are often necessary for growth, learning and change. As noted on page 35 an infinite variety of things can function as resources in a person's life and be considered as strengths. However, there are other resources that people may use to live their lives, to take a new direction, to meet challenges and overcome problems. These external resources can include people, organisations, services, information, knowledge, material resources and decision-making resources that are not or have not been part of people's lives.

Thinking about the people you are working with:

- Why is it important that external resources are used in a way that complements their own resources?

- What message might we give if we consider other resources before theirs?

- What message might we give if we consider other resources without reference to their strengths and aspirations?

In a strengths approach the external resources that might be needed to help change occur are mobilised in ways that complement people's strengths and goals. This is different from attempting to compensate for perceived deficits. As an example, out-of-home care in child and family welfare can be used as a way of compensating for perceived deficits in a family. A parent's 'inability' to cope with a child's behaviour can be compensated for by placing the child in care—a deficit-based response. In using out-of-home care as a resource to support and complement parents' strengths (rather than as the answer to the family's problems), placement can be used to assist them to make changes. Within the context of family goals, the carer becomes a resource as part of a team that includes the worker and family. Other members of this team complement and support the family's efforts at change, with resources being mobilised in a purposeful and complementary way.

This framework for adding value to people's strengths is clarified in the following sequence.

Adding Resources in a Strengths-based Way

> People's strengths and capacities are complemented as necessary by resources in their natural networks.
>
> If necessary,
> ↓
> commonly used community resources are added and,
> ↓
> only if necessary,
> ↓
> specialist resources are mobilised.
> ↓
> EMPOWERMENT

The way any additional resources are mobilised is extremely important. If specialist or other external resources are provided without reference to people's own strengths and resources, we can undermine their ability to learn and be self-determining. We can give messages such as: 'You have no strengths that are relevant' or 'You can't cope or change or manage your own life' or 'Only experts can fix this'.

Chapter Three

Power-over

'People's lives can be adversely affected by the behaviour of individuals acting as representatives of professions, organisations, institutions, ideologies and religions who espouse and often impose particular ways of being.'

~

'Dominant and prominent cultures, individuals and organisations often set and implement agendas and expect compliance from minorities, groups, communities or individuals who are less resourced or choose different ways of being and doing things.'

~

'We can use power over others when we act as experts about what's best for others and about other people's experience, capacities, and strengths. As the expert we can think we have all the answers, know what the problem is, what the solution is and how to go about getting to the solution. As the expert we tend to do most of the work, creating dependence and making it impossible for genuine empowerment, learning and growth.'

Many of the assumptions, conventions and taken-for-granted ideas about people and change are called into question by the strengths approach. It provides alternative, constructive and profoundly different ways to address life's difficulties and even the most serious of personal and social concerns. Some of these have already been discussed in addressing the strengths emphasis. However, this goes hand-in-hand with concerns about power and self-determination.

Relationships between and among individuals, groups, families, organisations, communities, nations and cultures—and even our relationship to the natural world—are subject to dynamics of power. Probably the most important principle of the strengths approach is the sharing of power, or what is referred to as 'power-with'. With the view to developing an understanding of 'power-with' this chapter explores its opposite—'power-over'.

I first came across the explicit use of 'power-over/power-with' terminology in 1990 among feminist friends and colleagues engaged in women's services. I thank them for this gift. Their reflective critiques examined the nature of gender oppression, and of liberation and empowerment; oppression equating with power-over, and liberation and empowerment with power-with. This simple but critically important conceptualisation from the women's movement extends beyond gender issues to every context of human interaction between and among individuals, families, groups, communities, organisations and social institutions and states. It is relevant to our understanding of oppression and disempowerment with regard to age, class and status, sexuality, race and ethnicity, health and ability, and the interactions between them.

American pioneer in organisational theory and behaviour, social worker, feminist, writer and management consultant, Mary Follett, is generally credited with the earliest use of power-over/power-with terminology. She used these terms as a way of differentiating between coercive and collaborative ways of running organisations; the former being a form of control that leads to serious or even disastrous consequences in organisations, and the latter that leads to cooperation, innovation and effectiveness.

Some writers also use the terms 'power-to/power-for' together with power-over/power-with in discussions of power and authority, but power-over and power-with, as I define and discuss them, correspond with meanings given by these writers.

Colonisation as a metaphor for disempowerment

Colonisation or colonialism, where a country or society engages in processes that make another country or territory into a colony, has become a metaphor in the strengths approach for 'power-over'.

In 1991 during studies of race and ethnicity and histories of colonisation through the centuries, I was suddenly struck by the parallels between patterns of human and institutional behaviour and contemporary social and political processes. Even social welfare practices (mostly undertaken by religious institutions) were no less colonising. Colonisation of the Indigenous people of Australia, including the policies that led to the Stolen Generations, were much the same as colonising processes anywhere in the world.

There are strong similarities between these processes and other injustices. They involve a central dynamic in which power is used with good or bad intentions to control the lives and determine the futures of countless numbers—often with little, if any, regard for human dignity. Examples include the removal of tens of thousands of children from their families in the United Kingdom, their forced migration to Australia, Canada, New Zealand and South Africa following World War II, and subsequent abuse of large numbers in institutions; the terrible abuse suffered over the centuries by people with mental illness; infants taken in their thousands from young mothers and adopted out because they were born outside marriage; the thousands of children removed from their families by child protection systems and placed in, and abused in, care throughout most of the twentieth century; the oppression of women; crushing discrimination based on sexual orientation and gender diversity, and the wide spread exploitation of labour.

Beside all this, social welfare, health and education systems, corporations and religious institutions (among others) were doing the same, to equal or lesser degrees; they were exercising power over others in everyday activities and practices while deeming these to be for people's benefit. Colonisation, it seemed, was not (and still is not) a part of our past. While colonisation devastates whole cultures and peoples its power-over dynamics can be seen reflected in contemporary realities. Thus the metaphor!

The metaphor highlights the parallel between the dynamics of colonisation and the part that social welfare practice and social institutions can play in people's lives. It alerts us to the dangers inherent in systems and in institutional and personal power.

When exploring what happens under colonisation we can identify genocide, murder, rape, the stealing of children, the destruction of the environment, the separation of families and communities, the removal or confiscation of land and resources, exploitation, slavery, the imposition of laws, culture, language, and authority, and all forms of coercion.

When considering the psychological and emotional impact on people we can identify the feelings of those who have this experience: fear, confusion, hatred, dread, sadness, depression, grief, anger, devastation, disempowerment and hopelessness. We can identify the various responses to this experience: rebellion, violence, division, migration, suicide, illness, conformity and resistance. People begin to doubt their own culture, knowledge, abilities, potential and sense of possibilities.

The justification for colonisation can be traced to a strong sense of superiority. We can identify underlying beliefs such as: 'Our way is best', 'We know what's best for them', 'They are inferior' and 'They must be saved'.

When we explore the beliefs of people who are colonised we can identify beliefs such as: 'We are inferior', 'We are not inferior', ' There's something wrong with us', 'They are wrong', 'We can't change this', 'We have to go along with them' or 'We must fight this'.

Power-over occurs when an individual, group or institution assumes the right to colonise and control others. There is an over-arching sense of superiority found in beliefs that negate or limit the right to resources, participation and self-determination.

Power-over in the contemporary world

The colonisation metaphor enables us to identify the visible and intentional ways as well as the invisible, unintentional or subtle ways, in which 'power-over' can characterise relationships between individuals or groups. Social institutions (such as the education system, the legal system, the mass media, corporations, police, governments, trade unions, religious institutions, the welfare system, and professional, community and national organisations) can, and often do, use power over others. People's lives can be adversely affected by the behaviour of individuals acting as representatives of professions, organisations, institutions, ideologies and religions who espouse and often impose particular ways of being. The use of power-over is not always violent nor aggressively coercive. However, it can, and so often does, disempower or even subjugate people. It profoundly affects the identities, prospects, aspirations and self-worth of individuals, families, groups and communities.

Fear, greed, a sense of superiority, professionalism or a range of other factors might motivate this position. In human services work, community work, voluntary helping and interpersonal relationships power-over can be motivated by assumptions about the need to protect or rescue and is built on the view that 'We know best'. The need to protect or rescue is, of course, often valid. The use of power-over can be justified in circumstances where people are unsafe. For example, traffic laws are imposed to keep people safe on the roads. Statutory services are designed to protect people. But we can intervene in ways that are disrespectful or even destructive.

Systems abuse is a clear example of the use of power-over. It is not always deliberate but the impact can devastate the lives of individuals, families or different social groups. People who use substances, families struggling to raise their children and make ends meet, young people in trouble, people with mental illness, disadvantaged communities, Indigenous people and many others suffer the stigma attached to the use of various welfare services in addition to disempowering social arrangements. They often then experience patronising, judgemental, blaming behaviour and processes. Even when relationships with workers and agencies are generally positive and helpful, people can still be 'kept in their place' by ignoring the wider structural, cultural, political, economic and social factors that impinge on their ability to take real control of their lives and futures.

The following example highlights the danger that human service professionals and their organisations can be to clients. It also illustrates the commonalities between the dynamics of some human service interventions and those of colonisation.

Sonia had a son, Jayden (ten years old), and a daughter, Chloe (eight years old). They lived with Marcus, Sonia's partner of three years. Marcus had perpetrated violence against Sonia on a number of occasions and often threatened her children who had witnessed the abuse. Sonia had attempted to leave Marcus on two occasions. On the second occasion Marcus physically constrained Sonia and forced her home from a friend's house where she and her children had been staying. Shortly after, Marcus began to abuse the children, locking them in their bedroom, verbally abusing them, and on occasions making Jayden stand on his head in a corner of their living room for extended periods. Sonia's protests and efforts to protect her children met with further abuse by Marcus, including burning Chloe's legs with cigarettes. Sonia and her children lived in terror for two weeks until members of the Community Policing Squad intervened following a notification by one of Sonia's friends who lived nearby.

The Child Protection Service was contacted and staff investigated the same day. A child protection order was taken out and Chloe and Jayden were placed in foster care in a nearby town. Marcus was charged with assault and Sonia was supported by a women's refuge. Sonia was in shock, not only because of the abuse she and her children had suffered, but because her children had been taken away.

Six months later Chloe and Jayden were still in care. Sonia and her children had been denied contact for the whole time. The children's behaviour in care had been difficult despite support from psychologists and other professionals. They were with their third caregiver. Marcus was in prison. During these and the following months Sonia repeatedly attempted to make contact with her children through the Child Protection Service. Time after time she was refused contact because, she was told, she had been unable to protect her children and it was considered unsafe to return them to her. She moved to another town in search of work.

Despite self-doubt as a parent, confusion and feelings of sadness, anger and disempowerment, Sonia contacted a family welfare agency to ask for help. The agency vigorously supported her efforts to see her children. After some months she was finally allowed to see her children. With the agency's support she gained regular contact with her children. The development of a plan to enable them to spend time with Sonia, initially for afternoons, then overnight, then for weekends, eventually saw the return of the children to Sonia.

Sonia and her children remained together without the need for further intervention by the Child Protection Service. They did, however, need professional support from time to time. Five years later, Jayden was in serious trouble and became a client of Juvenile Justice Services. He and Chloe had had significant difficulties throughout their schooling. Sonia entered into a new relationship, which endured.

The role of professionals in situations such as these—the power that they hold, the assumptions on which judgement is based and the way they provide services—is akin to the behaviour of colonisers, at least for those who are subjected to it.

(The following exercises were developed by the author and Bernadette Glass in 1991, and first published in *Communities of Hope*, McCashen W, 2004)

Values and beliefs affect everything we do. They play a crucial part in influencing and determining our way of communicating, relating, behaving and interacting with people. In the following exercise questions are designed to help explore the essential characteristics and dynamics of colonisation and to invite reflection on ways in which values and beliefs affect behaviour.

- What happens to people under colonisation? What is done to people?

- From what we know or from people we know, how do we imagine people feel as a result of this experience? How might we feel if we had these experiences?

- How do people respond behaviourally? What sorts of things do they do as a result of this experience?

- What beliefs are necessary on the part of those who are colonising, to justify their actions?

- What beliefs do people who are colonised take on about themselves and those who are colonising?

Answers to these questions can be recorded on a whiteboard for further consideration in the next exercise, using the following headings:

What happens under colonisation

How people feel as a result

How people respond as a result

Beliefs of those who colonise that justify this

Beliefs that people take on about themselves and those who colonise them

Cautions in using this exercise
In using this exercise facilitators should be careful to frame the questions in a broad context. That is, be considerate of colonisation in any number of past or present situations anywhere in the world. This is because we need to be respectful of, and sensitive to, people's experiences of colonisation (including those of friends and relatives), especially those of Indigenous people. Secondly, we cannot presume to know how people feel as a result of colonisation; we are simply asking people to consider, from what they know and understand, how they think people who are colonised might feel, and how they think they might feel in those same circumstances.

EXERCISE – *Colonisation as a metaphor for disempowerment*

The purpose of this exercise is to explore the parallels between the characteristics of colonisation and ways in which our dominant culture and social institutions can engage in colonising practices.

Given the exploration of colonisation in the previous exercise, participants in the discussion are invited to think about colonisation as a metaphor for disempowerment. They are asked to consider parallels between the dynamics inherent in colonisation and the dynamics between social institutions and their representatives and the community. The following questions are used to assist this reflection:

- Do present-day institutions colonise?

- If so, which ones and in what ways?

- Can individuals colonise?

- In what ways?

- How might the people you provide services to experience colonisation?

- What connections do you see between the deficit focus and the colonisation metaphor?

Dominant culture and power-over

Using the colonisation metaphor we can identify ways in which social institutions, organisations and individuals can (and do) use power over others. Dominant groups carry powerful beliefs that are treated as the only truth. This is evident in prejudice, discrimination and marginalisation on the basis of race, ethnicity, religion, social or economic status, gender, age, sexual orientation, health status or psychological, physical, intellectual ability/disability.

Dominant and prominent cultures, individuals and organisations often set and implement agendas and expect compliance from minorities, groups, communities or individuals who are less resourced or choose different ways of being and doing things. This heightens our awareness of the dangers inherent in the ways we relate to people. It alerts us to avoid colonising practices even where there are good intentions.

Eduardo Galeano (1992), using the term 'colonialism' rather than colonisation, makes this point:

> Blatant colonialism mutilates you without pretense, it forbids you to talk, it forbids you to act, it forbids you to exist. Invisible colonialism, however, convinces you that serfdom is your destiny and impotence is your nature: it convinces you that it's not possible to speak, not possible to act, not possible to exist.

Power-over is characterised by violent or non-violent coercion, but other forms of power-over can involve processes that are deliberately or inadvertently driven by workers. All of them can constrain self-determination. They include the following:

- Knowing what's best for others (assuming one truth or knowledge is correct and following its path to a solution prescribed by that truth).

- Telling people what's wrong with them (pathologising, labelling, blaming, making value judgements).

- Telling people what to do and how to do it (bossing, forcing, prescribing solutions).

- Blaming, labelling or classifying people (assuming to know the truth based on dominant ideas without consideration of unique circumstances and contexts).

- Deliberately or inadvertently excluding people from decision-making or limiting their participation (blocking choice or jumping in and taking over).

- Giving unsolicited advice (imposing views and ideas based on assumptions about what's best for people).

- Telling people what their strengths are (being patronising, condescending or imposing views that assume we know what people's strengths are).

- Isolating and marginalising people (excluding people from decision-making, treating people as incapable).

- Imposing views, plans or strategies for change.

EXERCISE – *Our responses to power-over behaviour*

In pairs or small groups discuss each of the power-over behaviours specified
in the first column of the table below, and how you feel about and respond to each.
Then share your thoughts and reflections.

BEHAVIOUR	HOW YOU FEEL WHEN OTHERS TREAT YOU LIKE THIS	HOW YOU REACT OR RESPOND
Not listening		
Assuming to know what's best for you		
Telling you what's wrong with you		
Routinely telling you what to do and how to do it		
Blaming you		
Labelling you		
Excluding you from decisions about yourself		
Giving you advice you didn't ask for		
Assuming to know your strengths and telling you what they are		
Imposing plans or views on you		

EXERCISE – *Our responses to power-over behaviour* (Continued)

Suggested questions for reflection after the exercise:

- What strikes you most having done this exercise? What stands out for you?
- Which power-over behaviours did you have the strongest responses to?
- Was there any pattern that emerged for you?
- What has all of this got to do with your practice as a worker or manager?

Power-over and labelling

Labelling and classification can be forms of power-over. They are extremely powerful in the way that they can affect people's identities and behaviour. For example, when family members label a child 'the black sheep' a value judgement is made. 'Evidence' of any underlying behaviour is repeatedly noticed and cited so that the child begins to internalise negative ideas about herself. She then comes to believe that's the way she must be and finds it difficult to act differently.

EXERCISE – *Labelling*

- What are some of the labels that can do people harm?
- What are some of the labels that can get in the way of change and empowerment?
- What are the problems associated with labelling?
- How might labelling colonise or disempower people?
- What cautions should we be aware of in using labels?
- What impact do labelling and classification have on people?
- How can we describe and talk about people in respectful ways?
- What can we do to be respectful of and hopeful about people?
- What do we know of the strengths and capacities of people who are stereotyped or labelled?
- What can we do to avoid framing people as the problem?

Labelling is not always consciously or intentionally used to disempower people but the 'truth' that labels hold is still powerful. Labels such as 'schizophrenic' or 'dysfunctional' or 'hopeless', 'lazy', 'selfish' or 'bad', 'addict' or 'alcoholic' and thousands of others are all based on classifications or constructs determined by the dominant culture and dominant 'knowledge', whether deemed right or not. Labels can profoundly affect people's identities. They can define people and therefore confine what is possible for them. The following table underlines problems with labelling and cautions regarding their use.

Taking Care with Labelling

LABELLING AND CLASSIFICATION CAN:	IF LABELS ARE USED WE NEED TO ENSURE:
<ul><li>blame us</li><li>describe us in ways that frame us as the problem</li><li>feed the problems that we experience</li><li>reinforce what we believe is wrong with us</li><li>assume bad intentions</li><li>focus on what's wrong and ignore the possibility that there's something that's right</li><li>ignore exceptions to problems</li><li>oversimplify issues and hide the real issues in our experience</li><li>create a 'them and us' attitude</li><li>entrap us in the problem</li><li>bring confusion and disempower us</li><li>lead us to unnecessarily rely on experts rather than our own capacities.</li></ul>	<ul><li>they are respectful, bring hope and are validating</li><li>they recognise uniqueness and at the same time expose our commonalities and similarities</li><li>they expose people's expertise and reflect people's strengths and capacities rather than reinforce constraints</li><li>we avoid framing people as the problem by recognising the wider structural and cultural context of people's lives</li><li>we open up other possibilities and solutions, create greater understanding and accept that we may be wrong.</li></ul>

Sourced from McCashen 1996; Deal & McCashen 1998.

Labelling can also include those attributes that are considered positive, such as 'responsible' or 'cooperative', because these labels can also keep us in our place. A classic example is the quality of caring which has been socially constructed as admirable but can lead to the disempowerment of the carer. Women in particular are encouraged through their socialisation to be caring. But caring can be the very quality that works against their ability to meet their own rightful needs and can often lead to the creation of unnecessary dependence rather than self-sufficiency or interdependence.

Labelling can affect the esteem, identities and attitudes of individuals and families. It can also affect communities as a whole. The stigma attached to living in particular communities, or being a part of a particular community of interest affects how people see themselves, what's possible for them and the way they relate.

Power-over and experts

Experts and expertise are important. Specialised knowledge and skills are often essential resources for assisting and supporting people. However, the way we use our expertise can disempower people. We can use power over others when we act as experts about what's best for others and about other people's experience, capacities, and strengths. As the expert we can think we have all the answers, know what the problem is, what the solution is and how to go about getting to the solution. We can rely on assumptions, labels and classification based on what we assume is the truth. We can assume to know why things are the way they are and what to do about it. We can even assume to know what people's strengths are and tell them that too! As the expert we tend to do most of the work, creating dependence and making it impossible for genuine empowerment, meaningful learning and growth.

This is an hierarchical approach that uses assumptions based on dominant knowledge to diagnose and describe people (individuals, families, groups and communities) and define what is or isn't possible for them. Such an approach acts as a means of social control by getting people to fit particular models or ideas. It creates passive dependence on services and institutions. It leads to blaming people for failure and framing them as resistant, hopeless or uncooperative when they don't fit with or accept the dominant culture's models, values or ideas. This occurs despite the fact that goals, agendas and interventions are set by anyone other than the people concerned. It defines and confines people and stifles self-determination in the process of helping.

Structural and cultural constraints to change

Just practice, as noted in chapter one, acknowledges and addresses structural and cultural impediments to personal and social change. These impediments or constraints originate from dominant social structures and culture.

A social structure, in simple terms, can be defined as the way social groups organise to do things. Social structures include families, community organisations and associations, government and government departments, trade unions, churches, mosques, corporations, the media, the legal system, the education system, political parties and so on. Social structures can be resources for people—for instance, through social security, workers' rights, education and information. Social structures can also impose constraints or prevent access to resources, such as employment, housing, public transport and so on. In the strengths approach we refer to these as structural constraints.

Culture consists of beliefs, traditions, assumptions, meaning, myths, and patterns of relating and behaving. These things can be deeply enriching for people. However, they can adversely affect people's capacity to learn, grow and change. In the strengths approach we refer to these as cultural constraints. When people internalise these constraints, they can become self-limiting or even oppressive. These are sometimes referred to as personal constraints because they are internally self-limiting. They originate from knowledge and assumptions found in psychology, sociology, religion, the interpretation of history, and many other ways of knowing and understanding people and the world.

Social structures influence the culture of families, groups, organisations and communities. But culture is also influential in shaping the way that social structures are established or maintained. Both social structures and culture shape ideas and carry powerful messages about human experience. The following diagram illustrates the connection between social structures and culture.

Social Structures and Culture

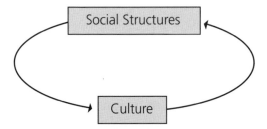

EXERCISE – *Exploring constraints to change*

Structural constraints

- Which social structures can disempower people or constrain change? What are some examples of how this happens?

- Which ones can enable change and empowerment? What are some examples of how this happens?

- Do any organisations and institutions in your community get in the way of change for people? If so, in what ways?

- Do any of them hinder or prevent growth and empowerment, and if so, in what ways?

- Do any of them contribute to growth and empowerment, and if so, in what ways?

- Which ones are a resource to people and in what ways?

Cultural/personal constraints

- What are some examples of how culture influences people's thinking and behaviour?

- What impact does it have on individuals?

- In what ways might culture constrain change and growth?

- How might it constrain self-determination?

- What beliefs and ideas do people or organisations have that are helpful to people and their empowerment?

- Do you or your organisation have any beliefs that might be preventing or hindering change and empowerment? If so, what are some examples?

Knowledge and meaning

People are meaning-makers. We are constantly engaged in a process of making sense of what we observe and experience. But the meaning people give to events and experience is always subjective. This subjective view uses values and beliefs from culture to judge what is happening and why. For example, if a man stays at home to look after his children while his wife goes out to work some people might say that he is liberated and being a real father to his kids, that his wife is liberated and independent and that all this is admirable. Others might say he won't work or his wife has him under the thumb. Others might think the couple is strange (because they break with important traditions and norms). Some might say he is not a man; that he won't earn a living or take responsibility for providing for his family.

Most often the beliefs and ideas of the dominant (or prominent) cultures and social structures around us (family, friends, peers colleagues, workplaces, the community, the media, schools and other social institutions) provide the points of reference we use to give meaning to our experience. These beliefs lead us to define what is normal or abnormal, possible or not possible, good or bad, and right or wrong. In this way they can define people and try to determine what is possible for them.

The meaning we give to experience is more significant than the experience itself in determining our responses to it. There are numerous ways of interpreting the world and seeing others and ourselves; many meanings that can be given. They can be powerful in marginalising, dividing and discriminating against people, or connecting, including and respecting people. Therefore, exploring meaning and the myriad of ways of interpreting our experiences can shed different light on events and open up new possibilities.

Chapter Four

Power-with

'The strengths approach brings hope by making explicit connections between stories of strengths, growth and change, and aspirations for a brighter future. It is a practice of respect. Respect requires a high regard for people's intrinsic worth, the right to self-determination and the right to participation and inclusion.'

~

'Using power-with means the development of collaborative partnerships where the expertise, knowledge and resources of all parties are valued, shared and developed in a team approach to change.'

~

'The strengths approach uses power-with not only to help ensure that interventions do not inadvertently keep people in their place, but also to assist people to become liberated from the problems at play in their lives.'

It's difficult to imagine what can be more respectful and generous than human beings sharing their power and resources for the good of others. The great advances in social justice have been founded on respect for human potential, dignity and fairness. None of these could have been achieved without cooperation and shared power. They can be found not only in historical events, however, but in everyday activity, in families, workplaces, organisations and communities everywhere when people connect with each other. Sharing power is part of our humanity. It is noble and a great strength.

The strengths approach brings hope by making explicit connections between stories of strengths, growth and change, and aspirations for a brighter future. But as discussed in previous chapters, the strengths approach is not simply about strengths and aspirations. Nor does it ignore or minimise problems, or simply give them a positive spin. It faces and confronts problems and challenges colonising practices. So how can we work for change in ways that are not colonising? What helps to create change that is liberating, empowering and self-determining?

The opposite of power-over is of course power-with—the essence of the strengths approach. Power-with involves values, beliefs and actions that do not colonise. Power-with is the means by which empowerment is achieved.

Some conventional definitions of empowerment describe the giving of information, skills and resources to others, or delegating or giving authority or permission. This definition involves power-over because it inherently implies that the 'receiver of empowerment' is passively reliant on a 'giver of empowerment'. Doing these things may free people of certain constraints. This is valid and worthwhile and often necessary. But it does not necessarily follow that people will be empowered as a result.

Other definitions, especially in social work, describe processes that involve growth, learning, becoming stronger, and gaining control of one's life, circumstances and future. The process of empowerment involves the individual, family, group, community or organisation actively tapping their own resources, skills, knowledge and information, and engaging those of others as necessary in order to learn, grow, change things and take control. Power-with processes are processes that enable empowerment. They involve collaborative effort and workers become facilitators of these processes.

Respect and power-with

Power-with is not possible without respect. Respect requires a high regard for people's intrinsic worth, the right to self-determination and the right to participation and inclusion. It requires belief in people's potential—honouring and valuing their strengths and seeking to learn from them. Being respectful means believing in people's rights, the right to safety and the right to resources.

Respect also involves a high regard for uniqueness and diversity. Respect for uniqueness is crucial in understanding experience. While we have much in common with others each of us is unique. Our experiences and the meaning we give them are unique to each of us. This understanding helps to avoid the dangers inherent in generalisation. Solutions to problems should therefore be individually tailored to people's specific circumstances and aspirations.

While respect for uniqueness is essential, so too is respect for the commonalities between people. Despite our uniqueness, our common experiences enable us to connect, understand, empathise with, learn from and support each other. This is reflected in the view that there are more similarities between people than there are differences. For example:

- We all make mistakes.
- Blaming makes things worse.
- We can all get trapped by thinking and behaviour that prevents change.
- We can all do things that aren't good for us.
- We can all have difficulties changing.
- Everyone needs resources.
- All people have strengths and resources, both known and unknown to them.
- How we see ourselves and the world influences how we relate and behave.

Keeping such commonalities in mind can lead us to genuine empathy. It can also enable us to get in touch with our own imperfections as well as our strengths and is less likely to lead us to be judgemental. Remembering our commonalities can be a humbling experience. It can remind us of ways in which we overcome adversity and what is possible in terms of human potential. It can also help us stay in touch with our humanity by reminding us of the ways that we become discouraged or feel hurt or hopeless. It can build connectedness and enable power-with.

Reducing power imbalances

Taking action to address imbalances of power is crucial to just, respectful practice. People come to services already disempowered by the problems they face. In the human service context these imbalances are even greater because of the power inherent in agency, community, legal and professional mandates, and the 'knowledges' of the helping professions. These substantially increase the personal power of workers. Furthermore, the view that neutrality and objectivity is possible has been a powerful influence in the helping professions as elsewhere. Michael White (1994, p. 1) addresses this view:

> The therapeutic context is not exempt from the structures and from the ideology of the dominant culture. The therapeutic context is not exempt from the politics of gender, class, race and culture. The therapeutic context is not exempt from the politics associated with the hierarchies of knowledge and the politics of marginalisation.

Knowledge can be a formidable force in the way that it characterises and defines people, behaviour and possibilities. This, of course, includes labelling and classification. Thinking of knowledge as being made up of exact and definable facts can lead to the categorisation and classification of people, events and experience. It can exclude or dismiss information that is not favourable to the ideas or beliefs of the dominant culture. People's unique contexts, experiences, aspirations, motivations, circumstances and histories can be ignored. If we think of knowledge as 'ways of knowing' instead of indisputable fact we are more likely to be considerate of a range of possible ways of interpreting experience. Recognition of this changes the way professionals respond to people who engage the services they provide.

Using power-with means the development of collaborative partnerships where the expertise, knowledge and resources of all parties are valued, shared and developed in a team approach to change. In the following table, distinctions are drawn between various characteristics of power-over and power-with.

Power-over and Power-with

POWER-OVER:	POWER-WITH:
• relies on dominant knowledge to diagnose and describe people	• avoids imposition of dominant knowledge, stories and labels
• validates and acknowledges people's experience but interprets experience according to particular models	• validates people's unique experience and honours the meaning they give to their experience
• tends to ignore or minimise structural and cultural contexts and under-value people's knowledge and meanings	• acknowledges the structural and cultural contexts of people's lives and the uniqueness of their experience
• ignores or minimises the value of people's strengths and capacities relying primarily on the worker's skills and expertise	• seeks to recognise and mobilise people's strengths and capacities as a central focus in change efforts
• is driven by organisational, state and professional priorities	• values people's aspirations and goals over other agendas
• expects people to meet workers on their ground and expects people to adapt to their context	• enables professionals to form partnerships and adapt to people's contexts
• relies on professional interpretations, concepts and language	• enables professionals to enter into people's worlds and landscapes, and honours their language
• confines practice to therapeutic or social work models, conventions and traditions	• creates a context of discovery and action, improvising and trying new things
• relies on worker expertise and gives weight to professional knowledge and skill	• relies on the shared expertise and knowledge of all stakeholders and gives priority to inclusive, transparent and consultative practice
• believes in objective knowledge	• values diversity of knowledge and acknowledges subjectivity
• relies on having to know the answers and tends to blame people for failure, framing them as uncooperative, resistant or hopeless if things don't work out	• relies on the finding the right questions and a team approach where responsibility is shared
• enables processes and outcomes to be determined by professionals.	• enables processes and outcomes to be determined in partnership.

Doing power-with and social justice

Another way of thinking about the exercise of power with others is through principles of social justice—sharing resources, information, knowledge and skills; participating in decision-making; and addressing equity and access to resources. The strengths approach invites us to go beyond efforts that help people make improvements in their lives to working towards addressing oppressive realities.

Socially-just practice requires the building of interdependence and community. It requires a commitment to people's right to self-determination and to resources. It also requires that we identify and address the power imbalances that inherently exist in relationships.

Lobbying, campaigning, advocating, taking direct action, and protesting are important forms of action for social justice. But social injustice is not only something that we can address in the external world. The principles of social justice can be brought to daily life in our relationships, workplaces, communities, families, groups, and organisations. We can do justice by doing respect, inclusion, collaboration, consultation, transparency and self-determination, and by keeping alive our focus on people's strengths and capacities.

Transparency

A core principle of social justice and power-with that needs to be underlined is transparency. Transparency simply means having things out in the open, being up-front and honest. The use of power-over often requires secrecy and hidden agendas, which can so easily lead to unjust practices. Transparency helps keep workers accountable to those they provide services to. In the human service context this means:

- all information is openly and fully shared

- rights, roles, responsibilities and confidentiality are explored and made explicit

- meetings should include everyone receiving services

- records are not hidden but openly used for the purpose of change, with people's full participation

- we are honest about our misgivings, short-comings and joys.

Self-determination

Self-determination means people have control over the processes they engage in to address change as well as their lives and future. Commitment to the principle of self-determination is critical to power-with. Self-determination is about 'ownership'. It involves genuine choice and the right to participation, inclusion and consultation. People own their vision of what they want things to be like. They decide on and participate in action to address their concerns and interests. In casework, counselling and support services this is referred to as 'client-directed practice'. This term emphasises the principle of ownership and, therefore, people's right to take an active lead in the service delivery process. Various elements of client-directed practice are specified in the table opposite.

When the conditions for self-determination are met, people's motivation and confidence increase. They gain experience and learn skills that enable them to take greater control of their lives and to gain access to the resources necessary for reaching their goals.

Self-determination

PEOPLE'S EXPERIENCE	WORKER'S RESPONSIBILITY
People's unique experience is acknowledged and validated. People become aware of commonalities and similarities with others.	The worker listens, helps validate and explore the context of the issues.
People have control of the change process as much as possible	The worker does not jump to solutions or attempt to move ahead of people.
People identify and define the issues, strengths, goals and steps towards change.	The worker assists the identification of issues, goals, strengths, exceptions and steps.
People's strengths and solution-finding ability are the focus of work.	The worker enables a focus on strengths and resources and supports people to mobilise them.
People have the right to additional resources.	Additional resources are accessed, when necessary, in ways that complement people's strengths and resources.
People are always aware of achievements and progress.	The worker assists in noticing and measuring change.
People are colleagues and have the right to participate in every aspect of the change process.	Workers ensure that practice is transparent, honest and participatory: • Workers enable ownership of, and participation in, recording • No records are hidden from people • Meetings are inclusive • Confidentiality, rights, roles and limitations are explored and made explicit.
People are their own experts.	Workers do not know the answers. Workers share their skills and knowledge and act as facilitators of change. Workers actively seek feedback and evaluation throughout the change process.

What makes a good worker?

An extensive community consultation into ways the provision of human services could be improved identified strong and unambiguous messages about what's important for those receiving services (McCashen 1999). A key theme to emerge was that no matter how good or bad a service was perceived to be, what makes the difference for people is the way in which individual workers do their jobs. The experiences and views captured in the lists below (McCashen 1999, pp. 9-10) identify the essence of good practice and reflect the underlying principles of self-determination and power-with. They are important because they come from the wisdom of clients themselves. The various services they were involved with included child protection, police services, local government and various non-government counselling and support services.

GOOD WORKERS LISTEN

- They genuinely listen
- They let you have your say
- They remember things; you don't have to keep going over stuff
- They try to understand
- They help clarify what you are saying
- They help you feel normal
- They consult you about things
- They don't impose their view.

GOOD WORKERS DON'T PLAN THINGS FOR YOU

- They make sure they help, not criticise
- They help you identify your goals
- They see what you need to make things happen
- They help you with your own plans
- They help set tasks you can manage
- They get clear about what you want and help you look at all the options
- They don't tell you what to do.

GOOD WORKERS DON'T JUMP TO CONCLUSIONS

- They try to understand your circumstances (past and present)
- They don't assume you've done the wrong thing
- They assume people are doing the best they can
- They are aware of what else is happening
- They don't make false accusations
- They don't judge you even if you've done something wrong
- They don't generalise
- They don't blame.

GOOD WORKERS COME TO HELP

- They are not intimidating
- They go with you to do things if you need them (e.g. meetings, transport, etc)
- They let you find out things for yourself, try things and make mistakes
- They encourage you to contact them if you need help
- They want to listen and help.

GOOD WORKERS EXPLAIN THINGS	GOOD WORKERS FOLLOW UP

GOOD WORKERS EXPLAIN THINGS

- They don't walk in and take over
- They don't hide things from you
- They explain about confidentiality
- They explain what's happening and why
- They tell you what they can and can't do
- They let you know you can have a support person
- They share their knowledge about what resources are available
- They don't talk about you without your knowing
- They use plain language.

GOOD WORKERS FOLLOW UP

- They keep appointments
- They check to see how you are going
- They follow up even when they're not involved any more.

GOOD WORKERS ARE PROFESSIONAL

- They share their experience
- They don't let their personal problems interfere
- They remain professional but are human.

Focussing on solutions not problems

Solution-focused therapy has been influential as part of 'the third wave' discussed in chapter one. It sees people as their own experts and solutions as resting with them and their networks. It therefore relies on people's strengths, capacities and goals, rather than worker expertise and knowledge, to bring change. In order to do this it is necessary for the worker to create a collaborative partnership with people where power is shared.

Solution-focused (or solution-oriented) practices bring something significantly useful to the strengths approach. 'Solution-focused therapy' is a commonly used term that has its origins in the work of American social worker, Steve de Shazer (1985, 1988, 1991). Many have adopted the term 'solution-focused practice' in order to highlight the usefulness of its ideas in settings other than the therapeutic (such as community development, management and staff supervision). In essence, solution-focused work is concerned with how solutions work rather than with how problems work. It informs the strengths approach with simple but profound ideas:

- All problems have exceptions that expose strengths and capacities, and give clues to solutions ('exceptions' means exceptions to the problem—times when the problem is absent or not as bad).

- It's more useful to know what will be different when a problem is absent, or less of a problem, than to understand the causes of a problem.

- It's more useful to focus on what people are doing when the problem is absent, or less of a problem, than on what people are doing wrong.

Solution-focused practice helps people develop a preferred 'picture of the future'. It draws on skills, strengths, resources and exceptions to find ways to move towards their picture of the future. In this way it is future-oriented rather than past-oriented. It is more concerned with what people want to be different in their lives than with what is wrong. It emphasises the idea that people can construct their own solutions based on what they are doing well and have done well in the past (Walter & Peller 1992).

For example, if stress and not having enough time to myself is the issue, using a solution-focused approach would invite me to get in touch with and describe what I want to be happening instead—a picture of the future. This might consist of qualities in my life such as feeling contented and rested, being relaxed and happy, and having time to myself.

It then involves describing what contented, rested, happy and relaxed would 'look' like. This might be things like going to the gym three times a week, watching a movie once a week and taking an hour each day to read. I would then be invited to think about times when I have been contented, rested, relaxed and happy in my life before, and what I had done, and what conditions had been present that enabled this to happen. This would then give direction as to what I might do to reach my picture of the future. The diagram below illustrates a solution-focused process of change.

Solution-focused Cycle

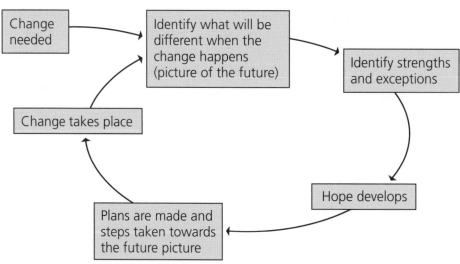

the strengths approach

Solution-focused practice provides a framework that emphasises and respects people's ability to be their own agents of change. Through this framework people can emerge as their own experts. It moves away from pathology and relies more on people's strengths and expertise than on worker expertise and knowledge. In its 'pure' form, however, it does not set out to address the social, political, structural, economic and cultural realities of people's lives.

Hearing and responding to people's stories

Narrative therapy (sometimes also referred to as narrative practice) is another major contributor to the third wave. It is concerned to ensure that power is addressed not only in the relationship between the practitioner and those seeking support but in the lives of those seeking support as well. It is an approach that uses power-with.

It begins by listening to people's description of the problem stories that dominate their lives ('I am no good'). It then supports them to explore alternative positive stories ('At least I mostly managed to do the right thing by my kids') and then develops new possibilities for the future based on the alternative story ('I will be a worthwhile person again').

Narrative therapy is directly and explicitly concerned with issues of justice and power. It positions itself to ensure that these issues are addressed as a result of therapy, using people's own language and way of describing things to explore their experiences ('The idea that women should do what they are told seems to have a strong influence on your life'). It is concerned to ensure that interventions do not inadvertently keep people in their place and that they are actually liberated from the problems at play in their lives ('When you are living a life free of violence, what will you be able to stand up and say about your rights as a woman?' rather than simply 'What will be happening when you are safe?').

It is beyond the scope of this book, and not its purpose, to properly describe narrative therapy. However, an attempt is made is here to briefly capture its essence and the core strategies used by narrative practitioners.

Narrative therapy was pioneered by social workers Michael White and David Epston. Like solution-focused practice, narrative therapy focuses on people's skills, experience, knowledge, values and aspirations to resolve problems. It moves away from pathologising, viewing problems as separate from the person. The worker forms a collaborative relationship with people and treats them as their own experts. Narrative therapy avoids advice-giving and does not impose ideas and opinions.

Narrative therapy as noted, however, differs from solution-focused therapy in that it explicitly concerns itself with issues of justice and power by challenging the dominant ideas that negatively affect people's lives. It is concerned with the wider cultural and political context of people's experience and considers issues relating to class, race and ethnicity, gender, age, ability and sexuality and how 'dominant discourse' around these negatively impinges on people's lives and identities. In this context it looks at stories that can be told about the ways in which problems influence people's lives.

'How has homophobia affected your life?'

It explores the patterns or themes that emerge in people's experience over time and the contexts in which these have unfolded.

'So this has made you constantly anxious and lonely and unable to be yourself all through your adolescence and into your adulthood?'

The meaning people give to the stories they carry about themselves affects their relationships, the way they see their past, themselves and their future. This also affects what people believe is possible or not possible for them.

'I feel so lonely most of the time. I guess I was always a loner. Even when I was a kid I had trouble making friends. Other kids would bully me and I'd retreat to protect myself. Then I was too anxious to make new friends. I suppose that's just how it is and I have to live with it.'

Problem stories have a way of gathering their own momentum where certain events and experiences are given weight and importance and others are neglected, ignored or not even noticed. A narrative emerges over time that consists of a dominant story so powerful (for example, 'homosexuality is disgusting') that it affects every aspect of the person's life; where some experiences, knowledge and preferences that would otherwise counter this are subjugated or made invisible (for example, circumstances where the person has not let fear of homophobia stop them being who they are, or noticing when others respect gay people just as they do anyone else). So narrative therapy assists people whose lives have been adversely affected by dominant negative stories to 're-author' their lives; that is, create an alternative story out of the ways in which they have been able to cope, manage, beat the problem, create positive differences and so on.

'I had a cousin and we were really close. I loved every moment we spent together. And my Aunt Joy loved me to death!'

This also involves giving new meaning to past experience.

'So your cousin and aunt and the German people next door — they really loved you regardless? What does that say about you?'

This alternative story, created by people themselves, is then used to help create a different future to the one the problem had planned for them.

'How might knowing this help you overcome the fear of homophobia?'

In this way, a far richer alternative to simply 'solving a problem' is created:

Narrative Therapists [sic] are interested to work with people to bring forth and thicken stories that do not support or sustain problems. As people begin to inhabit and live out their alternative stories, the results are beyond solving problems. Within the new stories, people live out new self images, new possibilities for relationships and new futures.

Freedman & Combs, 1996, p. 16

The worker asks questions to link times when the problem had less or no control, to new possibilities in the future, for example:

'Would it be true to say that these were times when anxiety and loneliness weren't in your life? Can you tell me more about the closeness to your cousin and aunt? How might this closeness figure in your life again?'

(The story of the women's group on pages 83–86 is another example of how this process can work.)

Separating the person from the problem
The idea that 'the problem is the problem; the person is not the problem' is given special practical meaning through what is known as externalising. The concept originates from the work of Michael White and David Epston (1990).

It involves 'naming the problem' by carefully listening to the way in which people refer to the problem; the way the person describes the problem and the meaning they are giving to the experience; how it is affecting the person's life and the language they use to describe it.

Narrative therapy focuses on how the problem operates in the person's life and their relationship with the problem. It invites the person to name the problem ('the homophobia', 'the violence', 'anxiety', 'loneliness'). This externalisation separates the person from the problem. When the problem is viewed as being a part of the person (or family or community) it frames them as part of the problem. When it is located outside the person it suggests the opposite, showing deep respect and making change more possible.

Narrative therapy uses externalising as a matter of course as a means of separating the person from the problem (Morgan 2000, pp. 17-20). The therapist explores how the problem influences and controls the person's life ('What happens when homophobia takes over?'), its history and development over time ('When did you first notice homophobia controlling your life?'). (See pages 135-138 for further discussion of externalising).

Unique outcomes and alternative stories

The narrative practitioner then proceeds to support the person to develop an alternative story (the closeness to cousin and aunt, for example). The alternative story is different to the dominant negative story that people carry about the problem and its effects. Alternative stories come through looking for unique outcomes. At a simple level these are much like exceptions in solution-focused therapy.

Alice Morgan (2000, p. 78) refers to a unique outcome as something 'outside the problem's influence'. So anything that's happening or that people are doing when the problem has no control or less control—where the person has been able to be in control rather than the problem being in control—can be understood as a unique outcome. This could be, for example, when the loneliness, anxiety, violence, or homophobia was not in control, and what the person was doing then that made a difference.

These unique outcomes have a history, context and meaning so when this is explored an 'alternative story' emerges. 'I used be really confident then' represents an alternative story to the dominant 'problem saturated' story ('I've always been hopeless with relationships'). Deficit descriptions are changed or reframed in this process.

Finding 'unique outcomes' or exceptions is a key strategy used to help people change the dominant negative story. Positive qualities and strengths can also be externalised to enable the person to create an alternative story to the dominant problem-saturated one ('Would it be true to say that when 'closeness' is around anxiety goes away?').

This can open up rich descriptions of what people value and hope for. It supports them to create futures that are different to what the problem had planned for them.

Narrative therapy is often supported by the use of documents such as letters, awards, certificates, greeting cards, journalling and so on to support the process of writing an alternative story and to support change efforts (see, for example, Morgan 2000, pp. 85–114).

What the strengths approach can look like
So far we have explored the strengths emphasis and its importance in bringing change, the concept of power-with and the essence of just practice. We have also considered the contribution of solution-focused and narrative ideas to the strengths approach.

The following story illustrates the dynamic application of the principles and ideas of the strengths approach in a therapeutic practice setting. This story reflects just practice, belief in people's strengths and capacities, self-determination and the sharing of power.

Workers who provide support services to women with mental health issues noticed that many of the women didn't seem to progress. From the stories the women shared about their lives, it seemed that they were unable to get beyond the issues they were confronted with from day to day. The workers wondered about the effect and effectiveness of support, treatment and case management. They felt that services were inadequate in addressing the issues in these women's lives and wondered whether there was a way that they could be more helpful. On consulting with the women they found that they saw things the same way and decided to start a group. They promoted the group by describing it as 'an opportunity to share stories of your life with other women and think about new possibilities'.

The women were keen to meet and share their experiences, despite a level of anxiety about what the group experience might bring. For the first three to four weeks most of the women had to be transported to the group meetings or take convoluted routes for fear of a panic attack on the way. In the first meetings they simply shared their experiences. It emerged that all of the women were suffering from 'clinically diagnosed depression'. All of them except one had suffered sexual abuse as children, all of them except another had experienced (or were still experiencing) family violence. All of them experienced fractured relationships with partners, husbands, their children and friends. All of them believed that they were 'bad mothers'. It emerged that all of the women were receiving professional mental health care and were on medication—and had been for as long as twenty-five years.

As time went by the women were assisted to explore the meaning of their experiences. They discovered how much they had in common with each other and with many other women. Some of them had questioned their position as clients of mental health services and now the group began to 'unpack' that experience as well as their experience as women. They began to question the meaning they had given to their experiences. Where did the labels, diagnosis and prognosis come from? Why was it that they had learned to believe that much of what they had experienced was their own fault; that there was something wrong with them; that they could do very little if anything about their situation; that they would never be 'cured'; that life would never be any better?

The women identified origins of the powerfully influential ideas they had about themselves—sexism and patriarchy that gave way to the abuse they had experienced as children and women; ageism that gave way to their silencing as children; and 'healthism' that gave way to the prejudice and marginalisation they'd experienced as a result of their diagnosis and the prognosis that arose from it.

The women in the group were able to identify and describe their personal experiences and the specific sources of the ideas and beliefs that they had taken on. They could see the influences that schooling, peers, the media and their families had had on making these beliefs so powerful.

In addition, professional 'knowledge' had defined their 'problem'—depression—and what was possible for them. Despite good intentions this definition and everything it entails had inadvertently kept the women in their place. It added to already deeply entrenched ideas that affected their identities to such a degree that they felt powerless and hopeless about any alternative life or future.

During this time the women felt validated and started to feel 'normal' in their circumstances. They began to get in touch with their strengths and share stories of the positive aspects of their lives. This enabled them to see themselves in different *ways. They were able to begin to imagine new possibilities for their lives; to describe a new future and decide the steps they would take to get there. The group met for eight months. After only a few weeks, each and every woman was able to get to meetings without support.*

By the time the women stopped meeting, profound change had occurred in their lives. They had built strong relationships and a sense of community among themselves and they continued to share their lives in friendship. They had mended relationships with partners and family members. One had separated from a partner and in doing so, freed herself from a life of emotional and physical abuse. All except two of them were free of the need for medication.

The following example is an indication of the depth of change that occurred for the women: One member of the group had not hugged her children since they were toddlers. As a result of her time with the group, she decided to share her changing story of the past with her adult children, her hopes for the future and her love for them in ways that she had never been able to do before. She and her family established a new tradition that none of them would ever have imagined: a family group hug every week!

Stories of this nature may not be uncommon. But what does it take to enable processes that lead to such outcomes? What was the role of the workers in this story and what did they do to assist the changes that occurred?

The workers believed in the women; they believed that they had the capacity to make changes despite the odds. They held a deep respect for the women's intrinsic worth and their right to self-determination. They knew that they did not hold the answers for the women; that the answers could only be found within the women themselves.

They opened the way for the creation of a safe, trusting and inclusive environment where power imbalances and transparency were addressed at every level. The women and workers established the 'rules' for the group together, based on the principles of respect, respectful listening and confidentiality. The workers made no assumptions about how the group should be run and set no agenda for the group other than to create a safe and positive environment for sharing stories and aspirations. This meant that, right from the start, the women themselves determined the agenda for the group, its meetings and every aspect of its sharing and activity.

The women responded to an invitation to give evaluation and feedback. They constructed an evaluation tool that they used after every meeting. The workers did not ask the women to undertake any task or activity that they did not undertake themselves. The group was introduced to the workers' supervisor. The workers also reported back to the women what they discussed and learnt from their weekly meetings with their supervisor.

The respect embodied by the workers in engaging with this group of women was given expression in ways that reflect the essence of the strengths approach. They demonstrated:

- listening to, validating and responding respectfully to people's personal stories
- helping people to explore the meaning of their experiences within wider social, structural and cultural contexts
- helping people to describe their experiences in specific and concrete terms so as to respect uniqueness
- helping people to identify commonalities in their experience so as to develop a 'big picture' of the experience and help normalise it
- helping people to identify their strengths and the stories that can be told about those strengths. This generates hope and enables stories other than the dominant, problem-saturated ones to be told
- helping people to explore their values, aspirations and dreams and assisting them to describe them in specific and concrete ways
- helping people to build new experiences based on the stories of their strengths and aspirations
- helping to identify and mobilise resources that can support and complement people's aspirations and strengths, and their efforts toward change
- helping people to develop plans and identify steps that can be taken, based on their strengths, resources and aspirations.

For the women, it was the experience of validation and a growing appreciation of their commonalities that built trust and opened the way for further exploration. It was the stories of the women's strengths that enabled them to start to see themselves differently and become hopeful. It was the exploration of the dominant cultures surrounding them that enabled the women to explore their experiences from different perspectives and 're-story' their experiences. Their 'strengths stories' enabled the development of enough hope for the women to begin to make different plans for themselves, to become agents of change in their relationships and roles, and to take control of their lives.

Some cautions

There are some risks associated with being purist in the way we apply these approaches. I remember the story of a lone father of five children going to see a counsellor who happened to be a narrative therapist. He told me how the therapist kept asking about the past and 'playing games' by trying to get him to name his problems. He said that all he wanted was a few ideas about how to deal with some of the difficult behaviour of his children and some support with bringing up five kids. He was clear that he was not feeling oppressed by his circumstances. While an experienced practitioner would know not to go down this path so easily it is clear that in such circumstances a narrative approach was not the way to go. It may well be that a solution-focused response would be more appropriate with a confident dad who does not find his circumstances oppressive. He, in fact, engaged some practical help from a local government service whose worker simply began by asking him about what he wanted to change, what he could do himself and what else would help.

At the same time, when it comes to being strictly solution-focused, there is a risk that problems may be considered and discussed only in so far as is necessary for engaging people, without sufficiently attending to their story, normalising their feelings or validating their experience, and missing an important opportunity to explore meaning. The emphasis on solutions and exceptions can lead to a pragmatic goal-setting process that ignores power dynamics and political realities. This emphasis on solutions can over-ride the importance of deep listening—of acknowledging people's experiences and the meaning they give to them.

Hart (1995, p. 185), in evaluating narrative therapy and the contribution of Michael White, makes comparisons between White and de Shazer.

> De Shazer will not return to discussions about problems and concerns and will focus only on 'solution talk'. He states that it is not necessary to talk about

problems or concerns and one only does so far as it is essential to engage the client. White is different in this respect. He uses the new story that the person has discovered through the unique outcomes [exceptions], to talk about ways that the person can then defeat the influence of the problems or concerns and its meaning in their lives. From working with the solutions they go in different ways; White focuses on meaning, narrative and power while de Shazer focuses on behaviour, goals and pragmatics.

De Shazer has eschewed the debates on gender, race, culture and power in therapy. This denies the reality of power in the context of people's lives and the way that defining the problem is subject to the mechanisms of power. This refers to both overt power (i.e. the person is in danger if they speak about it, frequently the case in domestic violence situations or where there are secrets in the family) and covert power (where knowledges about particular aspects of a person's life do not gain privilege and receive any validation). Both these mechanisms will cause the process and the content of problems to be subjugated i.e. hidden from view.

Without serious attention to the wider context of people's realities strengths-based practice can become a ritual of positive thinking. This may make people feel better and bring improvements but does not lead to liberation from the constraints that keep people in their place.

> ...solution-focused therapists steer the conversation toward hypothetical solutions, exceptions to the problem, and solution descriptions. Narrative therapists elicit descriptions of a client's agency in relation to the problem, and deconstruct the discourses that support the problem. While a respectful solution-focused therapist would not shut down conversations about larger cultural constructs, SFT [solution-focused therapy] would not go there by default. On the other hand, a key focus of narrative therapy is examination of the effect of discourses, and clients' responses to them.
>
> Chang & Nyland 2013, pp. 73–4

In the strengths approach, both solution-focused and narrative practice are seen as highly important and valuable approaches. They integrate with principles of just practice and power-with.

In summary, the strengths approach is a power-with approach which:

- invites us to acknowledge and address the power imbalances between workers and agencies, and those who access services.

- leads us to identify and explore the entrenched messages that define people, keep them in their place and prevent them from being the best they can be.

- challenges us to be cautious about the way our own knowledge and other 'knowledges' can disempower and colonise people.

- challenges us to be honest, open, transparent, consultative, inclusive and collaborative and gives us ways to do this.

- enables us to identify and address the social, personal, cultural and structural constraints to people's growth and liberation.

These responses make genuine choice and self-determination possible because people's real aspirations and choices cannot otherwise be truly considered and freely chosen.

Chapter Five

Processes and Skills of The Strengths Approach

'The strengths approach invites us to listen for three essential things: people's lived experience, their aspirations and their strengths and capacities.'

~

'In the strengths approach—in any interaction, at any point in our relationship with people, and throughout the whole of that relationship—we will be engaged in processes and ongoing dialogue about the worries in people's lives, about how they feel and see things, about their strengths, about their aspirations, hopes and dreams, and about their resources, plans, and progress.'

~

'Questions that presuppose people's ability to find their own answers are very powerful. They embody the belief that people are their own experts. Workers become facilitators and colleagues, not experts on other people.'

The strengths approach is a values-based approach to empowerment and self-determination. Its values affect everything we do in our work with people. These values have practical expression. Every principle articulated philosophically and theoretically can be put into practice through respectful, considered thinking and reflection, and skillful, just, empathic action. They come together in a practice framework that shares power, is inclusive, collaborative, and strengths-based; that validates people's experience and honours their strengths and aspirations.

A practice framework provides a clear understanding of what underpins and informs our work. It consists of an accessible mapping of practices that are grounded in a set of values and principles that are ethical, defensible and explicit. It provides a clear understanding of the principles, values, knowledge and skills that guide practice. These, when articulated as processes, provide logic and guidance for professional judgement, critical decision-making, action, reflection and learning. They provide a conceptual 'mind map' for undertaking our work.

In this chapter, a framework for using the strengths approach will be established. It will incorporate all of the principles discussed in previous chapters. Processes and skills of the strengths approach and the relationship between them will also be explored.

Relationships and engagement

It has long been established that a relationship of trust and respect is essential for effective practice and successful outcomes (Rogers 1951). Building a relationship of trust is the foundation for all respectful and constructive helping processes. The quality and effectiveness of all human service interventions depend on how well workers engage people they work with. Relationship building is inseparable from engagement. Engagement can be defined as a connection with others to form and sustain a constructive working relationship. Without engagement there can be no working relationship. Partnerships cannot be formed and goals cannot be established. This is no less true for managers and their relationships with their staff and peers.

Building trust is facilitated by genuine interest in, and validation of, people's experiences, perspectives, strengths, capacities and aspirations. Engagement is more likely to occur when we listen, consult, establish common ground and work as part of a team. It is also facilitated by transparent practices and assisting people to take ownership of their own change process. It is richly enhanced by a genuine and abiding interest in people's strengths.

These components of engagement are not only facilitated by the worker, but are also the responsibility of the worker. In other words it's the worker's job to create the conditions necessary for people to engage, not the other way around!

 EXERCISE – Engagement

Imagine that you are at a function or activity where you don't know anyone.

- What can others do to help you engage?

- What can you do to help yourself engage?

- What other factors help you engage?

- What does this mean for practice?

Listening

> When you talk you are only repeating what you already know.
> But when you listen, you may learn something new.
>
> Dalai Lama

Listening is the skill most critical for engagement. The desire to be helpful can sometimes get in the way of good listening and therefore engagement. Sometimes our enthusiasm for finding strengths and positive stories can get in the way of listening to people's hardships and worries. Equally, our interest in the problem can blind us from seeing strengths. It's important to remember that listening is not the same as problem-solving, although essential to it. The skills of active listening are important (summarising, checking, paraphrasing, acknowledging, appropriate body language, eye contact and so on). These skills help ensure that we:

- seek to understand and clarify what is communicated

- do not interrupt, judge or interpret

- do not seek to change what people are saying or alter their meaning

- acknowledge and validate experiences and perspectives

- seek to hear 'the whole story' including the issues, feelings, context, constraints, strengths and aspirations

- are able to describe people's experience, feelings, concerns, strengths, aspirations, goals and plans in the same way they do.

Good listening is an essential skill in working with people. The strengths approach invites us not only to listen well, but to listen for three essential things:

- people's lived experience, the meaning they give it and the context in which the experience takes place
- people's aspirations, preferences and goals
- people's strengths and capacities and the stories behind them.

Strengths-based listening assists people to reframe their realities and experiences, establishing a springboard for ways forward. The following practice story comes from an interview by Andrew Shirres (2016a) with Phil Watson, a family services team leader. Reflected in this story is the power that acknowledgement, validation and listening in a strengths-based way have to create change. Strengths can be found even in negative experience and behaviour, and the way we frame people's behaviour can profoundly affect change.

Phil:
I worked with a family recently and the guy had a background with the gangs. [He] was inclined to be quite explosive and had a history of being quite angry. One of the things from strengths-based [practice] that made it really easy was just to sit ... and when he got angry ... say to him, 'Hey look, I really appreciate how much you care because your anger is evidence of the fact that you care very, very deeply about this.' And what that really did was gave him an opportunity to actually be validated. For actually having a strength of feeling and concern about his family ... not being judged about the way in which he behaved or demonstrated that. That then gave him an opportunity to sit back and think, 'Yeah, actually ... It's actually OK for me to care. Maybe my behaviour isn't the best.' So it really then gave us an opportunity to have a conversation about ... it being OK for him to feel those things really deeply but was there a better way that he could manage, that actually wouldn't impact or make people around him frightened?

Andrew:
So rather than tell him how he should manage something like that kind of behaviour his participation in that process, in designing the actions himself, if you like, made a difference to your working relationship?

Phil:

Oh, absolutely because it then meant that he understood for the very first time that his getting angry was not necessarily a bad thing 'cos it demonstrated to him that he really did care about things. And previously he had been told that obviously he didn't care 'cos all he did was get angry. And strengths-based [practice] allowed him to see things in such a way that he could address his behaviour. He really just needed someone to acknowledge the fact that he cared. And for someone to actually identify that just because we behave badly doesn't mean we have bad intentions. And once he could distinguish the difference between his belief and his behaviour, he was then able to act in a way in which he could begin to match his beliefs and his behaviour. And I think that is one of the great things about strengths-based [practice]. It allows people to be empowered to match their beliefs and behaviours in a positive way.

Acknowledgement and validation

Acknowledging and validating people's experiences are primary characteristics of listening. They involve gaining a clear picture of what's happening by checking our understanding and the meaning people are giving to their experiences. It can be difficult for anyone to move beyond the problems facing them unless they feel heard and validated, as the following example illustrates.

Maura came to a counsellor because of various difficulties she'd been having with her daughter's behaviour. She told the counsellor that she had experienced family violence for some years until her husband took his life six months earlier. Just three months ago she and her daughter had lost everything when their house burnt down. Family members and friends had supported Maura but the counsellor was struck by Maura's strength in being able to survive the experiences she'd had. She simply acknowledged and validated Maura's experience and shared her admiration of Maura's ability to cope despite the serious trauma she had experienced. She asked what had helped her get through. Maura said she was still recovering and that she would be for a long time. She said the thing that helped most was people just being there and listening to how she was feeling.

The counsellor asked Maura what sort of support her daughter, Phoebe, had had. Maura started to cry and said that it was something she hadn't really given enough attention to. Two weeks later when Maura returned for her next appointment, she reported that things had changed for the better already; that she'd been spending a lot of extra time with Phoebe lately and just listening to her and acknowledging her sadness and anger. The counsellor asked her what she thought had made the difference. Maura said that when she came last time it helped a lot to have someone understand and appreciate her situation. She'd realised that Phoebe hadn't really had the same opportunity.

Part of the process of validation involves exploring the social, cultural and structural context of experience. Identifying external factors that impinge on experience and behaviour can help remove self-blame and alter the way we perceive our reality and ourselves. Normalising enables people to see that others have such experiences and respond in similar ways in similar circumstances; that given their reality, their responses are understandable. This is an important characteristic of validation because it enables people to discover common experience and feel a sense of community with others facing similar challenges and reactions. The skill of normalising is discussed in greater detail later in this chapter.

Stages of the strengths approach and a mind map for practice

In the strengths approach—in any interaction, at any point in our relationship with people, and throughout the whole of that relationship—we will be engaged in processes and ongoing dialogue about the worries in people's lives, about how they feel and see things, about their strengths, about their aspirations, hopes and dreams, and about their resources, plans, and progress.

A simple but consistently useful guide that incorporates these processes and associated skills has emerged from principles discussed in previous chapters. It was pioneered in 1990 at St Luke's (now merged with Anglicare Victoria) in Bendigo, Australia and has been widely adopted since then. This guide represents a framework or 'mind map' that consists of six key stages for reflection, learning, planning, action and review:

1. Listening to people's stories, exploring the context and meaning they give their experience, and identifying the core issues (including cultural and structural constraints)

2. Developing a picture of the future and setting goals through an exploration of people's aspirations

3. Identifying and highlighting strengths and exceptions to problems

4. Identifying additional resources that complement people's strengths and goals

5. Mobilising strengths and resources through a plan of action

6. Reviewing and evaluating progress and change.

The following table, known as the 'column approach' (also pioneered at St Luke's in 1990—see O'Neil & McCashen 1991), illustrates the use of questions for conversations based on the first five steps of this framework. The column approach is a paperwork tool that is used to record, in summary point form, conversations and reflections between workers and those accessing services. (Using the column approach as a paperwork tool for practice is discussed further in chapter six)

The Column Approach

STORIES AND ISSUES	THE PICTURE OF THE FUTURE	STRENGTHS AND EXCEPTIONS	OTHER RESOURCES	PLANS AND STEPS
Ask questions that invite people to share their stories and enable them to clarify the issues, such as:	Ask questions that help people explore their aspirations, dreams, interests and goals, such as:	Ask questions that help people explore their strengths and the exceptions to the issues, such as:	Ask questions that help people identify resources that might help them reach their goals, such as:	Ask questions that help people specify steps towards their goals, such as:
What's happening? How do you feel about this? How long has this been a problem? How is it affecting you and others?	What do you want to be happening instead? What will be different when the issues are addressed?	What strengths do you have that might be helpful? What do you do well? What's happening when the issues aren't around?	Who else might be able to help? What other support or resources might be useful?	Given your picture of the future, strengths and resources, what steps can be taken? Who will do what, when, how?

The following example illustrates the use of the framework of stages outlined above.

Miang's husband died five years ago. She has three teenage boys. Two of them, Jonah, 16 years old, and Toby, 14 years old, refused to go to school and spent much of their days on the streets. Her third son, Patrick, 19 years old, had left school and was trying to find work. He and Miang would argue a lot because he would lie around the house a lot. Miang was struggling financially and suffered back pain, making many day-to-day activities difficult. Miang's worker, Poh, had been providing support to her for around four weeks. She had visited her a number of times and they had talked a lot about her situation. Poh had tried to engage the boys but had not been successful.

Using the strengths-based mind map as a guide, Poh had helped Miang talk about the things that were worrying her and how these were affecting the family's life. They had talked a lot about the strengths in the family, the good things about the boys, what Miang hoped for and needed to happen, what she wanted for her boys and herself. They identified resources and supports that could help and plans that could make things different.

The following column approach captures a summary of their conversations including initial steps that could be taken. Step six is not included. Reviewing efforts and progress is the focus of following meetings.

Miang's Five Column Plan

WORRIES	PICTURE OF THE FUTURE	STRENGTHS AND EXCEPTIONS	RESOURCES	STEPS AND PLANS
• Jonah and Toby not at school.	• A job for Patrick.	• I love my boys.	• Thomas, my brother, and my sister Lucy always look out for me.	• First priority – get some exercise. See if Lee could come walking with me.
• The boy's future.	• The boys are back at school or some other education.	• Patrick finished school and keeps looking for work.	• The Chinese community – Paulina and Lucy are still involved.	• See Lucy and Paulina about some of the Chinese Association's activities.
• The boys might get into trouble.	• I have a job too.	• Jonah and Paul look up to their Uncle Russell.	• Uncle Russell does Tai Chi.	
• The boys coming home late.	• The boys are doing things they like.	• I have good friends – Paulina and Lee.	• Tai Chi Association.	• See if Russell can motivate the boys to get back to Tai Chi and take them.
• Arguments with the boys.	• I know where the boys are and that they are safe.	• Jonah looks after the garden and likes it (takes after his father).	• The gardening club.	• Thomas could help.
• Paying the bills.				
• Can't afford things for the boys.	• Lots of good times with friends and family.	• My community and family stopped me going downhill in the past.		• Find out about job training for Patrick.
• I want to work but have had no job for twenty years.	• I am involved with my community again.	• Jonah and Toby enjoy Tai Chi.		• Ask family about some moral support for Patrick.
• My back stops me doing things.	• I feel good about myself and enjoy life more.	• My back is better when I get exercise.		• See if the gardening club could help with plants and ideas for Jonah if he's interested.
• Losing connections with my community.		• When the boys are happy we don't argue.		
• I sometimes get depressed.		• The boys have stayed out of trouble so far.		

Each of the six parts (the five columns above plus the subsequent reviewing of progress) is a process in itself, valid in its own right and can make up all of a given interaction (for example, listening to the concerns and worries). Each part of the process can be used in relation to any or all of the other parts depending on what is being shared by people (for example, when discussing the picture of the future, drawing on examples of good things in the past to get ideas about what's possible for the future). A worker may, in one moment or interaction, be asking about a person's experience and in the next responding to a strength implied or mentioned by the person. In another moment or interaction, they may be talking about the person's concerns again, then in the next moment asking about the person's hopes based on remarks they made.

Whatever the case, ongoing dialogue about the worries in people's lives, about how they feel and see things, about their strengths, about their aspirations, and goals, resources and plans, can be aligned over time to make useful sense of experience, bring hope and gain direction for the way forward. (For discussion of the relationship between exploring strengths and exceptions and developing a picture of the future, see pages 129–130).

The framework provides a versatile map for conversation, reflection and planning and should be used according to people's readiness. The process is meant as a guide to be used flexibly in responding to people's sharing over time. Too much structure can lead to the worker driving the process. At the same time, too little structure can be unhelpful.

There are dangers in being too prescriptive or simplistic in using this strengths-based mind map. Sometimes people are not able to get in touch with their aspirations or describe a picture of the future because they don't feel hopeful enough. They can feel so overwhelmed by the problems they face that it is difficult to imagine that things can be different. This is typically the case in instances of abuse, depression, or trauma. Taking people down the path of 'future picture exploration' in this situation can be disrespectful, unhelpful and counterproductive. In this case giving priority to validating experiences and exploring strengths and exceptions is more likely to help bring enough hope to describe a picture of the future. At the risk of being too simplistic, this can be seen to align more closely to a narrative practice process. In these circumstances the process looks like this:

1. Listening to people's stories, exploring the context and the meaning they give their experience, and identifying the core issues (including cultural and structural constraints)

2. Identifying and highlighting strengths and exceptions to problems

3. Developing a picture of the future and setting goals through an exploration of people's aspirations

4. Identifying additional resources that complement people's strengths and goals

5. Mobilising strengths and resources through a plan of action

6. Reviewing and evaluating progress and change.

Sometimes people do not need to explore and analyse their past. They may already be sufficiently in touch with positive experiences or take little to get in touch with strengths and exceptions. In this case priority is given to exploring people's aspirations. Consideration of strengths and exceptions occurs within the context of these aspirations. The process in these circumstances is like the one outlined on page 97.

The implications and usefulness of the framework for service delivery, support work (including planning and management), staff supervision and community work are explored in following chapters.

Strengths-based skills

The single most important challenge in the strengths approach is ensuring that each and every part of the change process is owned and directed by the people accessing the services. Workers become facilitators of change as opposed to drivers of change. They do this via a range of skills that are particular to strengths-based approaches. These skills are founded on values and beliefs of the strengths approach. They are based on faith in people and positive attitudes to them. They arise organically from strengths-based ways of thinking that awaken curiosity about people's experience, context, strengths and aspirations. They also develop over time through practice and reflection.

Strengths-based skills reflect the various principles and beliefs of the strengths approach and are inseparable from the strengths-based mind map discussed above. Each of these skills in themselves can be understood as a process when put into practice. They include:

- acknowledging and validating people's experience and feelings as we listen to identify the problem, and understand its context and impact (discussed at the beginning of this chapter)
- strengths-based questioning
- developing concrete description
- identifying and mobilising strengths, resources and exceptions
- reframing
- normalising
- developing a picture of the future and establishing goals
- noticing and measuring change
- externalising
- identifying steps and strategies.

Conditions for change and empowerment

Exercising power-with in conjunction with an emphasis on strengths contributes significantly to creating the conditions necessary for change and empowerment. These conditions are absolutely critical to change that aims to be self-determining and empowering. They are also strengths! To make change people need to:

- feel safe, confident
- share their stories and experiences
- feel heard and validated
- know what works and what doesn't
- notice and appreciate change and progress
- be open to other truths, meanings and possibilities
- have a sense of hope
- have a picture of where it is they want to get to: a picture of the future
- be sufficiently motivated to engage in change and be able to address the cultural and structural constraints that get in the way
- be aware of, appreciate and be able to mobilise their strengths
- have sufficient resources
- know what to do and how to do it
- be a full participant in the processes of change including decision-making
- be connected with others who will support and appreciate their efforts and progress.

It is the worker's job to help create these conditions. These conditions are embedded in the strengths-based mind map discussed on previous pages. This is illustrated in the following table.

Conditions Needed for Change and Empowerment

ISSUES	THE PICTURE OF THE FUTURE	STRENGTHS AND EXCEPTIONS	RESOURCES	PLANS AND STEPS	REFLECT AND LEARN
• Feeling safe and confident in the relationship. • Able to share stories and experiences. • Feeling heard and validated. • Knowing what needs to change.	• A sense of hope. • Sufficient motivation. • Openness to other possibilities. • Having a picture of the future.	• Being aware of and appreciating strengths and positive stories. • Knowing what works and what doesn't.	• Sufficient support and resources.	• Knowing what to do and how to do it. • The ability to mobilise strengths and resources.	• Knowing what works and what doesn't. • Noticing and appreciating change and progress.

EXERCISE – Conditions for change

- What helps change and empowerment?
  (Think about what helps you to grow, learn and become empowered.
  What do you need?)

With regard to your current job role:
- What conditions are currently present that enable change, growth and empowerment?

- Can you identify the conditions for change that are present in your relationships with people you are working with?

- What conditions for change are present in their lives?

- Can you identify any conditions that aren't present in your relationships with people you are working with?

- What can you do to address these?

Incorporating the beliefs of the strengths approach into the strengths-based mind map

In the following table various underlying beliefs of the strengths approach are incorporated into the strengths-based mind map for practice. This illustrates ways in which beliefs of the approach contribute to the various stages of practice. They rest on and affect power-with practices.

Beliefs of the Strengths Approach and the Strengths-based Mind Map

ISSUES	THE PICTURE OF THE FUTURE	STRENGTHS AND EXCEPTIONS	RESOURCES	PLANS AND STEPS	REFLECT AND LEARN
• The problem is the problem, the person is not the problem. • Problems can blind people from noticing and appreciating their strengths and their capacity to find solutions. • People can change.	• Focussing on possibilities helps people take responsibility. • People need to have a picture of what they want things to be like. • The solution is more important than the problem.	• All people have strengths and capacities. • Problems have exceptions that expose strengths and expertise and give clues to solutions. • Positive stories bring hope • Focussing on strengths and exceptions encourages people to take responsibility.	• People need support and resources. • People are interdependent. • Resources should be added in ways that complement people's strengths and capacities, not as a way of compensating for deficits.	• People can change. • Small change leads to bigger change.	• People can learn from mistakes. • Change takes time. • Noticing change generates hope. • The power for change is within us.

People are their own experts.
POWER-WITH: Respect, Inclusion, Collaboration, Teamwork, Transparency, Empowerment, Self-determination

Questions as the basis for skills

The importance of questions in strengths-based practice cannot be over-emphasised. Questions that presuppose people's ability to find their own answers are very powerful. They embody the belief that people are their own experts. Workers become facilitators and colleagues, not experts on other people. Strengths-based principles and frameworks rely primarily on finding the right questions as opposed to knowing the answers—an impossibility when it comes to assisting empowerment and self-determination! Assuming the role of expert can get in the way of empowerment. Questions open up possibilities and enable ownership of the change process.

Strengths-based questions are characterised by:

- not knowing (suspending assumptions and using open questions)

- curiosity about and appreciation of experience, context, constraints, strengths, exceptions and aspirations

- open invitations to share stories and explore values

- the belief that people are their own experts

- the belief that people can change and grow

- expansiveness (room to move from specific descriptions to exploring the context of experience, feelings and meaning)

- concrete description (clearly and specifically describing the issues, strengths and aspirations)

- positive framing

- respectful and context-friendly language.

More specifically there are many sorts of questions that can be asked that are purposeful for change and empowerment. Note that they are inherent in the strengths-based mind map. They can be categorised as questions that:

- explore the problems and their influence on people's lives

- identify and explore constraints

- externalise the problem

- find exceptions/unique outcomes

- explore positive differences and experiences

- find and story the good things in people's lives, past and present

- find and story strengths and build confidence and self-esteem

- explore meaning, values, aspirations, hopes and dreams

- explore possibilities

- develop a picture of the future

- identify supports and resources

- invite people to make their own decisions and decide on steps and plans

- help people notice and measure change.

Some strengths-based questions
for empowerment and self-determination

Before moving on to explore the skills of the strengths approach, here is sample set of strengths-based questions derived from the stages specified in the strengths-based mind map.

About the concerns, difficulties and constraints – to understand feelings, experience and the influence of the problem:

- What's happening?

- How are you feeling about these things?

- What does this mean to you?

- How do you see things?

- What is there in common with the experience of others?

- When did the problem come along? How long has the problem been around?

- How does it operate in your life?

- Where did it come from?

- Which part of your life does it affect (work, home, relationships, hopes for the future, thoughts and so on)?

- How does it work against you?

- How does it work against others?

- Has this or anything like it happened before?

- What are the trends that are evident?

- How often do these things happen?

- Where do these things happen?

- When do these things happen?

- How bad do things get?

- What's happening then?

- Between 1 and 10 with things at their worst at 1, and at their best at 10, where are things now?

- Is there anything that's getting in the way of managing the problem?

- What do you say or think to yourself about the way things are?

- Are there things that are keeping you stuck?
- What control do you have over these things?
- When are these problems and feelings not so bad?
- What's happening then?

About what works to make things better – to get clues and ideas about what to do to change things:

- What's kept you going despite the difficulties?
- What was happening before these difficulties came along in your life?
- When were things better than they are now (even if only a little bit better)?
- What was happening then?
- What were you doing?
- What else was different then?
- Can you think of times when things have been above 5?
- Can you think of times when they have been at 10?
- What was different then?
- What's stopped you from slipping below 1?
- Are there times when the problem isn't there?
- What's happening then? What's different?
- What are you doing differently?
- What are you thinking that leads you to do things differently?
- Can you tell me about times when the problem didn't get the better of you?
- What were you doing then?
- Are there times when you have been able to stand up to problem?
- What was happening then?
- How did you go about that?
- Can you think of times when the problem doesn't have/hasn't had as much control?

- What's different then?

- What are you already doing that makes a difference (even if only a small difference)?

About exceptions/unique outcomes that are uncovered – to help create a new story:

- How did you prepare for these positive differences and the things that work?

- What do you think was the turning point?

- What exactly did you do?

- What were you thinking then that led you to do this?

- Did you plan this? Did you make the decision?

- Did others play a part?

- What was the response of others?

- What does this say about you as a person?

- What might others say if they knew you were able to achieve this?

- What personal qualities does it make evident?

- What have you learned from this?

- What does this say for your hopes, plans and dreams?

- What are the other positive events, experiences and circumstances in your life?

- If you were to put the stories about the good things together what would you be able to tell others?

- Given this 'new story' (the trend suggested by these good things) what do you think could be different in the future?

- What seems possible?

- What would be different to what (externalisation) had planned for you?

About strengths – to identify and 'story' the skills people have that they can draw on to build confidence and self-esteem:

- What do you care about?
- What are you interested in?
- What do you like doing?
- What are you good at?
- What do the special people in your life think you are good at?
- What do they like about you?
- What would they have to say about you in this situation?
- What can you rely on about yourself?

About the good things in people's lives — to find hope in other contexts and times:

- What are the good things in your life?
- Tell me about the good things in the past.
- What were you doing/what was happening that made things this way?
- What have been some of the positive experiences you have had?
- Can you think of times in your life when things have been above 5?
- Can you think of times when they have been at 10?
- What was happening then? What was different?
- What have been the special times; even the little things?
- What have been the best times?
- What have been the special relationships?
- Who are the important people in your life, now and in the past?
- How do they see things?
- Tell me about the things you have achieved or done well; even small things
- What aspects from the past would you like to have in your life again if you could?
- What's at least one thing you are really proud of?
- How have you handled or overcome problems in your life before?

- How have you managed to get through difficult times?

- What helped you to do this?

- What helped you get through?

- What were you thinking that enabled you to do these things?

- What have you learned from these things about yourself that is helpful?

- What do all these things say about you?

About values and aspirations – to explore possibilities, help build a picture of the future and establish goals:

- What do you want things to be like instead of the way they are?

- What would that look like?

- What do you want to be different in your life?

- On a scale between 1 and 10, with 1 at their worst and 10 at their best, where would you like things to be?

- If things were at 10 what would be happening?

- If things stayed above 5 what would be different?

- What do you want for yourself and your life?

- What do you really care about?

- If things were going really well what would be happening?

- What would you notice?

- What would others notice that would be different?

- If you could change just one thing, what would it be?

- What would you be doing differently?

- What do you really value in life?

- What's most important to you?

- What are your hopes?

- What have you hoped for in the past/before these problems came along?

- How would you be feeling if things were going well?

- What would you be doing that would enable you to feel this way?

- What else would be happening?
- What would others be doing?
- What would things be like if the problem were not in control anymore?
- What do you want for your life instead of what the problem has decided?

About supports and resources – to help find support and sustain change efforts:
- Who else cares about you?
- Who else cares about these problems?
- How can they help make a difference?
- What have people done already that has helped?
- What resources have you used to help overcome problems before?
- What information and knowledge have you used/can you use?
- What's been useful?
- Who has supported you in the face of difficulties?
- What organisations or groups have been supportive?
- Who else is supportive and in what way?
- How did you involve these people?
- What is it about you that they value enough to help you?
- What organisations and services in the community have been helpful in your life?
- How did you go about involving them?

About plans and steps to take – to help make things happen:
- What are you going to do?
- What resources will you use?
- What do you know that you could use to change things?
- What information will you use?
- What skills and strengths will you use?
- Who will help and how will they help?
- When will it be done?

About progress and change – to notice and celebrate change:

- What's changed since we last met?

- On a scale between 1 and 10, where are things now?

- How does this compare with the previous rating?

- What's made the difference?

- What's kept you above 1?

- What have others noticed that's been different?

- What else is different to usual?

- Has anything positive happened that you didn't expect?

- How did these things come about?

- What were you thinking or doing?

As shown in these questions, strengths-based concepts, principles, processes and skills become the points of reference for the questions we ask. Questions are used transparently in strengths-based practice; workers give context to their questions by explaining why they are asking them. Every conversation takes place within the context of informed consent; workers seek permission to enter into any exploration and articulate the reason for the questions. This helps to ensure choice and ownership.

Developing concrete description

As mentioned earlier, questions are of critical importance in the strengths approach. They invite reflection and when used carefully, they support deep and meaningful learning. One of the key skills of the strengths approach is to assist people to describe events, behaviours, experiences, strengths, goals and plans in specific and concrete terms. This is referred to as developing concrete description. Questions are used to help define issues, strengths, exceptions, goals, plans and steps in ways that are immediately measurable, 'see-able' or 'do-able'.

When we feel overwhelmed by problems we tend to feel less hopeful. A problem-saturated view can stop us from feeling we can do something about our situation. For example, Faye describes her situation like this:

It's always been like this. The kids never do what I ask them. They just keep demanding things and when I give in they ask for more! I never get time to myself. I'm really tired and can't cope with all this. All I seem to do is yell at them.

Concrete description helps clarify people's experiences and the issues they are confronted with. It challenges beliefs and perceptions that have their roots in generalisations. Questions are essential for developing concrete description because they help clarify and specify the extent of the problem. These kinds of questions typically include ones such as:

- What's happening? What are people doing?

- Where is it happening and when?

- How often does it happen?

- How long does the behaviour or difficulty last?

- How intense or powerful is the experience, feeling or behaviour?

- Over what period of time has it been happening? How long have these issues been around?

In Faye's situation, snippets of conversation would look like this:

Worker: How long has it been like this? When did it all start?

Faye: About three years now, since Dan and I separated.

Worker: And you don't remember having the same difficulties before then?

Faye: Nothing out of the ordinary.

Worker: You've told me about the kids never doing what you ask. I've been wondering if there might be times when any of them actually do? Can you think of any exceptions to this?

Faye: Well ... sometimes Jordan tidies up after himself but the others don't.

Worker: Are the kids always messy?

Faye: Not always, it's mainly on the weekends. They're not so bad during the week.

Worker: What about in other situations, like when you're out somewhere together?

Faye: Well, they're pretty good when we go out.

Worker: What about at school? How are they at school?

Faye: They don't seem to get into trouble at school.

Worker: You said last time that all you seem to do is yell at the kids. When does it happen? How often do you reckon you yell at them?

Faye: I've thought about that. I only yell at them when I'm tired ... maybe two or three times a day on average.

Faye's descriptions expose a number of differences and exceptions that can be explored. More specific and concrete details tell a different story from Faye's first account: the kids don't get into trouble at school, Faye only yells at them when she's tired, Jordan sometimes tidies up after himself, and so on. Developing concrete description is also a means of reframing (see pages 121-126) because it exposes people's strengths and solution-finding skills as is evident in the example above.

As the example shows, questions for developing concrete description can be very useful in helping to identify strengths and exceptions. For example: When the problem is not there, what are you doing? Where? When? How often? What might it look like to others? What do they see happening? In your picture of the future, what will you be doing? What will others see? Where? When? How often?

Concrete description of goals and plans enables people to see specifically what they are aiming for. This makes achieving the goals more likely. In relation to Faye's situation goals such as 'Having the kids do what I ask' and 'Being able to relax and cope' can be described in specific terms such as: 'I'm helping Jordan tidy his room each Sunday evening and Kate comes home for dinner on time' and 'I have time to read each day; an hour or so in the afternoon'.

Concrete description also makes it easier to measure change. For example, 'Jordan helps with the dishes when I ask' is easier to measure than 'Having the kids do as I ask'.

Cautions for developing concrete description

However, simply developing concrete description can lead to oversimplification of issues, strengths, goals and solutions. People's feelings can be ignored. The context and the meaning of their experience can be minimised or overlooked. All experience has meaning and as meaning-makers people can distort, confuse or interpret experience in different ways.

Exploring meaning is essential in strengths-based conversations. It enables other ideas, beliefs and interpretations of experience to be considered. This makes it possible to confront any cultural or personal constraints that may be hindering change. This process typically involves reframing, normalising, and other skills discussed later in this chapter.

Identifying strengths and exceptions

One of the most important concepts of the strengths approach is that of exceptions. Exceptions can be defined as anything that's happening or anything that people are doing when a problem is absent or less of a problem. This notion and its power for change can be traced to the early work of Steve de Shazer (see, for example, de Shazer 1985, 1988 and 1991) and Michael White. In narrative therapy the term 'unique outcomes' is used (see, for example, Elliott 2000, pp. 66–8; Freedman & Combs 1996, pp. 67–8; White 1995). It may be useful at this point to revisit the discussion of unique outcomes on pages 82-83.

When the problem is absent or not as bad, people are doing something differently or there is something else that is different in the context in which the problem exists. Exceptions exist in the present or the past. They expose people's strengths and capacities, and tell stories that are different from problem-saturated ones, as evident in Faye's situation described above. Exceptions give clues to possible solutions and inform steps that can be taken to overcome problems.

A simple way of understanding what is meant by exceptions is to think about what people do 'that works'; what they do that brings them closer to a solution. Exploring exceptions opens opportunities for reflection on the things that people do that makes a difference in their lives.

Exceptions do not necessarily relate directly to the issues of immediate concern. For example, in the context of parenting difficulties, the strengths and capacities required to build and maintain friendships (such as communication, trust, compromise and acceptance), can help resolve the parenting issues. Any strengths and the stories behind them can be understood and valued as exceptions. When people are not controlled by the problem, they are doing something that exposes their capacity to do things differently. Every strength and exception exposes stories of what people do despite problems; what they do to overcome problems; what they do well and what they do to meet dreams and aspirations.

The following examples illustrate how strengths and exceptions can help expose capacities and lay the foundations for change.

James (13 years old) has been under a child protection order for the past three years. He has spent time in secure welfare, residential care, and family-based placements. James has a history of difficulties at school including refusal to attend school much of the time. He also has behavioural difficulties including running out in front of cars, climbing and threatening to jump off buildings and outbursts of violence against his parents. His parents want him at home.

The family has had counselling and various unsuccessful attempts have been made to return James home. James' mother has been retrenched from her job and they are concerned about keeping up their rent. His father is on a pension after a serious motorbike accident, often drinks heavily and complains about having to help with housework. Despite wanting to be home James tends to revert to unwanted behaviour including hurting his younger brother when they play together.

 EXERCISE – Finding strengths and exceptions

Before reading on, take another look at the situation described above.

- What strengths can you identify and why do you think each of these is a strength?

- What exceptions can you identify and what do each of these suggest about the family?

At first glance, this is a somewhat bleak situation. But you will have identified a number of strengths and exceptions that change the story of this family. James' mother can hold down a job. The family wants James home. James wants to be at home. They keep trying. They have tried counselling. James' father helps with the housework. He doesn't drink heavily all the time. James has been at home for periods. James plays with his brother. James and his brother don't fight all the time. Ron learned to ride a motorbike. The family has a home. They can manage despite a low income.

These strengths and exceptions tell a different story from one saturated with problems and negativity. They indicate numerous strengths and capacities and shed light on underlying hopes and aspirations: the desire to be a family and the ability to keep trying despite the odds, the innumerable skills inherent in keeping house, interactions with professionals, employment and interests that they have. Looking at this family's story through a strengths-based frame exposes enormous determination, strong emotional ties and a deep aspiration to be together as a family. These strengths and exceptions come together to tell an *alternative story*.

Aileen expresses her disappointment and frustration with events in her community:

'The council planted trees in the street and within a week a row in one street had been snapped off at the bottom. The local store closed three months ago. Then new people reopened it. They were a gay couple who had developed a coffee shop with outdoor seating. Now they're leaving because the shop has been vandalised and their flat at the back of the shop stoned on numerous occasions. The police have done nothing even though a few of us got together to make a delegation. Last year the local priest stopped coming to do services and now they send a church leader instead who visits for readings and an afternoon study circle. It's not the same anymore.

'When the woollen mills closed two years ago so many people were out of work that it had a bad effect on things here. Some of the houses are vacant and have been taken over by squatters. The local employment training program gets some of the young people involved, but a lot of them are only interested in computers. The Technical and Further Education College (TAFE) is impossible for people to get to, it's so far from here. Over at the community house all they seem to do is run social functions. What hope have we got?'

In this description there are numerous strengths, exceptions and resources. Local government obviously has some interest in the neighbourhood. Not all of the trees have been destroyed. People have joined in collaborative ways: making a delegation to police, organising functions at the community house, and meeting for a study circle. There is evidence of respect for diversity in action relating to the gay couple's experience. Action taken by various people suggests a range of strengths, skills and aspirations that can form the basis for further activity. There are a number of resources potentially available to the community: a church leader, community house, the mills, the TAFE College, vacant housing, local government interest and a coffee shop.

Off-hand or passing remarks and stories that don't seem relevant can contain significant exceptions or unique outcomes. While these are easily overlooked, they can so often be pivotal in the change process. To revisit the story of James and his family:

In the course of a conversation with their worker James' parents mentioned that James wanted to cook. They said that they would not let him cook because he would make a big mess and wouldn't clean up after himself. They also said that in any case he would probably light the house on fire! Refusing to let James cook had led to a major argument the day before. In the context of the volatility and numerous issues facing the family, James' desire to cook was quickly forgotten.

Over the next four weeks they tried different ways of addressing James' behaviour with little success. Out of the blue his parents reported that James had done some cooking while they were out and that they were annoyed with him but didn't say anything. The worker was struck by what he perceived as a significant difference: James had cooked and cleaned up after himself and his parents did not enter into any arguments about it.

The worker asked whether they believed this was significant; whether they thought it was an achievement. They said they hadn't thought of it in that way but seemed intrigued by the thought that James had done something different to the usual—he'd actually cleaned up after himself! The worker asked whether they would feel more confident allowing James to cook. They said that they weren't sure but that they'd be prepared to give it a go. As a result they did let James cook. James' mother and James even prepared a meal together. This significant shift opened the way for thinking differently about James. They identified a number of strengths and skills that James had and in doing so discovered strengths in their parenting that they had not been aware of.

Questions for identifying strengths and exceptions

Here is a snippet of a conversation about exceptions:

Maria: The voices are giving me hell.

Worker: I've been wondering if there are times when they are quieter?

Maria: No they're always there.

Worker: So they are constantly chattering?

Maria: Well, when I go canoeing they seem to stop.

Worker: Really? Totally?

Maria: Pretty much totally.

Worker: That's really good.

Maria: Yeah, I love the river.

Worker: That's interesting – the voices slow down then. I wonder if it's worth doing a bit of a survey over the next few days of other times when they might be less 'noisy' in your life?

(Pugh & McCashen 1999, p. 22)

There are hundreds of questions that can be asked to invite people to reflect on strengths and exceptions, such as:

- What do you do well?

- What do you consider as your strengths? What do others consider as your strengths?

- What are your skills and interests?

- Who are the special people in your life and what would they say about you and this situation?

- What was happening before these difficulties arose?

- When were things better than they are now?

- What are the good things you have done in the past?

- What have you done that has made a positive difference?

- Are there times when the problem isn't there?

- What's different then? What are you doing differently?

- Are there examples you can think of when the problem didn't have as much control? What was different then?

- What does this say about you? What is it about you that enabled you to do this?

- What other resources are there?

- How might they help?

- What resources in the community might be helpful?

Questions that invite reflection on people's ability to overcome or lessen the impact of the problem are important in exploring exceptions. They help challenge personal constraints and expose skills and expertise that affect people's positive sense of self.

Reframing

As meaning-makers people are making sense of what they see and experience. As noted earlier the meaning given to experience is more significant in determining our responses to it than the experience itself.

The meaning we give to experience is embedded in the way we frame it. In other words, changing the way we frame experience involves changing the meaning we give to it. When the women's movement described women subject to family violence as 'survivors' as opposed to 'victims', it reframed experience. It created an alternative story. This is profoundly powerful because the change of language and meaning, while not in any way minimising or ignoring the seriousness of the reality, frames the women in a most respectful, empowering way and opens up the possibility of a different future for them than the term 'victim' does. Change one word and we can change the world!

In chapter three labelling and various relevant cautions were discussed including the harm it can do, how it can disempower people and get in the way of change and empowerment. The labels used to describe people are in effect one way of framing perceived reality. Reframing changes the way we think of any given reality, the way we think about people, and the way people think of themselves and their prospects.

Reframing involves changing our view. Watzlawick, Weakland and Fisch (1974, pp. 38–9), describe it this way:

> To reframe, then, means to change the conceptual and/or emotional setting or viewpoint in relation to which a situation is experienced and to place it in another

frame which fits the 'facts' of the same concrete situation equally well or even better, and thereby changing its entire meaning.

We make meaning from the world around us by taking a limited number of facts and inferring or assuming other detail to be able to make sense of things. Reframing leaves the facts alone but may well challenge the assumptions. With care, you can change the other person's reality without causing conflict.

Beyond personal perception, all ideologies from political systems to religions are frames for creating meaning. Cultures, likewise, embody methods of interpreting and shared ways of making sense of the world, as are the models by which we perceive ourselves and others. When we share frames with others, we share meaning. When we have different frames we can easily fall into conflict if we consider the frames of others to be non-legitimate.

Reframing helps people think differently about themselves and the problems they are facing. The purpose is to redefine problems in ways that promote existing strengths and solution-finding skills and thus open the way for change. It does not aim to try and change facts or evidence but to explore alternative perspectives on the same event, story or experience and enabling genuine choice of a preferred description. Reframing is aimed at creating possible positive descriptions.

The term 'dysfunctional' could be used to describe James' family. But his family is functioning. It is troubled, concerned and stressed, but it is functioning. The strengths and exceptions evident even in such a problem-saturated reality reframe James' family as concerned, surviving despite the odds, committed and determined, responsible and as having numerous skills. Their aspiration to be together as a family is a profoundly important aspiration and an exception that became central in bringing about change.

Labels and negative descriptions can be reframed by pre-supposing good intentions, considering strengths and exploring contexts. Labels such as 'over-protective', 'lazy' or 'unrealistic', are all based on value judgements. They can be replaced respectively with 'caring', 'laid-back' or 'imaginative'. These, of course, are value judgements as well but people are enabled to take responsibility when strengths and aspirations inherent in their intentions are valued and made evident. When parents hit children, for example, they usually do so not because they want to do harm but for reasons such as wanting to correct unwanted behaviour or get some peace and quiet. This is not to ignore or excuse dangerous or difficult behaviour. When there is risk of harm, the issues must be clearly named but the way we do that can critically affect outcomes. A conversation that also explores and validates good intentions is more respectful than one that is stuck on blame or what people are doing wrong. It is also more likely to encourage other means of addressing the issues at hand.

Anita is 14 years of age. She has been in trouble for shoplifting and was recently charged with assault. She has not attended school for three months. She left home following incidents in which her parents physically abused her. This involved the use of inappropriate discipline in response to finding out she had been sniffing substances and engaging in sexual activity. She was placed in residential care following an investigation three days ago. Since coming into care Anita has been generally cooperative and workers have been able to develop a connection with her. This morning Anita began arguing with another young person, Davis, about him having the TV on too loud while she was trying to sleep in. The argument escalated to a point where Anita grabbed a broom and was about to hit him when a worker walked in. The worker asked Davis to leave the room while he talked to Anita.

The worker could respond like this:

'You know the rules around here, Anita. I hate to think what would have happened if I hadn't come into the lounge room when I did. It's totally unacceptable to use violence to get your way. Don't ever do anything like that again.'

Alternatively, the worker could respond like this:

'When I came into the room and saw you about to hit Davis with the broom I was really concerned. You must have been really angry. I know things must be tough for you after everything that's happened. You seem to have settled in quite well so far so let's see if we can find a way to make things right. We don't want you getting into trouble. We want things to be as good as possible for you here. Tell me what happened.'

EXERCISE – *Reflecting on reframes*

Which approach is most likely to engage Anita?

How is she likely to respond to the first response to her behaviour?

How is she likely to respond to the second response?

In the following example Jodi and her husband are subject to a child protection investigation. Their newborn baby was placed in care when Jodi and her husband left hospital at her husband's instigation and failed to make contact for three days. The first statement was made by a protective worker to Jodi's husband.

'You decided that Jodi would be better resting at home. Leaving the baby and not contacting the hospital for three days is cause for great concern. We can't be sure something won't go wrong so your baby won't be returned to your care until we're certain you can take responsibility. Jodi will probably need to stop expressing milk.'

This statement comes from another worker:

'When you and Jodi left your baby at the hospital and didn't make contact for three days we became quite concerned. Jodi must be committed to your baby, to be expressing milk all this time and you must care a lot to have taken her home to rest. Your commitment and sense of responsibility suggests that you care. We'd like to work with you to find a way to get your baby home as soon as possible.'

Each of these statements captures concerns for the baby's welfare. The second statement however reframes the reality by considering other aspects of the reality without ignoring the issues of concern. It does this by considering strengths and good intentions and is more likely to enable Jodie and her husband to engage in efforts to address concerns.

Reframing can be assisted through:

- exploring strengths and exceptions despite the problem (What do these positive things say about the way you have been able to deal with the problem?)

- inviting reflection on other possible perspectives (What other ways are there of seeing this situation? What would special people in your life say about the way you have coped? What difference would it make if we looked at the situation from another perspective? (for example, gender)

- considering the context of the behaviour (Do you mean this never happened before your mum died?)

- questions that pre-suppose good intentions (What were you hoping to achieve when you did that?)

- exploring the wider social and cultural context (How many others do you know who have a hard time bringing up kids on their own?)

- developing concrete description (as discussed on pages 113–115)

- conversations that normalise people's experience (see below).

EXERCISE – Reframing

1. Reframe the following labels and negative descriptions of people.
   What are some possible descriptors that reframe the situation?
   You will need to imagine possible contexts in which the labels are used.

   - Inconsiderate
   - Dysfunctional
   - Uncooperative
   - Interfering

   - Manic
   - Over-protective
   - Lazy
   - Attention-seeking

   - Unrealistic
   - Untidy
   - Impatient
   - Bossy

2. What enables you to reframe these labels? What are you thinking that enables you to reframe?

3. What are some possible questions you could ask that might help people reframe these?

4. Why is reframing important? What are the benefits of reframing for:

   - people receiving services?

   - the worker?

5. Read the following description.

   'People just don't care anymore. I feel like giving up. I've put everything into this project. I thought I was doing the right thing. People put a lot into the community and somehow managed to achieve so much. I've supported them as much as I can.

   It seems so wrong. There's the church and community centre but companies are closing down and the kids around here have no hope now. It's just fortunate that there are people who will continue their commitment and keep things going.'

6. Consider anything that indicates possible exceptions, strengths or positive contradictions. Reframe it in a way that might be helpful. What questions might you ask that might help this person reframe the situation themselves?

Normalising

Normalising is a process of reframing problems by identifying the commonalities between people's experiences, feelings and responses to problems, and the meanings they give to them. It occurs through the sharing of people's common experience in the same or similar circumstances and consideration of social and cultural issues that contribute to these circumstances.

Normalising can happen through the use of questions and the sharing of knowledge and information that enables people to think about the commonalities between their circumstances, experience, feelings and responses and those of others in similar circumstances.

Sharing our own experience or our knowledge of the experience of others in the same or similar circumstances can be a powerful way of helping to normalise experience. For example, most parents are able to identify with the challenges that other parents face, so sharing stories and experiences as parents can be normalising. It does, of course, also have the benefit of strengthening collaboration and trust.

Normalising enables people to view the problems they face as understandable. This helps 'de-pathologise' and remove blame or guilt. It helps bring a sense of relief and raises self-regard. This way of reframing the problem challenges personal beliefs that can get in the way of change and can free people to take responsibility.

The principle of ownership is a crucial characteristic of reframing and normalising as much as it is in the identification of strengths and exceptions or developing a picture of the future. The worker, in assisting reframing or normalising, uses questions and propositions to help people look at their realities from different perspectives so as to enable a genuine choice of a preferred description, even if that description remains a negative one. In strengths-based practice, workers are not attempting to talk people out of the problem or 'frame it away'.

Developing a picture of the future and goal-setting

As noted in chapter two, aspirations drive change. Our strengths and capacities are the fuel we use to get where we want to go, but without aspirations and dreams our direction can be unclear and motivation diminished. When workers invite people to share their aspirations they are inviting them to share deeply held values. Exposing and articulating aspirations and the meanings they hold helps increase motivation and provides inspiration and a meaningful context for the articulation of clear goals.

Developing a picture of the future helps people get in touch with and describe their aspirations. It consists of two inter-related processes:

1. Exploring future possibilities and ways of being (exploring aspirations, hopes and dreams)

2. Developing concrete description of what people will be doing/what will be happening when the problem no longer exists (setting goals).

The picture of the future is people's vision of what they want things to be like. It is a description of what will be happening when the issues are resolved, including how they will be feeling and what they will be doing. This provides a meaningful context for change efforts. The picture of the future (people's values and aspirations) becomes a point of reference or theme for setting goals. Goal setting is the process of describing (and recording), in specific and concrete terms, the desired outcomes that arise from the picture of the future.

Questions for developing a picture of the future

Questions that assume positive change are characteristic of questions that help develop a picture of the future. Some questions for developing a picture of the future might include:

- What do you want to be different?

- What do you want to be happening instead?

- How will that make a difference?

- What are your hopes?

- What do you want for yourself and your life?

- What do you really value in life?

- How would you be feeling if these issues were not in your life?

- What would you be doing that would help you to feel this way?

- What would others be doing?

- If you could change one thing what would it be?

- If there were a miracle and things were different what would you be doing?

Using the scenarios from James' family and Aileen's community discussed earlier, here are some examples of a picture of the future that can emerge at an aspirational level.

James' family:

'James is living at home and he is happy. We are happy and relaxed because he is not scaring us with his threats to hurt himself or anyone. We don't need welfare anymore and we are able to pay the rent and manage. James and Thomas are getting on well. Ron isn't drinking heavily. We are a family that can get on together and cooperate and have fun.'

Aileen's community:

'People feel proud of the community and are hopeful. Our streets are beautiful, lined with trees. The church is working with the council and the local community to redevelop the area. A cooperative is operating and the houses have been renovated for low cost accommodation. The local shop serves coffee and cake on the deck and opens at night to serve affordable meals. People gather there at any time of the day to enjoy each other's company. The police come to play sport with the young people once a week and a community group is formed to stop vandalism with support from the police.

'People are using the mills to develop skills and hobbies and the young people have a sense of purpose. Employment training is run there and the TAFE College and a local business run computer training and some of the older people are helping out. Our study circle has expanded and people have joined who we didn't expect to. It discusses the community's potential and things that can be done to make a difference and takes action to help make people feel secure and have needs met.'

Framing the picture of the future as if it were achieved can increase motivation and make goals manageable. For example: 'I am taking a half-hour walk each day' can be more powerful than 'to take a half-hour walk each day'. It helps makes goals 'do-able'. It enables people to project themselves into the landscape of their aspirations as illustrated in the vision of Aileen's community described above.

These pictures of the future are not simply dreams or idealised views of what is possible. They are based on strongly held values as well as on exceptions, strengths and resources found in the realities described. People's picture of the future may include things that don't appear to have any direct relationship to the problem. These are just as important in their own right because they are what people value. By honouring them workers validate people's aspirations, and help tap motivation that can contribute to resolving the issues of concern.

It's difficult to make change if we are not clear about where it is we want to get to. Clear, well-defined goals give a clear indication of what steps we need to take. They also enable us to get a clear sense of what we are achieving and what difference our efforts are making.

The picture of the future and goals are crucial in the change process because:

- they honour people's aspirations and help increase motivation

- they give concrete expression to people's hopes and aspirations, making change more achievable. This helps people to take responsibility

- they provide a context for the exploration of strengths and exceptions making them more relevant and meaningful

- knowing what will be different when the problem is absent gives helpful direction as to what steps need to be taken

- progress towards concrete goals is easily measured in comparison to general or vague hopes

- achievements and exceptions are more easily noticed and appreciated.

The relationship between the picture of the future, strengths and exceptions

The picture of the future provides a context for exploring strengths and exceptions: for what works and what doesn't work. This is evident in the following example.

Julia and Mario have nine children. They live in an isolated rural community and rely on social security benefits and odd jobs to bring up their family. Their six-year-old son, Anthony, was removed from the family by the Child Protection Service after he had told his teacher that his father had been hitting him. Julia and Mario agreed to cooperate in an intensive family service intervention to work towards having Anthony return and remain at home.

In a lengthy conversation about what they wanted for their family, they described wanting to be happy and to get along well together. They said that Anthony was a good boy but misbehaved a lot and wouldn't do anything he was told. They said that they wanted him to behave like the others do and that what mattered most to them was having cooperation and love in the family because it was hard struggling to bring up so many children with so few resources. Cooperation and love mattered most because it meant they could be organised and meet all their children's needs.

When discussing the sorts of things they had tried to get Anthony to behave, the worker asked them what had worked. Mario, without hesitation responded: 'Giving him a bloody good whack and sending him to his room!' The worker remembered the genuine and meaningful sharing of their picture of the future for the family and related what she had heard: 'You told me yesterday about how important cooperation and love are for you. I'm wondering how hitting Anthony has helped with that.' Mario paused and thought for a moment and then laughed and said, 'It doesn't!' He laughed more and said, 'I suppose I have to find a different way!'

Defining what we want clarifies what is really important to us. In the example of the women's group discussed in chapter four, the women began with the hope that they could make change in their lives; they each wanted a life free of depression and independent of medical intervention. As they developed their picture of the future they described positive relationships in their families, confidence in themselves, new or renewed friendships, revitalised interests and contributions to their communities. These aspirations provided a different context for exploring the strengths and exceptions in their lives—past and present.

On the other hand, people often find it difficult to imagine what things might be like without the problem. It's often difficult to get in touch with future possibilities when the weight of the problem is so great. Exploring exceptions and strengths provides evidence of what is possible. It also provides evidence of what people are capable of and gives clues about what steps might be taken to reach the picture of the future. This can inform or reinforce aspirations, enhance self-esteem and confidence and increase motivation.

The strengths, exceptions and resources evident in Aileen's community formed the basis for their picture of the future. For the women's group the uncovering of exceptions, alternative stories and strengths enabled them to see a connection between their strengths and aspirations and, therefore, new possibilities.

Rarely do we concentrate entirely on future picture development or on exploring exceptions only. Most commonly we move back and forward from one to the other, sometimes re-visiting the issues of concern, responding in a fluid way to whatever is shared. While this flexibility is important, too little structure can lead to confusion and lack of clarity. On the other hand, as noted earlier, too much structure can limit spontaneity and work against opportunities to share the richness of experience and aspirations. It can also lead to the worker driving the process.

Measuring and noticing change

Moi sits at her kitchen table with a social worker and talks of her concerns about her children and how she will ever get over the loss of her mother who died recently of cancer. She has lost motivation as a parent and complains at length about her children's behaviour. As they sit talking, Moi's children arrive home from school. They greet Moi with a kiss, go and hang up their school bags and come and ask if they can have something to eat. Moi tells them they can get some food but to make sure they clean up after themselves. The children get some food and tidy up, then ask for permission to go and play with a friend next door. Moi tells them they can but to make sure they are home by six o'clock. Moi then continues to complain about her children's behaviour.

Change doesn't happen unless it's noticed. This statement need not be taken literally—however, it highlights the fact that, while change is inevitable, its power cannot be harnessed unless it is noticed. Noticing and measuring change are essential elements of strengths-based work. They involve an active process of observation and reflection through which people see, value, and appreciate exceptions, positive differences in their realities, and progress towards change. Self-esteem and confidence increase when people notice what it is they did that made a difference to their reality. This brings about a consciousness in people of their power to make a difference. People begin to experience themselves as their own solution-finders. When people are aware of what makes a difference and their part in it they are more likely to be able to sustain the change they make.

Helping to notice and appreciate change can happen through:

- sharing observations and feedback

- celebrating efforts and achievements (parties, picnics, gifts, and so on)

- recording achievements and positive differences (awards, certificates, documents, and so on)

- finding appreciative audiences (discussed later in this chapter)

- asking people to observe specific things

- scaling (discussed later in this chapter)

- setting measurable goals

- writing letters, cards and notes to people that highlight change efforts and achievements.

There are a number of cautions relating to measuring change. Any measurement tool or tasks must be meaningful and relevant for the people using them. In sharing observations the emphasis again needs to be on ownership; feedback needs to be offered tentatively so that people can make a genuine choice about whether or not they agree and to what degree. Observations should also be supported by evidence rather than based on opinions or generalisations. Timing is also important. Attempting to draw attention to positive differences when people are experiencing pain can invalidate their feelings and perceptions.

Scaling

Scaling is a numerical tool for noticing and measuring change, exceptions and progress towards goals. It first gained prominence in solution focused practice (see Kowalski and Kral 1989). A typical scaling question goes like this:

- On a scale between one and ten, with one being when things are at their worst and ten being when things are at their best, where are things now?

Scaling is an easily accessible means of helping people measure how things are going over time. It helps make comparisons between when things are at their best, when they are at their worst and when they are somewhere in between. It helps people to identify exceptions because anything that is happening when things are above the number one exposes skills and strengths they are using when the problem does not have as much control as it otherwise can. Typically, scaling questions include:

- What's happening when things are above one? What are you doing then?

- Are there times when things are at three or four? What's different then? What are you doing?

- Are there times when things have been at ten? What's different then?

These kinds of scaling questions can shed light on possible ways forward. They help identify strengths and exceptions, giving clues about what might be done differently.

Scaling can also be used to assist people to develop a concrete picture of the future:

- If things were as high as ten what would be happening?

- What would need to happen for things to stay above five?

- What have you tried before when things were above five?

The following example illustrates the use of scaling in strengths-based conversations. In this example, Con, aged twelve, has been refusing to do his homework, and arguments with his father, George, occur every day. Con's mother, Thula, gets very upset about the arguments and is frightened George will hit Con. The worker asks each of them to rate on a scale between one and ten, with one being 'really terrible' and ten 'really good' (the family's words), what they feel things are like. Con says one and Thula agrees. George says they are at minus ten! The conversation unfolds as follows:

Worker: Where do you want things to be?

George: Ten.

Thula: Five or six would be alright.

Worker: Have things ever been above minus ten George?

George: When he behaves himself.

Worker: What's happening when Con behaves himself?

Thula: He's a good boy. He makes his bed and does his homework and he doesn't argue with his father.

Worker: Where would you put things between one and ten when things are like that, Thula?

George: Ten, but it hardly ever happens.

Thula: Yes, ten, of course, but he can't be perfect.

Con: If Dad doesn't yell and scream I don't yell at him.

Worker: If things were at ten what else would be happening?

Thula: George wouldn't be yelling at Con and Con wouldn't be yelling at George. No yelling!

Worker: What else?

George: We'd be doing things together, like a family. Going places more and play cards like we used to.

Worker: Can you remember other things that happen when things are at ten? What are you doing?

George: He does his homework and helps his mother and me and has his friends here.

Worker: What are you doing differently, George?

Con: Not yelling! He talks to me properly. He lets me have friends stay.

Worker: It sounds like there are times when things are really good between you. Is that true?

George: We used to have good times a lot. The boy loved his father.

Thula: And his father loved his boy.

This brief conversation gives an indication of a number of strengths, exceptions and aspirations. In work with this family the worker will be curious about more of the stories of 'good times', the love between father and son, what's happening when Con is doing his homework, what's happening when there's no yelling (or less yelling) and so on. He will be attentive to the family's aspirations and build on those that have already been touched on to help develop some concrete goals.

Appreciative audiences

An appreciative audience is made up of people who value the qualities and contributions of others. This way of identifying and affirming strengths and exceptions originates from the work of White and Epston (1990, pp. 155–63).

An appreciative audience:

- is a witness to people's struggles, strengths and skills

- understands people's stories and values their aspirations

- encourages people's efforts and notices their achievements

- provides positive feedback

- helps people to take steps towards their aspirations

- complements people's efforts by helping to make resources accessible

- helps sustain progress and change.

Appreciative audiences witness and support people's emerging stories. In the strengths approach workers become appreciative audiences to people's efforts at change and are often engaged in finding other appreciative audiences.

Publication of people's stories, thoughts and opinions can be a means of creating new audiences. The word 'publication' is not limited to formal publication in books; it can also mean letters, articles, notes and simple quotes in newsletters, minutes of meetings, reports and exhibitions. It can also take the form of song lyrics, poems, CDs, DVDs. Even things like murals, notice boards, invitations and menus can be vehicles for publication.

In group and community work, people can become appreciative of the efforts and achievements of other group members. In casework, counselling and support work, there are often networks of people who can be appreciative of the efforts of their friend, colleague or loved one. Those who have been held as special in people's past can be invited in as witnesses to the change. This can be undertaken by asking them to be literally present physically to support change efforts, or through invitations to people to reflect on the opinions of those 'special people' in their lives.

 EXERCISE – *Appreciative audiences*

- Who are some of the appreciative audiences in your life, past or present?
- Why are they important?
- What part have they played in your life?
- What part do they play in your life now?
- In what ways can appreciative audiences help change and sustain it?

Externalising

As discussed in chapter four, externalising is a key characteristic of narrative practice. When people are confronted with problems it is common for them to internalise unhelpful ideas about themselves, their past and their future, as noted in the discussion of cultural constraints in chapter three. The same can occur in relationships. That is, people interpret the problem as something that exists because of some deficiency or weakness in their character or, as the case may be, in their relationship. Externalising aims to challenge such assumptions and underlying beliefs. It does this by deconstructing the cultural and historical roots of the problem; by placing the problem in its cultural and historical context—thus moving the problem from inside the person or the relationship to outside the person.

The problem is treated as something that has a life of its own but at the same time as something that can be changed. Externalising separates the person (or family, group or community) from the problem. It helps people to see the problem as something separate from them; as something they can do something with. The problem is objectified. Difficulties such as the effects of a problem (feeling guilty, afraid, anxious) can be objectified (guilt, fear, anxiety) or responded to as people describe them (guilty, afraid, anxious).

So, externalising questions might include:

- How has guilt/fear/anxiety (or guilty/afraid/anxious) taken over your life?

- What would things be like if the guilt/fear/anxiety were not in control anymore?

- Can you tell me about times when guilt/fear/anxiety didn't get the better of you? What were you doing then?

In these questions we are simply exploring the problem and its effects, asking about a picture of the future and exploring exceptions or unique outcomes, but we are using externalising to do it.

Metaphors and other aspects of language can be rich supports for externalising. For example, we can talk about emotions or problems no longer 'pushing us around' or we can speak of 'keeping a lid on an issue', 'dissolving the ice', 'clearing the decks' or even of 'making friends with a problem.'

As noted in the earlier discussion of narrative therapy (see page 79–83) strengths can also be externalised. Picking up on the language and expressions used, we might ask about where the problem came from ('When did you first notice the grief and what it was doing to your family?'). We will be just as interested to know about the strengths the family has used to 'overcome the grief'. ('Sticking together seems to help overcome the grief, then?'). Other examples of externalising strengths are: 'Determination always wins out in the end', 'Pride in culture gets me through'.

But externalising, like all of the skills of the strengths approach, is not a technique to be pulled from a bag of tricks simply to help people change their behaviour. In conjunction with the other skills of the strengths approach it helps to address the structural and cultural constraints discussed in chapter three. It assists people to consider their experiences from a range of different perspectives, leading them to define the problem in a different way from when the problem is seen to reside within them. Carey and Russell (2002, p. 77) emphasise the significance of externalising in the following way:

> When it is understood that people's relationships with problems are shaped by history and culture, it is possible to explore how gender, race, culture, sexuality, class and other relations of power have influenced the construction of the problem. By giving consideration to the politics involved in the shaping of identity, it becomes possible to enable new understandings of life that are influenced less by self-blame and more by an awareness of how our lives are shaped by broader cultural stories ... This opens a range of possibilities for action that are not available when problems are located within individuals.

In contexts such as those referred to in the above quote we might ask questions like:

- How has sexism/racism/homophobia affected your life and your family?

- What do you want for your life instead of what sexism/racism/homophobia has decided?

- Are there times when you have been able to stand up to sexism/racism/homophobia?

The following process is a composite of ideas inspired by O'Hanlon, 1994, Freedman and Combs, 1996, Morgan A, 2000, and the author's own experience of strengths-based frameworks. It describes a process for externalising conversations and gives a possible structure for narrative therapy, following steps according to how it might unfold over time.

Like the strengths-based mind map discussed in chapter five, this process acts as a guide or mind map for conversation, reflection and learning. Each part is valid in its own right but can be joined up as a series of conversations over time. The externalisation used here is *anxiety*.

1. *The story as it is now:* Sharing experience and feelings. Exploring the social and cultural context of the problems or challenges. Sharing common experiences, interpretations and meanings given to these and similar events and experiences. Eliciting rich descriptions of experience. Listening for trends or themes in the story.

2. *Externalising the problem:* Naming the problem or issues *(anxiety)* based on the person's description, language and metaphors used.

3. *Investigating the problem's influence and history:* Exploring how the problem *(anxiety)* is influencing or has influenced the person's life. This can include trends and patterns that emerge in the story about the way *anxiety* is operating now or has operated in the past. Exploring the influence of the problem includes the problem's way of operating. This includes its tactics, intentions, rules, purposes, motives, techniques, allies, deceits, lies, plans, beliefs, ideas, ways of speaking (Morgan 2000, p. 25).

4. *Identifying exceptions/unique outcomes:* This involves exploring the events, experiences and circumstances that expose differences or trends in the way *anxiety* is operating or has operated in the person's life. (Stories are elicited of when the problem isn't there or hasn't been there, when it doesn't have or hasn't had as much control, or when it has or has had no control at all).

5. *Exploring preferred experience:* Conversation focuses on whether or not the stories that make up the exceptions or unique outcomes are 'preferred' stories. That is, does the person value these and is this how they want to live their lives?

6. *Exploring what leads to unique outcomes while highlighting the skills, strengths and capacities used:* Questions are asked that invite people to think about their own personal agency in bringing about the unique outcomes. (For example, How did you go about getting control in this situation instead of *anxiety* being in control? What exactly did you do? What are you thinking and doing when your *calmness* overcomes *anxiety*? What else is happening? What does this say about you as a person? What might others say if they knew you were able to achieve this?).

7. *Linking past and present unique outcomes to create a different/alternative story:* This process links the unique outcomes from the past and present to create a new story over time, an alternative story (a story of how *calmness* wins out over *anxiety*).

8. *Extending the story into the future:* This involves conversation about the new possibilities that the alternative story suggests (a life where the person is free of, or in control of, what *anxiety* does or tries to do). It invites people to consider a future alternative to the one 'the problem' had planned for them.

9. *Living the new story:* Efforts focus on seeking skills, strategies, situations, relationships and people who can help keep the new story alive.

Developing steps and strategies

In many respects this part of the strengths approach is the easiest. Identifying and exploring strengths, resources, exceptions, aspirations and goals provides direction for considering and deciding plans, strategies and steps. Care needs to be taken, of course, to ensure that the people workers are trying to help own any steps or plans decided on. In addition, the steps and plans need to be concrete and specific to help people feel confident enough to try whatever they decide needs to be done. In essence this is an action plan. It applies the strengths, resources and ideas informed by the exceptions, and consists of a specific and concrete description of what will be done, who will do it, how it will be done and when it will be done.

A Snapshot of the Strengths-based Practice Mind Map

As a way of summarising, the following table presents a snapshot of the strengths-based mind map for practice, and many of the relevant skills discussed in this chapter.

ISSUES	THE PICTURE OF THE FUTURE	STRENGTHS AND EXCEPTIONS	RESOURCES	PLANS AND STEPS	REFLECTION AND LEARNING
• Listen to people's stories and feelings, explore their context and identify the core issues, including constraints. • Seek to understand people's stories of their experience and their feelings and meaning. • Validate feelings and perspectives.	• Seek to elicit people's aspirations, values, hopes, dreams and goals. • Find out how this will make a difference to their lives. • Help develop a picture of the future. • Then develop and describe goals based on the values and aspirations.	• Identify and explore strengths. • Elicit people's positive stories, and strengths. • Explore exceptions to the problems and assist re-storying. • Look for clues and ideas about what might work to change things. • Think about how strengths might help.	• Identify resources and supports that can help people reach their goals. • Share your ideas, information and knowledge for consideration.	• Develop a plan of action which mobilises the strengths and resources towards the goals.	• Review and evaluate progress and change. • Validate and acknowledge difficulties. • Learn from mistakes. • Highlight and celebrate successes. • Find out more about strengths and what works. • Keep doing what works. • Make new plans based on what's been learnt.
Ask questions that invite people to share their stories and enable them to clarify the issues of concern.	Ask questions that help people explore their aspirations, dreams, interests and goals.	Ask questions that help people explore the strengths and exceptions, and develop new stories.	Ask questions that help people identify resources that might help them reach their goals.	Ask questions that enable people to specify steps towards their goals.	Ask questions that invite reflection and focus on learning.
This helps bring clarity.	This brings meaning and purpose and provides direction and a context for change efforts.	This brings hope, gives people ideas about what to try and encourages them to keep trying.	This supports efforts at change and complements people's own resources.	This provides a way forward.	This helps people learn and encourages them to keep trying.

What difference can the column approach make?

We've comprehensively explored the strengths-based mind map and associated skills in this chapter. Much emphasis has been placed on the importance of using the strengths-based mind map as a guide for practice. We have also looked at the use of the column approach as a tool for practice that matches the mind map. But what difference can it make to use it? Here is a story that highlights its value.

Rebecca, with four boys five years of age and under, had been married and experienced physical and emotional violence. In a second relationship she experienced more violence before leaving that relationship. She then parented alone. Her first two boys were traumatised as a result of exposure to the violence. The behaviour of her first child, later diagnosed as having Attention Hyperactivity Deficit Disorder, made it exceptionally difficult, if not impossible at times, to leave the house. Her second child did not verbalise until he was five years old. He was later found to have autism. He smeared regularly and had night terrors among other difficulties. Her third child was 'fine' at twelve months old, but her baby suffered from colic and reflux, did not sleep and was constantly screaming. Here is the story of her experience of human service intervention:

Rebecca reaches a point where she isolates herself in her house in the struggle to cope. She isn't sleeping, is highly stressed and anxious and feels she can't cope. On a visit to the doctor with one of her boys she reports that she can't cope any longer and that she needs help. The clinic nurse, with Rebecca's go-ahead, calls a close friend of Rebecca's and the child protection service. Child protection workers visit Rebecca at home the same day. Her good friend, who had always been a strong support to Rebecca, arrives just prior.

The child protection workers are supportive and help calm Rebecca. They explain their job and talk about options. They arrange overnight support from Rebecca's family and her friend, and a visit from a family support service the following day.

Rebecca is highly anxious and agitated because of lack of sleep. A young worker from the family support service visits and is friendly but does not engage with Rebecca. She takes out a book about parenting and begins to read it out to Rebecca. Rebecca feels affronted and asks her to leave. She contacts the service and asks for another worker. The service asks Rebecca what sort of worker she would prefer. Rebecca tells them she wants a female Aboriginal worker who understands her culture, who is older and who has kids of her own.

This worker visits a couple of days later. The first thing she does is ask Rebecca if she can make her a cup of tea. Then she sits and asks Rebecca about herself. She first asks about Rebecca the person, not the mother. She asks a lot about Rebecca, the person. She just chats and she listens to Rebecca and as she does she notices and highlights one strength after another, quite naturally. She does this in every conversation, noting and acknowledging the difficulties in Rebecca's life and the challenges. She keeps finding even the smallest positives. She asks Rebecca about the things she wants and needs to happen. Rebecca feels heard and respected and even hopeful. She finds she is able to trust this worker. The worker visits Rebecca three times over the next four days.

On the fourth visit the worker takes out a copy of the five-column approach and explains it to Rebecca. Together they write down Rebecca's worries; the things they had already talked about. The worker asks questions that help Rebecca clarify and prioritise all they had talked about, her hopes for herself and her boys, and they write that down. They sum up the strengths and things that Rebecca can do herself, the supports she has, the resources she could use and the role they could play and they write that down. Then they make a plan about what can be done, using those strengths and resources and write that down too.

Here it is! Laid out in front of her—this tangled mess of problems that had had so much control for so long—pinned down in ink, simplified, now manageable and in perspective. Here are her great skills, her values, hopes and aspirations, her goals shining back at her – crisp, proud, and saying, 'You can do it!' A plan that almost jumps off the page with excitement, joined up with her beautiful friend's encouragement and the support of her loving family. This can make her life and her boys' lives better!

The powerful visual impact of the column approach—seeing the strengths, resources, goals and steps—brings great clarity for Rebecca. All those profoundly helpful conversations that strengthened her make even greater sense. This is Rebecca's work, supported and respected by a worker using the strengths-based mind map to guide meaningful conversation and planning.

From this point with active practical support from family, friends and a range of specialist services, work is undertaken that involves help with sleeping routines, child care, speech therapy, occupational therapy and behaviour therapy, tutoring and homework help.

All is well now.

Today Rebecca is an Aboriginal community worker studying for her social work degree.

In strengths-based practice both the process as outlined and each of the particular skills of the approach challenge personal and cultural constraints to change. Every question that leads to an exploration of aspirations, hopes, dreams, strengths, skills, exceptions, alternative stories, meaning, and the origins of ideas that people have, has the potential to challenge and resolve cultural and personal constraints to change. Every effort to reframe, externalise or develop concrete descriptions can challenge those constraints because doing so changes the story of the problem.

 EXERCISE – *Using the strengths-based mind map*

The following exercise is designed to assist people to practise using the stages of the strengths approach; to get a sense of how the solution-finding process can work as a whole and the connections between each of its parts. The questions are based on the various key skills of the strengths approach using the strengths-based stages of conversation and planning explored earlier in this chapter. These are suggested questions to get the ball rolling. You may well use your own or refer to the questions on pages 107-113. You can use the column approach 'template' and the headings discussed in this chapter to record your progress through the exercise. It is particularly beneficial to have a colleague help facilitate the process using the instructions provided.

1. Take a sheet of paper and draw up a five-column approach like the one used earlier in this chapter. Write a heading at the top of each column from left to right as follows: Issues and Feelings; My Picture of the Future; Strengths and Exceptions; Other Resources; and Plans and Steps.
   (Or you can use similar headings using your own words)

2. Choose an issue currently affecting you in your professional, community or personal life. What's happening and how are you feeling about it? What are you doing? What are others who might be involved doing?

3. What are the structural and cultural/personal constraints that are relevant to this issue? Is this a structural or cultural issue or both? How do structural issues affect the situation? What beliefs do you or others have that might be getting in the way of change?

4. Describe the constraints, issues, what's happening and what you are doing in concrete and specific terms. Note your feelings, the issues and the constraints in the first column.

5. On a scale of 1 to 10 (10 = best; 1 = worst) give yourself a rating that indicates where you are now in relation to resolving the issue. Note this rating in the first column.

6. Discuss how you would be feeling if the issues were resolved. What would be happening to enable you to feel like this? What would be happening if you were able to give yourself a higher rating? What would be happening if you were able to give yourself a rating of 10? What qualities do you want to be present in your life? What would be happening if the issues were resolved? What would you be doing differently?

7. Frame this description of your future picture in specific and concrete terms. Try writing this down in the present tense. Note these desired feelings and goals in the second column. Give yourself a rating of where you will be in your picture of the future and note it in the second column.

8. What strengths do you have that you can use to achieve your goals? What are the strengths of others who might be involved? What do the special people in your life see as your strengths? Explain these concretely: how do you demonstrate these strengths? What do others see or notice you doing when you use these strengths? Who are the special people in your life and what would they say about your ability to overcome problems and meet challenges? What stories would they recall? Note these strengths in the third column.

9. What are the exceptions to the problem? What happens when the problem is absent or less of a problem? What are you doing? What else is happening when the issues are not around? In other situations like this, what have you tried? What works? Note these in the third column.

10. Think about any additional resources that you might have to assist you to reach your goals (people, organisations, information or knowledge, material resources, decision-making resources, and so on). Are there resources that need to be accessed elsewhere? Note the resources in the fourth column.

11. Given your picture of the future, the strengths, exceptions and resources available, what can you do to resolve the issues? What do the strengths and exceptions suggest you could try? What steps will you take? Will others have a role and if so what will it be? Be concrete and specific. Note the steps and plans in the fifth column.

12. Give yourself a rating that measures any movement towards your goal since you started this exercise. Is this a higher rating? If so, what has made the difference?

Chapter Six

Client-owned Recording

---------------------- FEATURED QUOTES FROM THIS CHAPTER ----------------------

'The need for recording is a valid one but why not make empowerment, self-determination and change the primary purposes of recording?'

~

'Ensuring every word, every document written was completely transparent, consultative and inclusive had a remarkable effect on the relationships with the families I worked with, in terms of trust, in terms of their sense of ownership of the work we did together, and in terms of their esteem and ability to affect change in their lives.'

~

'The intention of client-owned recording is to assist and complement the process of empowerment and self-determination.'

O n moving from community work to child and family welfare in 1989, I was struck by how common agency and worker control of recording was in social work and human services generally, even among those who were forging more inclusive, collaborative and transparent ways of working.

I wanted to do something that might change this state of affairs, at least in my own little corner of the world. With support from my manager (thank you, Di O'Neil) I began by ensuring every word, every document written was completely transparent, consultative and inclusive of the families I worked with. This was an easy change to make. And it had a remarkable effect on relationships with these families in terms of trust, their sense of ownership of the work we did together, their esteem and their ability to affect change in their lives.

In a radical departure from conventional approaches to recording, workers began using open file systems and developed a client-owned approach to recording. This consisted of using paperwork tools such as the column approach, scales (see pages 153-160), contact sheets and letter-writing, replacing the need for traditional case notes.

This represented a deliberate effort to move away from terminology that is prevalent in medical and legal contexts that has so strongly influenced much social work thinking in the past. People are not 'cases' and their lives cannot be reduced to files. Not surprisingly the idea caught on in organisations adopting strengths-based and anti-oppressive ways of working. Over the years numerous agencies have adopted a client-owned approach to recording or modified recording practices to make them more inclusive and transparent.

This chapter explores the concept and practice of client-owned recording that complements the various skills and processes of the strengths approach. It includes paperwork records, letter writing, the column approach and scaling.

The table below compares key characteristics of traditional and client-owned approaches to recording. A client-owned approach, in contrast to a traditional approach, is open and transparent. It helps make workers and organisations more accountable to the people accessing the services and is driven by the principles of empowerment and self-determination. Wherever possible clients are enabled to keep original records in a folder of their own and the agency keeps a duplicate copy. This has the added advantage of 'transportability'. People can take their own records with them if they use other services or move to other regions.

Comparing Traditional and Client-owned Approaches to Recording

THE TRADITIONAL APPROACH TO RECORDING:	THE CLIENT-OWNED APPROACH TO RECORDING:
• is determined by the need for accountability to organisations, funding bodies, bureaucracies, the law and community and professional standards	• meets accountability requirements
• 'hides' records from clients or makes them mysterious to clients	• assumes that objectivity is not possible and that there are many truths
• tends to use coding, symbols, language and jargon not accessible or friendly to clients	• is based on the principles of empowerment and self-determination and the goals of the intervention
• can leave confidentiality and client's rights open to abuse	• ensures clients know about the record and its purposes, and ensures open access to the record at all times—at the very least
• assumes objectivity is possible	• aims to enable client ownership of the record
• can create files that do not represent the whole story or the true story (worker-subjective)	• makes it possible for clients to write their own record or participate in the recording
• is written by the worker at the office away from the client	• enables the client to decide what will be done with the record
• is held by the agency	• makes workers more accountable to clients
• uses case notes as the norm for recording.	• enables the client's story to emerge and be included
	• assists the change process and good practice
	• uses client-friendly language and formats
	• enables the client to hold the record while the agency keeps a copy.

The conventional approach to recording

Workers keep records of all sorts of activity depending on their roles: case notes, case plans, reports, data collection, supervision sessions, occasional and annual reviews, records of meetings, community activities and so on. Recording has long been a convention in human service work for important reasons. Keeping a record helps meet accountability requirements. We are accountable to our agencies, our profession, funding bodies, government, community standards and statutory authorities. Keeping a record of background information and history can also be important for continuity of service delivery.

The traditions or conventions of recording in the delivery of human services have, however, often tended, and still tend in many cases, to be dominated and driven by the need for accountability with little, if any, attention given to transparency of recording. The right to own the client's file had been an assumption so entrenched in the helping professions that it had rarely been questioned (unfortunately still the case today in many services). The benefits of recording tend to be for the worker, organisation, funding body or government department. People who use human services may not know that records are kept or, if they do, are kept in the dark about what is written and why. They are often inaccessible because of coding, symbols and professional language or bureaucratic jargon (O'Neil, Deal & McCashen 1998).

When recording is hidden from clients there is a risk that a false story can be constructed, rights can be neglected and confidentiality left open to abuse. The file becomes the worker's or agency's subjective story despite efforts to be objective. Even when only 'the facts' are recorded workers can inadvertently omit important and relevant information or inadvertently give a slant that does not reflect the client's experience or perspective. All of these factors counter the principles of self-determination, collaboration, inclusion, consultation and transparency.

Making empowerment the purpose of recording

What we see as the purposes of recording changes the way we go about it. The need for recording is a valid one but why not make empowerment, self-determination and change the primary purposes of recording? In a client-owned, client-directed approach to recording, the purposes centre on transparency, the building of trust and the reduction of power imbalances. The principles of the strengths approach can be given clear and practical expression through the way we record. As a team, workers and clients collaborate in recording. It is transparent, open, participatory and inclusive. Recording and paperwork become tools conducive to learning, growth and change.

Requirements and Purposes of Recording

REQUIREMENT	PURPOSE
• Accountability • Organisational requirements • Government or funding requirements • Background information for continuity • History.	• To reduce power imbalances between workers and clients • To make work transparent • To enable client participation in, and ownership of, the record of work • To strengthen trust and positive relationships • To provide tools for the recording of issues, strengths, exceptions, goals and measurement of change and progress • To contribute to the enhancement of learning, growth and change.

Developing client-owned recording

Client-owned recording consists primarily of a set of paperwork tools that are used to assist change. In a client-owned, client-directed approach workers usually do not keep case notes. Letter writing and a range of paperwork tools usually replace these. If case notes are kept, they are written with the client. The paperwork tools used include information sheets, column approaches, letters from the worker to the client, contact sheets, measurement tools and a wide range of tools used during the course of work carried out. All paperwork is characterised by client-friendly and context-friendly language. Any additional reports by workers or others are included.

There are a number of considerations and cautions in developing client-owned recording. Service delivery contexts vary widely so paperwork is best tailored to the unique needs of different groups, individuals or service areas. Striking a balance between need and purpose can be tricky. In some contexts the need for accountability by funding bodies or government can overwhelm the purposes of empowerment and self-determination in this approach to recording. This is especially true for families and young people who are subject to statutory intervention or in mental health contexts where there are often significant 'needs assessment' and data collection requirements.

The following questions are useful in the development of client-owned, client-directed recording by an organisation:

- How will the paperwork enhance empowerment and self-determination?

- How will it support and enhance change efforts?

- How can rights and responsibilities be established?

- How can we ensure choices about which paperwork tools are used or included?

- Is the paperwork understandable to the client; is it client-friendly?

- Is the language strengths-based and respectful?

- How will it assist participation, reflection and learning?

- Can the paperwork be held by the client and what would need to happen to enable this?

- Which paperwork tools will need to be tailored to unique programs or contexts?

- Is there room for flexibility and responsiveness to unique needs and contexts?

- Can the paperwork replace case notes?

- Will the paperwork accurately reflect the work carried out?

- Will it enable a record of the issues, strengths, exceptions, resources, aspirations, goals, plans and efforts of clients?

- How will it measure change and progress?

- Does it enable evaluation?

- How can it meet statutory and other requirements in a client-friendly way?

- Is it desirable to have a common information-gathering system throughout the organisation?

The principles of ownership, inclusion, collaboration and self-determination invite us to use recording in ways that are empowering and purposeful for change. If values and attitudes are more important than skills and knowledge then our attitudes and values matter most in guiding our work and the way we use any tool.

As stated earlier, the intention of client-owned recording is to assist and complement the process of empowerment and self-determination. Using a client-owned approach to recording can still be as oppressive or colonising as traditional systems if we do not respect this intention.

The following checklist of questions can be useful for workers to consider in relation to client-owned recording—and when using any tool:

- Do I have informed consent to use the tool?

- Is the timing respectful of client-readiness?

- How can the tool be introduced and contextualised appropriately?

- Will the client understand its purpose?

- Is the tool or the way I am using it culturally relevant and respectful?

- Will it complement the client's self-esteem and meet their needs and choices?

- Is it enhancing self-determination?

- Will it help the process of change?

- What is the purpose of using this particular tool?

- How does it fit the current phase in the work?

- Am I playing the expert or enabling the client to emerge as the expert?

Using the column approach for recording

As noted in chapter five, the column approach is a paperwork tool based on the strengths-based mind map. It reflects the principle, discussed in chapter two, that additional resources should be added as a complement to people's own strengths. It is designed to record the unique work and planning that people do together, and to help make recording transparent and client-owned. As illustrated in chapter five, we are concerned with five key questions:

- What are you worried about? (The issues)

- What do you want to be happening instead? (The picture of the future)

- What are the good things despite the problem? (The strengths and exceptions)

- Who and what can help? (The resources)

- What are you going to do? (The steps and plans)

Using the column approach, responses to these questions can be captured in summary form during the course of our work.

Over the many years since the first work was undertaken using the strengths-based mind map (see O'Neil & McCashen 1992) the column approach has become a core framework for guiding strengths-based, power-with conversations in human services. Its generic nature is beneficial for goal-setting, planning, reflection and action in virtually any human service context. It has been used widely in casework services, for guiding community development work, in group work, in staff supervision and for team and organisational planning. It helps engage people in empowering ways by demystifying change processes; making them transparent, understandable and accessible. It thus helps reduce power imbalances and enables people's expertise to emerge.

As with all tools, the column approach should be used flexibly and tailored to meet unique needs and contexts rather than being used in prescriptive ways. The cautions for client-owned recording discussed above apply no less to the column approach. There is a wide range of possibilities in using the column approach. While this tool is commonly referred to as the 'Five Column Approach', the number of columns and the headings can be varied according to the different purposes of the work being undertaken. There can be three, four, five or six columns or, over time, a combination of different column tools. Possible options are illustrated below:

Variations of the Column Approach Tool

ISSUES	THE PICTURE OF THE FUTURE	STRENGTHS	GOALS	STEPS
WORRIES	WHAT I WANT THINGS TO BE LIKE	WHAT DOESN'T WORK	WHAT WORKS	WHAT TO TRY
WHAT I DON'T WANT TO BE HAPPENING	WHAT I WANT TO BE HAPPENING	WHAT I DO WELL	WHAT I'VE TRIED THAT WORKS	WHAT I WILL TRY

WHAT WE VALUE AND CARE ABOUT	WHAT LIFE WILL BE LIKE WHEN THINGS ARE LIKE THIS	WHAT LIFE IS LIKE WHEN IT'S ALREADY LIKE THIS	THE PEOPLE AND THINGS THAT HELPED	THE THINGS WE DO WELL THAT COULD HELP	WHAT WE'LL TRY

THE WORRIES	THE GOOD THINGS	OUR HOPES AND DREAMS	PEOPLE WHO CAN HELP	WHAT TO DO

WHAT I WANT TO BE HAPPENING	WHAT'S BEEN TRIED? WHAT'S WORKED WHAT HASN'T?	WHAT WOULD FEEL OK?	HOW WILL I KNOW IF IT'S HELPED?

The column approach can be easily adapted to integrate externalising (refer to pages 135–138). For example, with regard to using substances, the column approach could look like this:

WHAT *USING* IS DOING TO MY FAMILY	HOW I'VE TRIED TO BEAT *USING*	WHAT'S WORKED	WHO CAN HELP	WHAT TO TRY

WHAT LIFE IS LIKE WHEN *USING* IS IN CONTROL	WHAT LIFE COULD BE LIKE WITHOUT *USING*	WHAT LIFE IS LIKE WHEN *USING* ISN'T IN CONTROL	WHAT I'M DOING WHEN *USING* ISN'T IN CONTROL

The Signs of Safety Child Protection Practice Framework (Government of Western Australia Department for Child Protection 2011, pp. 13–5), which has been widely adopted internationally, takes a similar approach to assessment and planning. It asks practitioners:

When we think about the situation facing this family:

- What are we worried about?
- What's working well?
- What needs to happen?

Signs of Safety uses a three-column tool for working with families which asks the three same questions: What are we worried about? (The issues). What's working well? (The strengths). What needs to happen? (Goals and steps to be taken).

Signs of Safety also uses the headings—worries, strengths and goals—in another slight variation (Turnell 2012). The framework also includes the 'Three Houses Tool' (*The Signs of Safety Child Protection Practice Framework* 2011, p. 19) developed by Nicki Weld and Maggie Greening in New Zealand. This tool adapts these three key questions for use in assessment with children as follows: House of Worries [the issues], House of Good Things [strengths and exceptions], House of Dreams [picture of the future].

Art therapists use painting, drawing, collage or sculpture to assist children and adults to explore their experience, develop a picture of the future, and story their strengths and the good things. Collage, painting and drawing can also be used as an alternative to words in a column approach.

The column approach can be used successfully in community settings. For example, an Indigenous community in Far North Queensland adapted the tool by painting their stories, hopes, dreams, and strengths on canvas instead of using columns. Another Indigenous community in northern Australia used the column approach in groups to develop a plan for resolving difficulties they faced in their community.

Letter writing

Another useful and important tool for recording and supporting change is letter writing. In the strengths approach, letter writing refers to letters written by workers to clients in order to complement and assist their efforts to make change. They can also take the form of notes or cards. Over the years, narrative therapists have used letter writing as a therapeutic tool (see Epston 1994 and White & Epston 1990).

While writing letters to clients is not strictly speaking client-owned (clients do not usually directly participate in the letter writing) the same principles that enable ownership of the change process apply. Letters should complement people's efforts and reflect their experiences, stories, aspirations, strengths and plans and the meaning they give to them. In other words, what is written must acknowledge and value what is true for the client as well as invite re-storying.

There are a variety of ways in which letters can be used to support and assist change. They can help build trust and rapport by reflecting our understanding and connection. They can sum up any aspect of work undertaken—achievements, goals, strengths and so on. Any element of strengths-based practice can be complemented and extended through the use of letters. These can include:

- relationship building

- validating and acknowledging

- clarifying and developing concrete description

- inviting reflection

- summarising

- reframing

- externalising

- developing a picture of the future and goal-setting

- identifying strengths, exceptions and resources

- noticing and measuring progress and change.

Letters can be an enduring record; they can be referred to over weeks, months or years. They can also become an essential component of a client-owned approach to recording because they so readily replace case notes. This is especially true when used in combination with other forms of client-owned recording.

There are some important cautions regarding the use of any tool. In the case of letter writing there is always a risk that when we write letters they may fall into the wrong hands. Confidentiality may be breached or, worse still, someone might be put at risk. Family violence situations are a clear example. Secondly, letters should only be written following permission from the client to do so. This typically involves a conversation about the reasons for writing letters including the desire to be transparent in recording, the sort of letters that might be written (for example, to summarise work or to invite reflection), how letters should be addressed and how they might be used.

Other considerations include:

- using culturally-relevant language
- literacy issues
- layout
- being yourself
- being purposeful and clear about why any letter is being written
- ensuring the letter is open for feedback (for example from a supervisor) before finalising and sending it.

The following questions can be a useful as a checklist for preparing letters.

- Does the beginning of the letter clearly state what the letter is about?
- Is the language respectful, relevant and understandable?
- Does the letter affirm, encourage and validate the client?
- How might it strengthen the client's role?
- How does it strengthen a relationship of trust between the client and the worker?
- Are concrete evidence and examples used to support generalisation?
- Does it reflect the client's story, including strengths, exceptions and aspirations?
- Might it be interpreted as patronising or condescending?
- How can the letter contribute to strengthening the client's ownership of the change process?
- How might it help to clarify issues, goals, strengths, exceptions and plans?
- Does it invite reflection?
- How might it assist continuity in the work you are doing together?
- How might reflection on exceptions help the client to 're-story' the past and present?
- Are the client's aspirations and goals accurately captured and used as a point of reference for ongoing work?

So what might a letter that reflects principles of strengths-based practice look like? Here's an example for consideration:

Dear Margaret,

Thanks for the welcome into your home on Thursday. It was good to meet you and your kids.

As I said to you when we met, I often write letters to people I work with. This time I am writing to see if I can summarise our conversation and to ask a couple of things I've been wondering about regarding your picture of the future that we touched on.

The things you shared with me included the 'hard times', as you put it, since you were able to 'kick Maurie out'. You said it was like 'pushing shit uphill' trying to bring the kids up on your own, having so little time to yourself and always struggling to make ends meet. You also described how Marcus has been a 'handful' since he started school and that Tammy doesn't give you any peace because she's so clingy.

When I asked you what you wanted for yourself and your kids you were very definite about it. You said you 'wanted a life, the kids behaving themselves and no more trash coming to the house.'

As we worked through the five column form you were able to get quite clear about the issues. We wrote them down like this:

1. Tammy is clingy. She hangs onto me or follows me around most of the time and doesn't seem to be able to entertain herself.

2. Marcus gets into trouble at school and four times in the last five weeks he has refused to go.

3. I have no time to myself—people keep coming to the house who I don't want here.

You described these issues in very specific ways but we didn't get a chance to talk more about the idea of your 'picture of the future'. At the time, you said you weren't feeling all that hopeful because of people coming to your home that you didn't want there, and how you found it hard to 'kick them out'. You were clear about what you didn't want to be happening.

I've been wondering what things would be like if these people weren't coming. Whether it would make a difference in terms of the kid's behaviour and the time you have to yourself. Have you given this much thought? I've also been wondering what it would take for you to ask these people to stay away; how you might do that. I remember being struck by the skill and courage you used to assert yourself in asking Maurie to leave and how you persisted with this.

The other thing I've been wondering is what exactly you would like the kids to be doing differently when they are 'behaving'. It's clear that Marcus won't be mucking up at school and that Tammy won't be 'clingy'. But what sort of behaviour do you hope for instead? Have you thought about what you might be doing differently yourself when the kids are behaving? I've been wondering what's different on the days when Marcus hasn't refused to go to school. Is anything different at school on those days? Are you doing anything differently?

Anyway Margaret, I will finish here and look forward to seeing you next Friday and hearing what you think about these questions.

All the best,

Rani

On reading the first lines of this letter it is clear what the letter is about. This letter achieves a number of practice goals that are strengths-based. It summarises clearly what Margaret has shared. It uses her own language and evidence provided by her in relation to the issues she is confronted with and refers to her aspirations. Reference is made to a particular exception (asserting herself in getting Maurie to leave) that may help expose strengths relevant to current and future challenges in her life.

The letter tends to be framed in a tentative way and avoids assumptions. It relies primarily on questions that invite Margaret to think about her future and any exceptions that might expose other strengths and ways of doing things that already work. It is likely to lead Margaret to reflect. Since the worker cannot know the answers, and does not pretend to, the partnership rests on attitudes of respect for Margaret's potential, her aspirations and her right to be an active agent of change in her own right.

Journalling and other writing

Many people find journalling and personal writing very helpful. Encouraging people to write can assist their learning and empowerment. Here is one worker's story about how writing helped.

Jenny liked to ring several times a day to discuss daily issues. One time she became extremely upset because she was unable to get a response. She wrote to the worker about her frustration and commented that she had solved the issue without her. The worker wrote apologising for not being able to respond and complemented her on resolving the issue.

Keeping a diary and letter writing became a new way of working together. Jenny found writing down issues was a good way of dealing with what was bothering her (externalising) and she was able to use this instead of ringing daily. The worker would spend time weekly discussing the diary. Often there were days when there was nothing written in the diary. The worker encouraged Jenny to write about what was happening on these days (exceptions).

Jenny found this helpful as she was then able to explore what she was doing on good days and this assisted her in finding strategies for bad days. Jenny uses her diary for many purposes now and finds it a useful tool in dealing with her life.

Jenny no longer uses the service. She sometimes writes to the worker to let her know some of the good things that are happening in her life.

Cooper 1999, p. 24

Scales

In chapter five 'scaling' was introduced as a skill for noticing and measuring change. Below are examples of tools that can be used for scaling. These are among a set of tools developed and published by Innovative Resources. They are available as an interactive DVD called *The Scaling Kit* and contain ten digitally interactive scaling masters with moveable components and text bubbles. These visual metaphors include such images as a temperature gauge, a water tank, a balance, a pathway and a ladder. They can be used by individuals, organisations and community groups to measure and evaluate feelings, progress, wellbeing, satisfaction, hope and so on.

Here's an example of how scales can be used to help people evaluate their own progress, set their own goals and find exceptions.

Bronwyn came to see her worker saying she was feeling confused and 'down'. She described her situation in terms of running 'hot and cold' but was unable to identify why she was down and found it difficult to distinguish good and bad times in her life.

The worker suggested it might be possible to get a better idea of any changes if she had a simple means of recording her feelings each day and any associated events. She wasn't sure. The worker showed her the 'scales' and explained how they could be used. Bronwyn chose a scale that depicted a thermometer and decided she would take some copies and mark each day with a different coloured pen for the morning, afternoon and evening, on a scale of 0 to 90 degrees, how she was feeling. The worker also asked her to note beside the corresponding rating any particular thinking or event which might explain her chosen rating.

On each visit Bronwyn brought along her ratings. By the third visit a clear pattern began to emerge. The higher the rating the more likely certain positive conditions were to be present. This provided lots of examples of exceptions and positive experiences which, over a couple of months, proved to be useful in helping Bronwyn to move forward.

Other paperwork tools

Myriads of tools are used by workers in human services every day in their work. Often they can be altered or enhanced to bring an emphasis on strengths and aspirations. For example, goal attainment sheets (using a rating scale) are useful in measuring change or a simple graph can be useful for tracking progress and the 'ups and downs' that naturally occur when people are attempting change. By focussing on the times when things are going well, these tools can expose exceptions and strengths that might not otherwise be noticed. Other tools such as the family tree or relationship map, rejuvenated by the strengths approach and by the creativity of the worker, can serve many strengths-based purposes beyond their original intent.

The principles that underlie client-owned recording are no less relevant in contexts such as group work and community development. The same strengths-based principles for recording apply inside an organisation, for example, in the context of staff supervision and within teams. Of course, the tools for recording vary according to the context and the purpose of the activities undertaken, but transparency, inclusion and self-determination should characterise the recording and sharing of written information.

Visual and tactile resources

There are, of course, hundreds of tools found throughout human services that have been used for many years to develop alternative stories, value strengths, name emotions, get in touch with aspirations and find ways of overcoming problems. Alongside those discussed so far in this book are an inspiring collection of card sets, stickers, paperwork and tactile tools developed by Innovative Resources, which was founded by Russell Deal in the early 1990s and grew to become the publishing arm of St Luke's (now merged with Anglicare Victoria). Operating as a social enterprise since its inception, Innovative Resources now has over sixty strengths-based, solution-focussed tools which take account of different learning styles and draw on the power of metaphors and visual elements such as cartoons, photographs, illustrations, paintings, collage, and font-based design to create meaningful conversations with children, young people and adults. The use of tactile resources such as cards, stickers, clay and squeeze-able figurines—things that can be sorted, shuffled, hidden, discovered, moved around, and randomly selected—opens up different neural pathways for people (especially kinesthetic and visual learners) to recognise and talk about strengths, feelings, goals, dreams and next steps in creative and inspiring ways. The capacity to bring an element of playfulness and colour into activities using hands-on resources is meaningful and significant; as it can quickly open up conversations that may not otherwise easily occur.

As digital technologies continue to open up new worlds of interaction and portability, many of these resources are finding their way into electronic formats where images can be stored, tagged, drawn on, labelled, circled, projected, sorted randomly, scrolled through, saved in personal galleries, posted and emailed with relevant messages or notes attached.

Technology and client-owned recording

The implications of technology for client-owned recording are far-reaching. Here are some thoughts from Andrew Shirres, practice development coach for Innovative Resources, on the ways in which technology can affect record keeping:

The fast developing world of technology holds particular implications for strengths-based recording practice. The move towards on-line databases that 'keep' client information is sometimes seen as an impediment to strengths-based recording practice due to the perception that it places a barrier between the client and the information held about her or him. Within the 'shadow-side' of this perception lies an opportunity, however, for a shift in emphasis towards greater client 'agency' and, consequently, ownership of information.

On a broad level, recent evolutions of 'client management systems', for example, include 'portals' that allow for client access to notes, funding, financial packages and staff rostering. Others go even further, allowing for clients to upload notes, images and comments to their on-line files.

To a lesser extent, client access to on-line files can be enhanced by remote access to client management systems in 'real' time through the use of tablets. This permits the client and their worker to collaborate on the record of a meeting while the meeting takes place in the home, office or even in a public setting. While, of course, collaboration in a public setting on progress notes is possible in a hard-copy format, the image of a client and worker using a tablet together does not as yet carry the same stigma as more traditional paper folders where a perception of a power imbalance appears more apparent.

In a similar vein, social media, email communication, and text messaging all provide new possibilities for client recording to break away from power-over implications of the worker-as-expert controlling the means of information collection. While normal cautions must be heeded in terms of confidentiality and intentional or unintentional public sharing, this should not diminish the very real, and exciting, opportunities that such technology provides for immediate, accurate and relevant recording of information.

We are left with a concept far removed from the 'norm' of a worker at a desk writing up the notes of a previous contact, sometimes days or even weeks later, trying to remember what they saw, heard or thought. A new norm could take its place, one where clients can choose where, when and how they can contribute to, or access, their information.

Chapter Seven

The Strengths Approach to Service Management

─────────── FEATURED QUOTES FROM THIS CHAPTER ───────────

'When human service professionals make a commitment to self-determination they take up the challenge to ensure that their work is characterised by an emphasis on people's right to control their own lives, decide their own futures and determine how they will do this.'

~

'From the beginning a central question pre-occupies workers concerned with self-determination: How will our conversations and decisions enhance people's ability to take control and resolve the issues?'

~

'The goal of service management is to create conditions that enable people to become their own service managers.'

f I needed support of any sort from a human service organisation I would want to be treated with respect. I would want to feel heard and understood, not judged. I would want to know what's going on and why, and be sure that nothing was hidden from me. I would want a meaningful say in what's done. I would want my resources acknowledged and valued, to be treated as capable and enabled to do as much as I possibly could myself. I would want to be able to trust the worker supporting me and be helped to decide my own goals and plans, and what needed to happen to reach them.

In the strengths approach to service delivery, workers collaborate with individuals and families to manage the delivery of services. They do not manage 'cases'. This chapter explores the implications of the strengths approach for casework, case planning and case management services. I use the terms 'service management' and 'service planning' rather than 'case management' and 'case planning' because they are closer to the spirit and intentions of the strengths approach.

Strengths-based assessment: responding to requests for service

'Assessment' is a term commonly used in social work and therapeutic settings to describe the initial intervention by workers to assess needs and decide on a response to people asking for assistance. In a deficit-based approach the focus is on establishing what the needs are and providing resources that are believed to meet those needs. Obviously, a strengths approach to assessment is something quite different.

Strengths-based assessment is a pro-active process aimed at:

- clarifying people's stories and the issues that need to be addressed

- specifying what will be different when the issues no longer exist (creating a picture of the future)

- identifying strengths and capacities

- exploring the resources needed to assist change

- deciding on a course of action in light of the future picture, strengths and resources that will assist the change process.

Assessment starts with the initial response to a request for service. This typically involves contact by phone or in person from the client or another party, and a meeting (or meetings) with the client to explore the request more thoroughly. Assessment is a process or phase rather than simply a one-off intervention and might better be described as a response to the request for service.

The request for service may come from someone other than the client, such as statutory workers, non-government services or family members. If this is the case the aim is to find out what the client knows of the request. It is important that the prospective client is aware of the referral and agrees to be contacted by the service. If the client has not agreed to the request it would be inappropriate to proceed unless there are sufficiently pressing safety concerns that require an immediate response.

Strengths-based assessment is characterised by an exploration and validation of experience, strengths, exceptions, aspirations and resources. It is not a needs assessment. It is not a psychosocial assessment.

From the beginning a central question pre-occupies workers concerned with self-determination: How will our conversations and decisions enhance people's ability to take control and resolve the issues?

In doing strengths-based assessments:

- people's experience is acknowledged and validated and issues clarified

- people are assisted to describe and define their picture of the future

- people are assisted to identify their strengths and the exceptions

- people are exposed to the experience of being experts on their situation

- people are assisted to identify resources from their natural networks that can be used to help reach their goals

- people are enabled to make informed choices about other resources that might help them reach their goals

- workers are clear about whether or not the agency should be involved, why it will be involved and what it will offer

- terms for working together are clearly established in a transparent way.

The following account illustrates a strengths-based assessment.

Andrea (30 years old) and her children are subject to a child protection investigation. Her three children have been arriving at school without having had breakfast. Her youngest, Kyle (nine years old), has been returned home by police late at night on two occasions recently. Her 14-year-old daughter, Stephanie, has been in trouble for shoplifting and, following another incident, has been charged with assault. Twelve-year-old Damian has been diagnosed with Attention Deficit Hyperactivity Disorder. Stephanie has been allocated a support worker through the Juvenile Justice system. The school welfare coordinator and teachers are concerned about Damian and Kyle's behaviour in the classroom and their lack of interest in learning. Andrea complains of being constantly tired.

John, from a family support team, takes a request from the Child Protection Service. The request is for intensive support and counselling for Andrea and support for her children to address concerns. John is careful to clarify the status of the request: Does Andrea know the request is being made and, if so, how does she feel about it? The protective worker states that there are protective concerns but no statutory order is being taken out at this stage. She also states that Andrea does not yet know that the request is being made. John hesitates to proceed with the request citing his agency's policy not to respond without prior consent by the family, adding that his agency is keen to provide assistance once Andrea has given clear agreement to the agency providing support.

He and the protective worker agree to arrange a meeting with Andrea and her children once this has happened. The protective worker contacts John again later that day saying that Andrea is in agreement with intensive support and open to John contacting her, and they arrange a meeting.

John, conscious of the impact of strangers intervening in Andrea's life, phones to introduce himself and the agency and to hear personally from Andrea how she feels about the meeting. He finds that Andrea is a little anxious and acknowledges how difficult things must be for her. He tells Andrea what he knows already and checks the accuracy of the information with her. Andrea confirms the information from the protective worker. John asks for permission to enquire more about her situation. He makes it clear that he and his agency will not be putting any pressure on her to participate and that he will respect her choice at all times. Andrea, at first reluctantly, tells John about her situation but gains confidence as he shows interest in her circumstances.

John asks Andrea what has helped her hold things together so far. Andrea seems taken aback by this question and says she doesn't know. He asks what she thinks are the good things about her children and her family. Andrea hesitates in response to this question and then tells John, 'We stick together'. Andrea comments that it's probably why things haven't been a lot worse. John asks Andrea whether she could think about other strengths in her family before the meeting—the good things about her children, what happens when things are going well for her and her children. Andrea agrees to give it some thought.

John asks Andrea what she hopes will change as a result of any work she and he might do together. Andrea says she wants child protection off her back but she needs support with the kids, mainly Damian, because, 'He's a real handful'. She also tells John that she needs some rest and that she wants Stephanie to stay out of trouble.

John and the protective worker meet with Andrea. Through discussion they clarify the key concerns. Andrea reiterates what she has told John and identifies other concerns:

- Kyle going out without permission and not knowing where he is

- Damian's difficult behaviour; constantly demanding attention and on the go all the time

- Stephanie getting into trouble

- Being tired

- Damian and Kyle misbehaving at school

- Child Protection being involved.

The protective worker specifies the following concerns:

- Kyle's safety and Andrea not knowing where he is

- The children not being provided breakfast.

With a commitment to strengths-based practice and an awareness that the issues presented provide only part of the story of this family John is keen to explore what strengths and exceptions are present. He cites Andrea's comment on the phone that things would probably be a lot worse if they didn't stick together as a family and asks her more about this. He also asks Andrea whether she's thought any more about what she considers as the children's strengths and her own. He helps her to describe what she wants for her family.

Through lengthy discussion and reflection Andrea is helped to describe the strengths in her family and a picture of what she wants for herself and her children. They also spend time discussing possible additional resources that might be helpful. John gets Andrea's permission to record the issues, strengths, resources and picture of the future explaining that this could be useful to refer to in the future and help keep him on track in his work with her if they decide to keep working together. He introduces Andrea to a column approach sheet and uses it to make a record of the main points.

Andrea's Five Column Plan

ANDREA'S CONCERNS	ANDREA'S FUTURE PICTURE	STRENGTHS	OTHER RESOURCES	THINGS TO TRY
Damian's behaviour.	Child Protection won't be involved.	We stick together as a family.	Kyle and Damian's principal doesn't judge me.	See if my sister can give me a break occasionally.
Not knowing where Kyle is.	I will be feeling energetic.	Stephanie looks after the boys and cares about them (gives me a break).	The school has been good with the boys.	Arrange to meet the school to see what I can do to sort things out (John will contact the principal and go with Andrea).
Damian and Kyle misbehaving at school.	I'll be getting the kids breakfast.	Stephanie stays out of trouble at school.	Stephanie's youth worker (she likes her).	
Being tired a lot.	Kyle and Damian are behaving at school.	Some days the boys don't get into trouble at school.	My sister is a support to me.	Arrange with Stephanie to meet her worker to see how things are going there.
Stephanie getting into trouble.	Stephanie is helping me a bit more and will have control of her behaviour.	I get the kids breakfast when I'm not too tired.	John [the worker]	
Child Protection being involved (breakfast for the kids).		Stephanie has never done anything illegal before.		See about some after-school activities for the boys.

The protective worker agrees that the goals set in the future picture are relevant to the protective concerns and that if Andrea agrees to work on these, and have John involved, then the Child Protection Service would be satisfied. John asks the protective worker what would satisfy Child Protection that they would not need to be involved any longer. The protective worker reiterates that if the kids are getting breakfast each day and Kyle is not at risk out on his own they would have no reason to be involved.

At this point John asks Andrea whether she would agree to working together to resolve the issues and she agrees. The initial assessment is complete and, at the same time, a client-owned plan is established as the basis for continuing work.

The following agreements are made and recorded in an open, transparent way: Child Protection's role is to monitor progress in relation to protective concerns. John's role is to support Andrea to reach her goals including the resolution of the protective issues. Andrea's role is to undertake action to reach her goals. John will report weekly to the protective worker on progress made and inform him of any protective concerns. They will meet in three weeks to review progress. John will visit Andrea most days for the time being and make contact with Stephanie's worker from the Juvenile Justice Service to make a time to meet with her, Stephanie and Andrea with the view to developing a coordinated plan.

John outlines commitments regarding confidentiality and rights that his agency makes. He gives a signed form to Andrea that addresses that commitment in writing. He will not receive or give information to anyone without Andrea's permission, unless someone is at risk. He will not meet with anyone about Andrea or her family without her being present unless she gives informed consent in writing.

The following questions can act as a guide for assessment:

- What are the issues? What are the reasons for the request?

- How does the person define the issues?

- Is there a crisis that needs to be alleviated and what opportunities are there for self-determination and participation in this process?

- Have issues of safety been sufficiently explored?

- Has the person's experience been sufficiently validated?

- What are people's strengths and resources?

- What resources are available in people's networks that can be mobilised to assist change or provide support?

- How might these be mobilised to help resolve the issues?

- What will change as a result of additional resources being provided by the agency?

- Are there other resources available elsewhere?

- Is there any risk of unjustifiably rescuing people in this situation?

- Are additional resources being mobilised in ways that value and respect people's strengths and resources?

- Are people's aspirations and goals clear?

- What can be done to enable the establishment of a client-owned plan?

Service management and service planning

In the strengths approach the practice goal is to create conditions that enable people to become their own service managers. Service management can be defined as the coordination of resources and services that assist people to reach their goals. It involves the collaborative management of services with clearly defined and agreed goals, roles, tasks, responsibilities and safety issues. It is an active process of assessing, planning and organising resources, and measuring progress. Service planning consists of conversation, reflection and action that lead to a client-owned service plan.

The following diagram illustrates this process. Service management begins with the formation of a partnership between stakeholders. This collaborative effort involves the development of a plan to meet the goals of the client while respecting bottom lines such as safety.

Service Planning Process

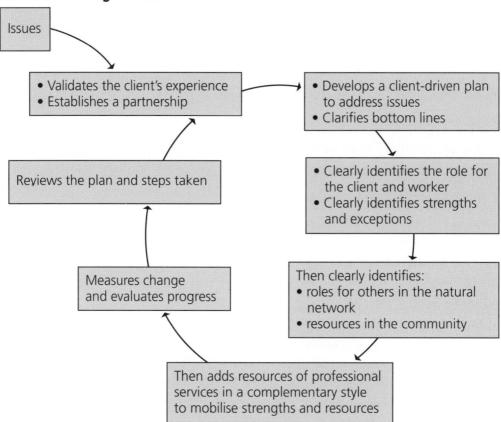

Issues

- Validates the client's experience
- Establishes a partnership

- Develops a client-driven plan to address issues
- Clarifies bottom lines

Reviews the plan and steps taken

- Clearly identifies the role for the client and worker
- Clearly identifies strengths and exceptions

Measures change and evaluates progress

Then clearly identifies:
- roles for others in the natural network
- resources in the community

Then adds resources of professional services in a complementary style to mobilise strengths and resources

The role of service manager

The role of service manager is to coordinate ongoing assessment, planning and evaluation. Service planning meetings become an avenue for sharing information and deciding tasks and action that will facilitate desired outcomes. The service manager has an essential role as facilitator in assisting and supporting stakeholders to plan, take action and evaluate, with particular emphasis on assisting people to become their own service managers. Service planning centres on establishing goals and plans, reviewing and evaluating what has worked (measuring change), and storying the exceptions and strengths.

In Andrea's situation the child protection worker has service management responsibility in the strict sense. This arises from statutory authority but John is taking a service management role. He does this by helping establish a plan that is 'client-owned', opening the possibility for Andrea to become her own service manager.

The column approaches prepared by John and Andrea (above) and Miang and her worker (chapter five) capture concerns, strengths, exceptions, the future picture and plans. They illustrate client-owned, client-directed service plans. These are Andrea's and Miang's service plans; each part of the plan was defined by them together with their workers as part of a collaborative effort. Such reflections and plans arise out of questions based on the stages of the strengths-based process. These plans are developed in partnership with clients and include the roles, responsibilities and tasks of others, including workers.

Stages of strengths-based service management

The stages outlined in the table below provide a framework for thinking about key steps in the service management process. The framework captures various characteristics of strengths-based, client-directed practice. Again, it is not suggested that things unfold in a neat progression. This table describes a process for service management in its idealised form. In the first phase of work (the process of assessment) a relationship of trust is built and clear terms for working together are established. These include clarifying rights, roles, limitations, ownership of recording and so on, as illustrated in the work with Andrea. Once these conditions are in place a more thorough exploration of strengths, exceptions, resources and goals can be undertaken (stages two and three).

Stages four and five involve action and reflection, experimentation, creativity, observation, measurement, and celebration of achievements as we uncover and mobilise more strengths and resources, and refine goals, plans and strategies.

Parts of the process are interchangeable depending on the circumstances. All stages are interrelated and involve overlap. Goal-setting begins in the first stage and revision of goals occurs regularly. Planning for the completion of service may begin in the first stage, although it is more likely to occur in the third, fourth or fifth stages. Enquiring about strengths and exceptions will often occur at the time of first contact as will exploration of the picture of the future. Workers take similar steps each time they are in contact: they connect, clarify the reason for the meeting, explore strengths and exceptions, review progress, set or revise goals, and plan steps and strategies.

Stages of Strengths-based Service Management

STAGE 1	STAGE 2	STAGE 3	STAGE 4	STAGE 5	STAGE 6
REQUEST FOR SERVICE: INITIAL ASSESSMENT	**ASSESSING FOR STRENGTHS**	**GOAL-SETTING**	**MATCHING RESOURCES TO GOALS**	**WORKING TOWARDS GOALS**	**COMPLETION OF SERVICE**
1. People's story is explored and their experience is validated.	1. People's story is explored more thoroughly.	1. People are assisted to develop a picture of the future.	1. Client resources, experience, capacities and skills are given priority.	1. Resources are mobilised to assist the attainment of goals.	1. Contact is completed when goals are reached, or, when agency or worker resources are not the most appropriate.
2. Issues are clarified.	2. Structural constraints and social inequalities are acknowledged and addressed wherever possible.	2. Specific and concrete goals are developed.	2. If necessary, additional resources are accessed to complement the client's resources.	2. Resources are used flexibly throughout the change process.	2. People are asked to evaluate the process and the agency's contribution.
3. Issues of safety are explored.	3. People's strengths and the stories behind them are explored more thoroughly.	3. The focus is on solutions rather than the problem.	3. The client is assisted to apply the skills and resources to reach their own solution to the issues.	3. People are supported and encouraged to keep working at the solution.	3. People have a record of the work carried out.
4. People's strengths, resources and the exceptions to the problem are explored.	4. Exceptions/unique outcomes are explored.			4. Progress is measured throughout the change process.	4. People's ability and right to a seek assistance in the future is encouraged.
5. Information about other possible resources is shared.	5. People's resources are explored.			5. New goals may emerge which require reassessment of the most appropriate resources.	
6. Initial goals are set.	6. Other resources are explored.				
7. Agreement is reached about terms for working together, or a request for a more appropriate service or set of resources is made.					

If change isn't occurring

Doing strengths-based work means creating environments in which people can grow, learn and thrive. If workers are putting in more effort for change than the people they provide services to, it is certain that empowerment is not happening. At times, this may be understandable. When people are experiencing crisis or trauma they can be immobilised to some degree. This can require extra effort on the part of workers to assist people to take control of their situation. However, if workers continue to work harder once people are strong enough to take responsibility, they can get in the way of empowerment and self-determination, thus reinforcing reliance on 'experts'.

Such situations call for workers to reflect on their practice and the relationship they have with those they are working with. The principles and frameworks of the strengths approach are the points of reference for reflecting on practice and the possible reasons why change isn't happening. People's own sense of power is enhanced by assisting them to define their goals and mobilise their strengths and resources.

If change isn't happening, the following questions can be useful:

- Has the problem been defined in a helpful way?
- Is the problem manageable; are steps small enough?
- Do the issues arise from personal or structural constraints, or both?
- Are we working on the right issues?
- Is the problem getting control of me too?
- Are the goals client-owned or are they someone else's?
- Are goals clearly defined? Are they concrete and specific?
- Is motivation sufficient?
- Are we moving too quickly for the client?
- Who is driving the change?
- Are we clear about who's responsible for what?
- Has change occurred that we haven't noticed?
- Are there sufficient resources?
- What have we tried before that has worked in this situation and in similar ones?
- Have we focused enough on exceptions and strengths?
- Are we doing too much for the client?
- Are we expecting too much?

If things are up and down

If things are going up and down throughout the change process (as they usually do), it's always important to acknowledge and validate the 'downs'. As noted in the discussion about validation in chapter five, people can find it difficult to move on unless their experience is acknowledged and validated. The downs can be framed as hiccups thus normalising the challenges in making change.

Life is full of ups and downs, but the 'ups' give direction about what to do. They expose exceptions that tell a great deal about what works and what doesn't work. This assists in knowing what needs to change and how.

Ups and Downs

Ups (Strengths and Exceptions)

Downs (Issues)

Can workers be directive in client-directed practice?

When human service professionals make a commitment to self-determination they take up the challenge to ensure that their work is characterised by an emphasis on people's right to control their own lives, decide their own futures and determine how they will do this. The term 'client-directed practice' validates and highlights people's role in the process of self-determination. It emphasises not only the right and capacity of people to participate in their change process, but their right and capacity to direct it.

Sometimes there are objections to this. Many workers engaged in work with statutory clients, people with intellectual or psychiatric disabilities, or children and young people, find it difficult—despite their commitment—to give expression to client-directed practice principles. Safety concerns can often work against people's confidence in the principle of self-determination, and mental illness or other disabilities can constrain people's capacity to be genuinely self-determining.

It is not unusual for people to feel so controlled by the problems they face that they are unable to be active agents of change. In other situations people are simply not motivated or confident enough to be active in the change process. Such circumstances lead to reliance on someone else deciding what needs to be done and how. It is in these circumstances that workers feel compelled, for understandable reasons, to be directive. So how can we know whether or when being directive is appropriate, respectful and empowering?

It's a worker's job to help uncover stories that focus on people's strengths. This brings hope and assists the emergence of people's own competencies. If workers are directive when people are capable or if they expect people to do things for themselves when they are not ready, they are likely to do harm.

In searching for the most appropriate form of action, primary tasks can be identified by reflecting on the underlying principles of the strengths approach. Each of the principles and processes of the approach cannot be lived in isolation from each other, although one or a number of them may be given greater weight than others in particular circumstances or at different times.

The following table captures a framework for guiding actions by workers that are respectful of people's readiness for change. How directive workers may need to be and how much they do for people can be determined according to the degree of empowerment or disempowerment they are experiencing. This can be imagined as occurring along a continuum. At one end of the continuum people's motivation, aspirations and perceived ability are low, while at the other end they are high. This framework suggests that people's ability and degree of motivation are integral to their ability to be genuinely self-determining.

The Empowerment Continuum

	DISEMPOWERED			EMPOWERED
	DIMINISHED ABILITY DIMINISHED MOTIVATION	**ABILITY** DIMINISHED MOTIVATION	**UNRECOGNISED ABILITY** SUFFICIENT MOTIVATION	**RECOGNISED ABILITY** HIGH MOTIVATION
Characteristics of the present experience	• Vulnerability • Blame • Sense of hopelessness • Blind to own strengths and those of others • Does not feel valued • Resources are limited	• Uncertainty • Confusion • Unable to use own strengths • Sense of hopelessness • Lacks confidence in self and others • Knows how to do what needs to be done • Resources are limited	• Open to change and learning • Willing to try new things • Hopeful • Doesn't know how to do what needs to be done • Resources and support are available • Feels valued	• Hopeful and optimistic • Open to change and learning • Sees problems as challenges • Knows what to do and how • Resources and support are available • Feels valued
World view	• Bleak picture of the future • Not aware of own strengths or capacities or those of others • Dominated by negative stories of the past	• Limited and uncertain picture of the future • Own strengths and those of others seem irrelevant • Has positive stories but negative ones dominate	• Lacks a concrete picture of the future • Aware of own strengths and able to appreciate those of others • Positive stories dominate	• Has a clear picture of the future • Aware of own strengths and those of others • Knows how to use own strengths • The positive stories dominate
Primary tasks	• Deep listening and validation • Assist reframing of the dominant story • Provide resources • Start with direction and small steps	• Deep listening and validation • Assist reframing of the dominant story • Build the picture of the future • Make resources accessible • Provide direction and take small steps	• Elicit and build on strengths • Ensure resources are accessible • Work with/enable • Strengthen the main story • Enable self-direction	• Facilitate/enable • Ensure resources are available • Co-visioning • Affirm the main story and build new ones
	Direction and 'doing for'	*Direction and 'working with'*	*Coaching*	*Mentoring*

When motivation and ability are diminished

When people are overwhelmed by problems, their picture of the future is usually bleak. This often corresponds with self-blame or blame of others. People can be fearful, blind to their own strengths and feel hopeless. Negative stories of the past dominate their lives. This is typically the case in circumstances of deep depression, trauma or crisis—especially where there is a serious threat to safety.

In these circumstances workers' primary tasks are to listen deeply, and to validate people's feelings and perspective. It is their job to assist a re-writing of the dominant negative story. It is their job to provide resources that the people they have been engaged to assist cannot provide for themselves and to invite them to take only those steps that they can at that time. Being directive or doing things for people is usually necessary in these circumstances, but it can only enhance self-determination if this 'directiveness' leads to increased motivation and the exposure of strengths. If people are at risk, it may be necessary to intervene in directive ways for them to be able to move along the continuum.

When people have the ability but their motivation is diminished

When people are dominated by a problem they can also lose sight of their strengths and those of others. They can know what needs to be done and how to do it but have a limited picture of the future. Negative stories of the past outweigh positive ones. This can be the case where there is crisis, depression, grief or hopelessness (such as failure to address risks arising from addictions or family violence, despite significant effort).

In these circumstances, workers' primary tasks are to listen deeply and to invite reflection on the exceptions to the negative stories so as to highlight the positive ones. It is the worker's job to help people build their picture of the future, provide resources in ways that complement their strengths and create opportunities to take small steps towards change. Being directive or doing things for people may be necessary but can only be respectful and empowering if it increases hope and complements people's own efforts.

When people are motivated but don't recognise their ability

Sometimes people are open and motivated to change and willing to try new things but can still feel uncertain about how to do what needs to be done. This is often because they lack a concrete picture of the future even though positive stories dominate. Examples of this can be found in a family situation where parents are having difficulty with their child's behaviour, know what they want things to be like in a general sense (e.g. 'getting on well') but are unclear about how to go about it.

In these circumstances workers assist people to notice and reflect on their strengths and exceptions. This can help people strengthen and build on their positive stories. When workers are directive or do things for people, they are likely to give the message that they don't think people can do things for themselves. The worker's primary role becomes that of coach and mentor. Once again, developing a concrete picture of the future and reflecting on strengths and exceptions can assist people to reach their goals.

When people are motivated and recognise their ability

People who are hopeful, motivated, open to change and trying new things tend to see problems as challenges. They know what needs to be done and how. They have a clear picture of the future. They have sorted the negative stories from the positive ones and they know how to use these. Sometimes people simply need to consult about an idea or are seeking some particular information. In these circumstances it is the worker's job simply to ensure that the necessary resources are accessible and to re-affirm the main story. A worker's primary role in these circumstances is one of mentor. It is unnecessary and unhelpful to be directive or do things for people.

People may not necessarily find themselves at the same point on the continuum, in all aspects of their lives, at a particular point in time. It is more likely that we find ourselves at different points on the continuum in relation to different issues, contexts or relationships. Sometimes we tend to see these different challenges in our lives quite separately and not see that the strengths we access in one area of our life can be applied very successfully to another. The strengths approach enables people to access and mobilise strengths and capacities by exploring the exceptions or stories of strengths found at other points on the continuum and in different contexts. This is powerful because it allows for the transfer of strengths and capacities from one situation in a person's life to another.

Duty of respect

There are many circumstances in which a specific framework or model of practice won't work. There are many circumstances in which workers can do very little. But they can always do something that can lead to empowerment. They can always 'do' respect and justice.

The first responsibility of people working in the helping professions is always duty of care. People have the right to be safe—a basic principle of the strengths approach. The use of power-over can be justified in situations where there is risk of harm although care needs to be taken in making such a judgement and ways found to respond with sensitivity. But workers also have a 'duty of respect'; a duty to use their power with others in ways that build the foundations for self-determination.

It's important to remember that for many people who access services their experiences of trauma, disempowerment and oppression have been so severe that to expect them to engage or make significant change without sufficient time and resources is simply expecting too much.

Most importantly, to reiterate what has already been said: The strengths approach is a philosophy for working with people. The term 'strengths approach' is used because it is a way of working with people that is dependent primarily on positive attitudes about people and change. It rests on values of respect for people's dignity, their capacities, rights, uniqueness and commonalities. It is an approach that rests on a set of principles and uses a range of frameworks in a flexible and responsive way to assist learning, growth and change.

The table overleaf (Deal & McCashen 1998) provides an opportunity for reflection that can be useful when dilemmas and challenges arise in practice.

Reminders for Doing Respect and Justice

WHAT WE CAN DO...	WHAT WE CAN'T DO...
Make ourselves available	Make others engage with us
Bring hope	Tell if someone is hopeless
Be respectful	Know what's best for others
Believe in people	Make others think like we do
Be honest	Make others trust us
Listen and consult	Rely on assumptions
Promote open decision-making	Make others join us
Share our resources	Determine how people will use resources
Make options available	Make choices for others
Offer another view	Impose our views
Be encouraging	Make people do what we want
Change ourselves	Change others
Change our beliefs	Impose our beliefs on others
Change the way we do things	Make others responsible for our failures
Try new things	Rely on old habits
Encourage change	Control processes or outcomes
Empower ourselves	Empower others
Be resilient	Be perfect
Have a vision of the future	Make others share our vision
Change the future	Change the past
Be careful	Guarantee success
Focus on solutions not problems	Ignore the experience of others
Learn from our mistakes	Stop others making mistakes
Change the world	Change the world

Chapter Eight

Parallel Practice: Building Strengths-based Organisations

'There are compelling reasons for parallel practice. Its humanity is one.
The seamless movement between the quality of practices and experiences taking
place inside an organisation and the quality of services it provides, is another.'

~

'Organisations with a strengths philosophy are concerned with social justice.
They work in ways that offer opportunities for transformation for individuals,
families, groups and communities and, at the same time, have structures and
processes congruent with just, respectful practice.'

~

'The way employees are supervised and managed has a direct and often
sustained impact on the way in which services are delivered. Employees who feel
valued, respected and empowered are more likely to be able to value and assist
the empowerment of the people they provide services to.'

have often thought that if I were looking for proof of the damaging effects of 'colonising' practices in contemporary modern life I could easily find it happening in the internal workings of a human service organisation somewhere nearby! Even in some organisations that claim to be strengths-based we can find instances of leaders using strengths-based tools and practices in power-over ways.

I am constantly surprised and inspired by, despite having witnessed it so many times, the magnificent success of employees of human service organisations, who achieve great things, and do so despite, not because of, the way their managers manage. This says a great deal about the strengths, values, imaginations and commitment of those employees.

Having said this, there is an equal truth: Good leaders who respect, value, support, encourage, consult, envision with, feel with, collaborate and share power with their employees achieve great things. These organisations not only 'reach compliance', 'meet the targets' and 'get the outcomes' but also create workplaces that provide respectful, inclusive, empowering services. People want to work in these workplaces because they are able to love their jobs. There is real dignity in this work. As Martin Luther King said, 'All labor that uplifts humanity has dignity and importance and should be undertaken with painstaking excellence.'

However, human service organisations exist in more and more politically complex and demanding environments. In response, a bureaucratic, top-down style of leadership has increasingly replaced more democratic and inclusive forms over the last couple of decades. Leaders are often overwhelmed by the demands placed upon them and are sometimes conflicted. Despite the desire to resolve challenges in constructive ways managers often find themselves inadvertently or deliberately using power-over. This can leave staff unsupported, disillusioned and even oppositional. This inevitably leads to poor staff retention. Both managers and staff become disillusioned and ineffective in their roles. The consequences for people who use human services are then poor, disempowering or even unjust.

What's needed are strong foundational frameworks grounded in values that are responsive, respectful and empowering for employees and, in turn, for the people who engage the organisation's services.

What is parallel practice?

If organisations want to develop and sustain the strengths approach they need to create a strengths-based culture. This requires commitment and leadership that reflects and models the principles of the strengths approach. Strengths-based organisations are those that 'do' power-with. This is what is referred to as 'parallel practice'.

I deliberately coined the term 'parallel practice' in the late 1990s as a term that specifically referred to the parallel between strengths-based, power-with practices with clients and strengths-based, power-with practices within organisations. This differentiates the term 'parallel practice' from 'parallel process'.

The term 'parallel process' emerged in psychotherapy in the 1950s as a concept that encapsulated the notion that there is a parallel between what happens in the worker-client relationship and the worker-supervisee relationship (Searles 1955, Sumeral 1994). The term 'parallel process' later came to be used to also refer to parallels between practice with clients and practices within organisations, particularly by supervisors and managers, whether good or bad. In other words, the way 'clients' are treated reflects the way employees are treated.

Parallel practice in organisations

Parallel practice in organisations reflects principles of the strengths approach to service delivery. It promotes 'power-with' ways of working with people where practice is guided by respect, inclusion, collaboration, self-determination, transparency, and finding and building on people's strengths. The concept of parallel practice is pertinent to organisational culture, supervisory and management styles, decision-making, quality of relationships, and support and development (McCashen 2013, p. 16).

Chapters eight, nine and ten explore parallel practice by considering the implications of the strengths approach for the way organisations are managed. The term 'employee' is mostly used because almost all of the matters discussed are relevant to all employees of organisations, including service delivery workers, supervisors, team leaders, managers, administrative support workers, directors and executive officers. Parallel practice is of critical importance.

The way employees are supervised and managed has a direct and often sustained impact on the way in which services are delivered. Employees who feel valued, respected and empowered are more likely to be able to value and assist the empowerment of the people they provide services to. In other words, outcomes for clients are inextricably linked to the culture of the teams and organisations that employees belong to and the way in which employees are supported (McCashen 2013, p. 16).

The concept of parallel practice is depicted in the following figure:

Parallel Practice

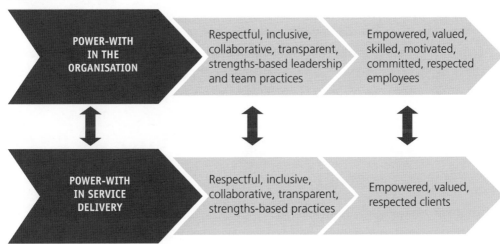

This does not suggest that organisations empower people, or that people are not their own agents of change. On the contrary, parallel practice involves a process that creates conditions necessary for change and empowerment. It does this for those providing services and for those receiving services. Notably the experience of those receiving services informs the practices of those providing services and the organisation generally.

Managerialism and power-over

At the beginning of chapter three, reference was made to Mary Follet's work and her use of the terms 'power-over' and 'power-with'. She used these terms to differentiate between coercive and collaborative ways of running organisations, the former being a form of control that leads to serious or even disastrous consequences in organisations and the latter leading to cooperation, innovation, and effectiveness. Her work is as relevant today as it ever was.

Much of the contemporary reality in human service management can be traced to the developments from the 1980s which saw a shift in the political landscape in Western societies where economic rationalism began to take a hold. This brought an emphasis on corporate management and what became referred to as 'managerialism'. This was a reaction to widespread and deep social change that arose from the great social movements of the 60s and 70s during which time social work broke away from an individualised and often pathologising focus (Ferguson 2008).

Asquith et al. (2005, p. 5) describes managerialism this way:

> Managerialism gives priority to the managerial and economic concerns of service funders and providers, focussing on service costs and efficiencies. ... The role of the social worker moves towards assessment of individuals' needs and the regulation of services delivered. Although the service user is seen less as a 'client' whose needs are determined by a professional perspective, there is nevertheless concern that managerialism as it applies to social work attaches more importance to budgets and targets than to meeting the particular needs of individuals.

The experience of power-over for employees

In conversations with employees of many human service organisations it doesn't take long for stories to emerge of power-over approaches in organisations, whether deliberate or inadvertent. These emerge alongside deep concern that people are not getting the services and respect they deserve. Experiences of job dissatisfaction, inadequate support and resources, not being heard, unacceptably high levels of stress, high staff turnover, disillusionment, low morale, disengagement, lack of meaningful consultation, and undervaluing staff are not uncommon in human service organisations. Managers themselves are not immune to these effects and many struggle to keep a human face in often exceptionally difficult circumstances.

These circumstances affect vast numbers of employees of human services around the world. There is no dignity in this! The very services that are established to support, respect and enable people must begin with regard for the people expected to do it. Every employee of every human service organisation deserves to be treated with respect and be valued. This is enough reason to 'do' parallel practice but the benefits flow on to those who receive services as well.

Rogowski (2012), in discussing the advent of managerialism, identifies the ways in which management now dominates what social workers do. Relationship-based work is replaced by a bureaucratic focus, which is driven by rationing of resources, risk assessment and risk aversion. This bureaucratic focus increases the administrative demands on workers in order to meet accountability, which when achieved is then equated with quality of service delivery. In this process the importance of human relationships, self-determination and empowerment, and value of professional social work ability, are overlooked, dismissed or even undermined.

A way forward

Large human service organisations everywhere, with good intentions, invest a great deal of time, energy, and often large sums of money, in developing vision and mission statements, slogans, strategic plans and the like (often with little or no meaningful consultation with staff). Grand statements are made about valuing communities, families and the individual, and claiming best practice approaches with neatly packaged statements and smart logos. Claims to empower, to bring hope, to show respect, often ring hollow not only to a great many people they provide services to, but to their employees as well.

In a well-researched and eloquent paper, Pamela Trevithick (2014, p. 1) argues that:

> ...managerialism has failed to recognise the importance of the emotional life of human beings and the importance of the relationships we build in social work and that this failure seriously hinders the quality and effectiveness of social work.

She explores the importance of affect, empathy and feelings and compares these with what she describes as 'the skewed representation of logical thinking as innately superior to emotional and intuitive reasoning'. She analyses 'the dangers evident in the more extreme and rigid forms of managerialism that can be found in some areas of social work...' and calls for a humanising of managerialism through 'emotionally-responsive, relationship-based practice.'

There is significant research that strongly advocates for emotionally-responsive leadership, not only essential for the wellbeing of employees but for effective practice (Gibbs et al. 2014, pp. 107–112).

Managerialism's prioritisation of economic imperatives, procedural administration and accountability occurs at the expense of employees and the people they provide services to. In the process, employees of human service organisations often become institutionalised under the weight of pressure to conform to their constructs and to 'toe the line' (a prime example is an over-emphasis on 'performance management planning', which is too often used as a method for controlling staff behaviour). In all of these circumstances there is a dearth of power-with values reflected in leadership styles. There is a seeming unwillingness or inability to prioritise and guide respectful, just practice. This leads to the loss of the extensive wisdom held by workers and those they provide services to.

The great wonder is that, despite all of this, the strengths movement has emerged and continually expanded and developed during the same decades as economic rationalism and managerialism. Many organisations have embraced strengths-based ways of delivering services during this time and many of these have also embraced strengths-based ways of organising and managing. The strengths philosophy is part of the culture of these organisations. They have experienced first-hand how the strengths approach and parallel practice can reclaim lost ground in the realm of just and respectful management and, as a result, provide more effective services.

Even government enquiries and their recommendations, policies and funding agreements more and more commonly require the embedding of strengths-based ways of working by their funded agencies and, in many cases, their own employees. This is to be applauded. However, how this is made to happen is of critical importance. Power-over approaches will simply not work in establishing strengths-based practices. Attempting to do so reflects a simplistic understanding not only of the strengths approach but what works to get the best from people and the best outcomes for people who engage services. Parallel practices are necessary for everyone's sake. Much of the discussion in the remainder of this chapter and the following two chapters is inspired by the great work of the managers, teams and organisations that embrace a strengths approach through parallel practice.

What parallel practice can look like in organisations
Parallel practice is not an add-on to strengths-based work. It needs to be modelled and lived so that a culture of respect, hope, collaboration, inclusion and the building of strengths can be developed. This is essential for sustaining strengths-based practices on the ground. Workers committed to working in strengths-based ways can find it difficult to sustain their efforts working for organisations that do not take a strengths approach. People commonly feel disillusioned when actions are taken by organisations that are not congruent with strengths-based principles. In a strengths-based culture staff commonly feel encouraged, appreciated, heard, supported and inspired.

Organisations with a strengths philosophy are concerned with social justice. They work in ways that offer opportunities for transformation for individuals, families, groups and communities and, at the same time, have structures and processes congruent with just, respectful practice. They use the principles of the strengths approach as their points of reference for their operation externally. They use the same points of reference for their operation internally; they 'live' these principles so as to become a model or microcosm of an inclusive, respectful, just society.

Strengths-based organisations take a strengths approach to decision-making, meetings, planning, supervision, administration, relationships with their communities and other organisations, and in responding to difficult internal and external issues. The implications of parallel practice can be challenging because many conventional and traditional management practices, structures and internal processes are thrown into question and hierarchy and the power and authority of individuals or groups is challenged.

The culture of a strengths-based organisation is grounded in an awareness and understanding of structural, cultural and personal constraints, and ways in which dominant knowledge and culture can lead to injustice and disempowerment. It values and celebrates diversity internally. It sees the problem as the problem, not the person as the problem. It is, therefore, always concerned with the political, structural, cultural context of the individuals and teams in the organisation itself as well as in the society in which it exists.

The strengths approach can be brought to life in any organisation or context: schools, welfare agencies, government departments, businesses, community groups and so on. What this looks like in any given organisation will vary according to the unique circumstances of the organisation, but strengths-based cultures share common features that are recognisable through parallel practice.

Parallel practice is immediately recognisable when we see strengths-based skills and questions being used in informal and formal contexts in organisations; in supervision, in meetings, in hallways, in annual reviews, in strategic planning and so on. It is recognisable when a team or committee of management uses a column approach to work their way through a dilemma or challenge. It is recognisable when we see a pack of *Strengths Cards* being used to prompt an exploration of strengths and exceptions. It is recognisable when we see a manager apologise to staff for an error of judgement and invite them to help avoid the same mistake again. It is recognisable when confidentiality is respected among staff and management, when bottom lines, responsibilities and rights are clear, transparent and agreed.

Parallel practice is recognisable when employees have a sense of belonging and ownership of decision-making and change processes, when there is a high level of participation and a feeling of being valued. It is recognisable when supervision uses strengths-based processes and skills to review practice. It is recognisable when staff are supported and encouraged to take initiative to explore new ground and test new ideas. It is recognisable when employees who are deemed to have 'done the wrong thing' are seen as having good intentions and affected by constraints rather than seen as the problem. It is recognisable when records of meetings, supervision and decision-making are transparent and owned by participants. It is recognisable when affirmative action and just and equitable working conditions are in place. The integrity of claims to just practice is compromised when such qualities are absent.

Strengths-based management and parallel practice

The term 'strengths-based management' implies a particular way of managing. Strengths-based management is an approach to management. It can be defined as a process that uses the principles, processes and skills of the strengths approach to lead and develop organisations and practices.

Strengths-based management involves parallel practice that:

- models respectful, inclusive, collaborative, transparent practice
- enables the sharing of power and responsibility for service delivery, internal decision-making and operations
- provides leadership in initiating, developing and sustaining strengths-based practice
- enables staff participation in, and shared ownership of, visioning processes
- focuses on the strengths and resources of staff
- acknowledges power imbalances in the organisation and works to address them
- encourages and supports participation in decision-making
- acts to address structural constraints to participation
- is mindful of cultural and personal constraints and how dominant stories and ideas can constrain change and learning, and is attentive to addressing them

- is committed to transparent practices and processes
- is clear about bottom lines and accountability
- enables the development of a clear picture of the future and measurable goals
- keeps a focus on exceptions and strengths stories
- sees the problem as the problem.

Strengths-based managers assume good intentions, recognise that people bring many strengths and skills, and value these by becoming appreciative audiences to their efforts.

Parallel practice is not always easy. The principles can be a two-edged sword. They provide a foundation for just and respectful practice. But they can highlight where we are going wrong! This is a good thing. The strengths approach is not something we adopt in one set of circumstances and shed in another. It is not something about which we can be selective. It is relevant in all situations, contexts and relationships. Respect means respect, belief in people means belief in people, just practice means just practice. How we are with each other is important in its own right. It also profoundly affects attitudes to service delivery.

The implications of parallel practice can be unsettling because they often expose contradictions, incongruities and vulnerabilities. But parallel practice does not mean being perfect. It means noticing, valuing and developing the examples and stories of just practice, just outcomes and empowerment. These examples can help to address the contradictions and build organisational integrity.

 EXERCISE – *What makes a good manager?*

Take a look at 'What makes a good worker?' on pages 76–7. Replace the word 'worker' with the word 'manager'.

- How do these statements reflect good management practices?
- How well do they parallel the strengths approach to service delivery?
- What examples have you observed, or perhaps experienced, of this sort of management practice and what were the outcomes?

Decision-making

Respectful, socially-just decision-making centres around values that recognise the intrinsic worth of others, the right of people to control their own destiny and their right to make real, life-enhancing choices. Participation, self-determination and empowerment are processes requiring ongoing articulation and reflection.

In parallel practice these principles are modelled and all stakeholders are considered. Inside the organisation this modelling means that managers, boards or committees avoid practices that marginalise or disempower. Principles of the strengths approach become key points of reference for decision-making.

Questions for consideration in decision-making (sourced from Deal & McCashen 2001) include those such as the following:

Questions for accountability:

- Is our decision open, public, able to be scrutinised and able to be challenged by anyone?

- Is our communication open, transparent and respectful?

- Is our decision and decision-making process legal, ethical, accountable and defensible?

- Have our discussions been active, challenging and robust?

- Does our culture contain 'blind spots' or 'skeletons in the cupboard' that are kept hidden?

- Is our decision-making limited because of personal agendas?

Questions for just practice:

- Are there social or organisational structures in place that maintain or contribute to inequalities and exclusion?

- Have values of social justice, respect, empowerment and self-determination informed our decision?

- Will anyone be disadvantaged by our decision? How have their views been taken into account?

- Is there any labelling or categorisation that blames people or frames them as the problem?

Questions for inclusion:

- Who needs to be consulted?

- Have we listened to, heard and respected minorities and quiet voices?

- Does our decision build on commonalities between people?

- Is our decision-making process disempowering of any individuals or groups?

- What are the alternative stories and viewpoints? Have we really heard them?

- Has our process been respectful of everyone?

- Is our language empowering, respectful, non-discriminatory and free of stereotypes and labels?

- Is our decision-making process based on generalisations that ignore unique experience and context?

Questions for hope:

- Does our decision build a spirit of hopefulness and optimism—with everyone?

- Have we identified and valued people's aspirations and dreams?

- How does our decision recognise and value people's strengths and capacities?

- Has anyone been disempowered or diminished by our decision or the process?

Questions for self-determination:

- How can our decision open up new possibilities and choices for those who are affected?

- What action do we need to take to ensure that people have maximum say over their own lives?

The following set of questions is developed from Ten Pivotal Questions for Strengths-based Managers (Laussel 2001). It attempts to capture key considerations for strengths-based planning and decision-making processes by management.

1. Have we considered the effects and implications for all stakeholders (clients, community, funding bodies, staff, board, committee of management)?

2. Is there transparency in our process? Do we need more input or involvement from any of the stakeholders? How will we inform others and involve others in the process?

3. Is the picture of the future clearly articulated? What are we aiming to achieve? Is it a picture that is shared by key people? Is it congruent with principles of the strengths approach? Are we clear about the bottom line?

4. Have we sufficiently considered the strengths, skills and capacities of everyone affected by this decision?

5. What are the exceptions? What has worked well before? How did we go about it?

6. Have we framed goals and strategies in achievable and measurable ways? Who will do what? How? When? How will these goals contribute to change for everyone?

7. What might get in the way of our goals? What are the current constraints? What resources can we mobilise to help address these?

8. How will we know if we have succeeded? What will be different and how will we notice? How will we acknowledge and celebrate achievements and with whom?

9. How will we demonstrate leadership in bringing this about? Are we using power-with or power-over? What will other people notice that demonstrates parallel practice?

10. Who will help support our efforts? Who else has a commitment that can help?

Introducing and developing the strengths approach

The strengths approach has a contagious quality so it's no surprise that organisations want to develop it. Introducing and developing the strengths approach requires learning, support and professional development processes that mirror it. This means that supervisory and management practices develop and sustain the strengths-based culture and structures. When organisations or individuals impose strengths-based practice they contradict and compromise its principles because this involves power-over. Strengths-based practice is encouraged and learnt through strong leadership, through seeing it modelled internally and applied in service delivery, as well as through learning and professional development processes.

Typically, strengths-based practice is introduced through formal or informal training and learning opportunities. It is often followed by training in strengths-based supervision and other complementary training that is tailored to respond to specific fields. But on its own, this will not create a fully functioning strengths-based culture. A whole-of-organisation approach is required to introduce, establish and sustain the strengths approach, not just training.

Building and sustaining strengths-based, power-with cultures involves a shift in paradigms for management. Above all else managers must re-assess their position and examine the ways in which they are managing and leading. Critical questions include:

- In meeting the organisation's agenda, how can I best serve those we provide services to?

- What does the way I manage and lead mean for my staff and for the people my organisation provides services to?

- How does my way of relating affect staff and how does this affect the way they relate to the people we provide services to?

- How can I reduce power imbalances and encourage shared responsibility?

- How do I model inclusivity and respect for human dignity?

As put by Gibbs et al. (2009, p. 16) in addressing what sustains good management practice and quality service delivery:

> Good modelling by team leaders and managers of thoughtful and reflective processes makes a vital contribution to a healthy collaborative culture. Most importantly, this leads to program improvements and to better service delivery processes and outcomes in the 'trickle down' process.

Next, employees need to be richly regarded, valued, supported and enabled to develop and learn. Good quality supervision day-to-day, week-to-week and year-to-year needs to be a feature of organisational practice. This includes formal supervision arrangements as well as mentoring and coaching, peer and group supervision, reflective forums, staff forums, meaningful learning opportunities and embedding reflective practice in all forms of supervision, problem-solving and planning.

An environment of strengths-based, solution-focused, narrative thinking and Appreciative Inquiry needs to be developed and sustained. In short, parallel practice is the key to the best organisational practice. Then the people who participate in the services the organisation provides get the most respectful, empowering services possible. These practices and the values they reflect lead employees to do the best they can, to be innovative, to be autonomous, to collaborate, to come to work excited, to feel they belong, to want to contribute and give to the organisation.

Strategies for doing all of this will reflect the philosophy of strengths-based ways of doing things:

- Collaborative and participatory processes

- Transparent and inclusive decision-making

- Responding to each individual's and each team's circumstances and context, strengths and aspirations in tailored ways

- Building on existing strengths, skills and aspirations of individuals and teams and the organisation as a whole

- Using resources in ways that add value to the resources that individuals, teams and the organisation already have.

Language in parallel practice

Just as deficit-based, power-over approaches in service delivery disempower people, so do deficit-based power-over approaches in organisations. Just as deficit-based, problem-focussed approaches rely on particular language for support, so do strengths-based, power-with approaches.

The language and discourse of managerialism is largely deficit-based or problem-focussed. It does not reflect belief in people. It is not a hopeful language. In these circumstances management practices are inclined to use power-over methods to keep employees aligned with policies, procedures and agency directions. Supported by a broad review of the literature, Appreciative Inquiry advocate, James Ludema (2001, p. 1) argues that a 'vocabulary of hope' is needed to replace the language of deficits in organisations:

> ...critical methods of contemporary organisational science have contributed to a growing cynicism about the future of human institutions by producing vocabularies of deficit.

> Vocabularies of hope serve as powerful catalysts for positive social and organisational transformation. They are ignited when organisational members (1) nurture cooperative relationships, (2) exercise a sense of optimism about their capacity to influence the future, and (3) inquire together into their most deeply held values and highest aspirations.

In conjunction with the notion of vocabularies of hope, implied here is a collaborative, positive and strong, values-based approach for organisational practice. It is evident that the language of the strengths approach is hopeful language. Parallel practice relies on the language of hope.

Appreciative Inquiry

Appreciative Inquiry, which emerged from early work by David Cooperrider, Suresh Srivastva and Diana Whitney in the 1980s, is highly relevant to strengths-based organisational practice and, in particular, organisational change. It can be viewed as a strengths approach to management and one strategy for building and sustaining strengths-based organisations. It moves away from traditional problem-solving methods that focus on deficits, which actually do not bring any real improvement. Cooperrider and Whitney (2001, p. 3) define Appreciative Inquiry this way:

> Appreciative Inquiry is about the coevolutionary search for the best in people, their organisations, and the relevant world around them. In its broadest focus, it involves systematic discovery of what gives 'life' to a living system when it is most alive, most effective, and most constructively capable in economic, ecological, and human terms. AI involves, in a central way, the art and practice of asking questions that strengthen a system's capacity to apprehend, anticipate, and heighten positive potential.

As such, Appreciative Inquiry involves action research to find and draw upon people's stories of when things are at their best in an organisation and create new possibilities for the future from these (Bushe 1998, p. 1).

Like narrative and solution-focused practices, Appreciative Inquiry emerged from post-modernist philosophy, which takes the view that social realities are constructed through words and language to give meaning.

> As we talk to each other, we are constructing the world we see and think about, and as we change how we talk we are changing that world. From this perspective, theory, especially theory that is encoded in popular images, is a powerful force in shaping social organisation because we 'see what we believe'. Creating new theories/ideas/images is, therefore, a powerful way of changing organisations. (Bushe 1998, p. 2)

Cooperrider and Srivastva (1995) argue that conversations are what create and change organisations and that these conversations are determined by what people can imagine and agree on. Furthermore, the questions asked in inquiring about any aspect of organisational life focus attention in a particular direction:

One of the most impactful things a change agent or practitioner does is to articulate questions. Instinctively, intuitively and tacitly we all know that research of any kind can, in a flash, profoundly alter the way we see ourselves, view reality, and conduct our lives ... if we accept the proposition that patterns of social-organisation action are not fixed by nature in any direct biological or physical way, that human systems are made and imagined in relational settings by human beings (socially constructed), then attention turns to the source of the ideas, our discourses, our researches — that is, our questions. Alterations in linguistic practices — including the practice of crafting questions — hold profound implications for changes in social practice.

Cooperrider & Whitney 2001, p. 15

The importance and irreplaceable value of asking the right questions to create meaningful change and empowerment has been well discussed earlier in this book. These sorts of questions are those that are conducive to Appreciative Inquiry and building strengths-based organisations.

Cooperrider and Whitney (2001, p. 29) distinguish between conventional problem-solving processes in organisations and Appreciative Inquiry as depicted in the following table.

Problem-solving and Appreciative Inquiry

PROBLEM-SOLVING	APPRECIATIVE INQUIRY
Felt need, identification of problems	Appreciating and valuing the best of 'What Is'
Analysis of causes	Envisioning 'What Might Be'
Analysis of possible solutions	Dialoguing 'What Should Be'
Action planning	Innovating what will be
Basic Assumption: An Organisation is a Problem to be Solved	**Basic Assumption:** An Organisation is a Mystery to be Embraced

Like the strengths approach, Appreciative Inquiry's focus is on positive potential. It is guided by a cycle consisting of four key processes:

1. Discover. Identify the organisational processes that work well.

2. Dream. Envision processes that would work well in the future.

3. Design. Plan and prioritise processes that would work well.

4. Destiny (Delivery). Implement the plan.

Cooperrider & Whitney 2001, p. 5

This process takes place over time, of course, and involves the whole of an organisation as well its parts. It is barely different to the processes of the strengths approach discussed in this book:

1. What are the strengths and things that work well?

2. What is our picture of the future?

3. What are our plans and steps based on what would work well?

4. Taking action.

There are compelling reasons for parallel practice. Its humanity is one. The seamless movement between the quality of practices and experiences taking place inside an organisation and the quality of services it provides, is another. The next two chapters look more closely at these parallel practices.

Chapter Nine

Parallel Practice and Staff Supervision

———————————— FEATURED QUOTES FROM THIS CHAPTER ————————————

'Respectful, trusting relationships between managers and staff are as critical in successful management and leadership as they are in service delivery.'

~

'Supervision plays an essential role in modelling practices of respect, listening, inclusion, collaboration, self-determination, transparency, and finding and building on people's strengths.'

~

'Good quality supervision must become a priority and wherever possible the scope of supervision must be widened to recognise and validate a range of strategies as necessary for employee support and development. These include mentoring, coaching, group supervision, reflective forums, peer support and reflective practice.'

Parallel practice is the heart and soul of good supervision. Good supervision is one of the most important aspects of organisational practice. It plays a crucial and fundamental role in the achievement of empowerment and self-determination for the people who access human services. It can play a crucial role in the provision of support and professional development for workers. It is also the conduit through which the management and decision-making processes of an organisation can be connected and become responsive to the experiences of the individuals, families and communities accessing services.

Experiences of isolation, marginalisation, discrimination and prejudice, and the impact of structural issues, are serious. The complexity of sociological, psychological, spiritual, cultural, political, economic and structural issues, and human and community relationships can be daunting. The risk of adding to already existing experiences of colonisation through the way in which we provide services and relate to people, is ever present. We can be dangerous to clients, even when good intentions, empathy and concern are present in our attitudes and practice.

This makes supervision a big responsibility. It is also a magnificent opportunity to model, develop and maintain a strengths-based culture and a means of influencing practices and policy. It deserves to be a priority in organisational policy and practice and, therefore, to have a policy in its own right. It deserves to be well resourced.

The functions of staff supervision

Staff supervision is essential to good practice and is a critical component of the social and community services landscape. It involves a range of activities designed to provide effective support and development for employees, and manage work undertaken by them. These activities most commonly involve one-to-one formal and informal (or 'on-the-run') interactions between supervisors and supervisees. However, other supervisory activities can be just as important. These activities are explored in the following chapter.

Alfred Kadushin (1976) introduced and set the tone for supervision practice in social work and other helping professions. He did this in clearly identifying and defining three core functions of supervision:

1. The managerial or administrative function which supports the supervisee to respond to the organisation's directions, priorities and responsibilities through planning, reviewing and managing their work

2. The educative function which supports the supervisee's development and learning

3. The support function, which provides any support necessary to help the worker deal with work related stress.

Others, notably British social worker Tony Morrison, have built on Kadushin's work. Adopting the terms 'management', 'education', and 'support' and incorporating 'mediation', Morisson (1993, pp. 19–23) defines the functions of supervision as:

• education that focuses on professional development and learning from practice

• management that focuses on standards set in supervision policy and adherence to (and implementation of) agency policy

• support that focuses on the wellbeing of the worker and the development of safe environments for supervision and support outside it

• mediation that focuses on advocacy and support for workers and clients, and representation of workers in relation to the wider organisation and other agencies.

While these functions are undeniably important, in an organisation that takes a strengths approach, emphasis is on the principles of the strengths approach and the relevant skills and processes. Workers are encouraged and supported to participate directly in policy development and organisational planning as part of a team.

The principles of the strengths approach provide clear points of reference for assisting just practice at personal, social and political levels. They are therefore crucial points of reference for supervision including the way in which supervisors go about addressing their own issues and concerns. Strengths-based supervision also uses the principles and processes of the strengths approach to help gain direction in decision-making and planning.

Key conventions in staff supervision

Morrison (1993, pp. 13–14, 19) provides a useful rationale and clear points of reference for staff supervision structure and content. Like Kadushin, his frameworks for supervision have been influential in shaping supervision policy in many social work and other human service organisations. Their work has resulted in the establishment of key conventions in staff supervision. Morrison (1993, p. 13) defines supervision as:

> ...a process in which one worker is given responsibility to work with another worker in order to meet certain organisational, professional and personal objectives. These are competent [and] accountable performance, continuing professional development and personal support.

According to Morrison, the purposes of supervision are to:

- ensure the worker is clear about roles and responsibilities
- ensure the worker meets agency objectives
- ensure quality services to clients
- develop a suitable climate for practice
- assist professional development
- reduce stress
- ensure the worker is given the resources to do the job.

Morrison (1993, p. 14) also emphasises that supervision is a partnership between supervisor, worker and the agency; that it is a shared responsibility and that the best interests of the client should always come first. The strengths approach, of course, gives priority to the best interests of clients and all supervision takes place in that context.

Supervisors are given responsibility, and indeed authority, to oversee workers and their practice. Many people committed to the strengths approach have difficulty with the term 'supervision'. Often this is because experiences of supervision have been unhelpful or unpleasant, or supervision has been carried out in a context where power imbalances have not been addressed. In the strengths approach to supervision, we are concerned to create an environment of 'power-with'. We refer to the principles, processes and skills of the strengths approach to guide supervision policy and practice.

Because there are many tasks associated with the supervisory role it can become problematic to settle on one alternative term. Some have tried the terms 'mentoring', 'consulting', 'coaching' or 'teaching' to describe this role; others have tried the term 'co-vision'. These terms simply describe what can be happening at certain times in the supervisory relationship or they describe the primary task being undertaken in a given context, moment, relationship or supervision session. The empowerment continuum discussed in chapter seven is just as relevant for supervision as it is for practice. How we define supervision becomes more important than what we call it.

While the rationales for traditional approaches to supervision are sound and often reflect elements of a strengths approach (for example, where Morrison emphasises shared responsibility and partnership) they can be influenced by, or get stuck in, a problem-focussed orientation or constrained by other organisational priorities. The issues discussed in the first pages of the previous chapter are pertinent in this regard. The shift in paradigm to a strengths approach to supervision can help overcome the problems associated with this but to be sustainable there needs to be a strong culture of parallel practice.

Concerns about supervision

The most commonly understood and adopted form of supervision is the arrangement for the provision of supervision to supervisees by allocated supervisors. This takes the form of formal supervision sessions and day-to-day on-the-run supervision. This arrangement can significantly limit the quality of support and learning for supervisees and can place stresses upon both the supervisor and supervisee, particularly in already stressed workplaces.

Staff supervision has become increasingly focused on the managerial function of supervision with little or no attention to the developmental and support functions. This is a concern expressed widely in the literature (Beddoe 2010; Bradley & Hojer 2009; Egan 2012; Noble & Irwin 2009). It is not surprising in contexts where managerialism has taken over!

Increasing emphasis is being placed on scrutinising the work of employees in order to minimise risk and meet targets. In this environment great weight is given to performance management, staff appraisal systems, professional development planning that centres on how well an employee fits with an organisation's priorities, how effective they are in meeting program targets and so on. The outcome of this sort of managerial supervision leads to job dissatisfaction, low morale, high staff turnover and other consequences such as stressed or even toxic workplaces, and poor quality or even dangerous practice.

While professional development and annual review mechanisms can have their place, regard for the dignity of work and the value of relationships of respect and trust are often overlooked, minimised or even dismissed. The literature on supervision is dominated by evidence that effective service delivery practice is dependent upon the quality of support and development and the valuing of employees. This makes for dignified, efficient, respectful, effective services, and innovative workplaces.

A major finding in a report on the results of research into the workforce of a large government social service agency in Victoria, Australia, that employs some thousands, emphasised the importance of support, supervision and professional development. The report found, not surprisingly, that lack of support and supervision seriously affected staff morale, retention rates, and quality relationships with children and families, so necessary to effective practice and positive outcomes (Department of Human Services 2011).

An excellent resource guide, developed by this organisation for child protection frontline and middle managers, cites literature which emphasises the importance of good supervision and its relationship to staff retention (in this chapter, I draw widely from this resource by Gibbs et al. (2009 and 2014) because it is so thoroughly researched):

> Good supervision is often the most important factor contributing to staff retention with a lack of supportive supervision being a reason for leaving child welfare. Other studies have cited the importance of supportive and informed supervision as a reason why child welfare practitioners remain in the job.
>
> Gibbs et al. 2009, p. 1

Good quality supervision must become a priority and wherever possible the scope of supervision must be widened to recognise and validate a range of strategies as necessary for employee support and development. While supervisors can act as coaches and mentors and, in doing so, assist the development of highly-skilled and confident workers, there is an inherent power imbalance between supervisor and supervisee. Those in supervisory roles are given responsibility to both direct and ensure accountability while at the same time assisting learning and providing support.

While there need not always be tension between the supportive and the developmental functions on one hand, and the management function on the other, there are a number of conditions that impinge on the provision of good supervision. These include factors such as:

- attitudes of supervisors to supervisees, their position and their job

- workloads of both supervisors and supervisees

- whether or not supervisors carry a service delivery load in addition to their supervisory responsibilities

- the level of service delivery experience of supervisors

- the level and quality of support and training provided to supervisors and those they supervise

- the modelling and leadership provided to supervisors

- staff shortages and staff turnover rates and subsequent demands on supervisors to provide more intensive support to new employees.

The forms of supervision discussed in the next chapter provide various means of support and learning beyond formal supervision. They include mentoring, coaching, peer and group supervision and staff forums which can be used strategically to share responsibility for the provision of support and development, both for employees generally and in supporting those in supervisory and management roles. This can help build a culture of meaningful support and learning, informed professional decision-making, innovation and excellence in practice.

Relationships and parallel practice

Strengths-based supervision is an essential means of doing parallel practice. It is essential because it can model and make such a significant contribution to the creation of a strengths-based culture in any organisation. The conditions necessary for learning, growth, change and power-with discussed in chapter five, are no less relevant in supervisor-supervisee/manager-employee professional relationships than in service delivery. Managers and supervisors play a critical role in creating these conditions in their relationships with staff and in decisions they make.

Relationship-based practice and the essential reasons for it in service delivery have been discussed in chapter five. Likewise, successful supervision relies, first and foremost, on the establishment of strong, trusting relationships. Positive workplace cultures are made possible by strong, effective relationships. As put by Gibbs et al. (2014 p. 150) as part of their review of the literature on this matter:

> Establishing a safe and effective supervision relationship at each level of the workforce contributes not only to individual good practice for that particular supervisee, it forms part of the culture of the workplace.

Wonnacott 2003 in Gibbs et al, (2014, p. 147) asserts:

> ...if supervisors can model clear, insightful and empathic relationships with practitioners, these same practitioners are far more likely to be able to adopt the same underlying values and skills with the [clients] they work with. Similarly, positive outcomes for [clients] are strongly related to the supervisor's reflective supervisory style.

Respectful, trusting relationships between managers and staff are as critical to successful management and leadership as they are to service delivery. This is not the case in unhealthy organisational cultures:

> ... dysfunctional processes, when not understood and managed, can ultimately result in heightened or dilution of risk when it is applied at case practice level with the child and family. Groups of practitioners may also replicate and mirror the same powerful, problematic dynamics ... These are largely unconscious processes but are readily recognisable in the way organisations reflect the same chaotic, conflictual, crisis-driven approach to problems that families exhibit.
>
> Gibbs et al. 2009, p. 16

All forms of supervision must be aimed at supporting and valuing employees, assisting learning and increasing knowledge, skills, confidence and motivation, and contributing to a safe and supportive learning culture. Supervision plays an essential role in modelling practices of respect, listening, inclusion, collaboration, self-determination, transparency, and finding and building on people's strengths. This assists learning, career development, staff retention and better outcomes for people receiving services. Supervision must also model critical, reflective thinking and support learning.

Respect for human dignity ought to be enough reason for managers to value, respect and support their employees. A close look at the evidence also tells us that it is crucial for good quality service provision. The flow-on effect of valuing staff ensures that the people who receive services experience respectful services and that successful service delivery outcomes are much more likely.

Supporting learning and development

As discussed, the developmental or educational function of supervision responds to the learning needs of the supervisee. Formal learning contexts such as classroom-based workshops and courses of study have long been dominant among learning methods in the human services. The literature on adult learning in recent years has thrown into question the effectiveness of these as a primary means of learning and emphasises instead the value and importance of on-the-job and informal learning methods.

In the '70-20-10 learning model' which has gained currency internationally, learning strategies are based on the view (supported by research) that:

> 70% of learning comes in an informal, on the job, experience-based sense without any formal learning event.

> 20% of learning comes from informal learning, sharing ideas and experiences through methods such as coaching and mentoring.

> 10% of learning comes through the actual learning event, such as structured courses, workshops, seminars and tutorials.

Kajewski & Madsen 2012, p. 4

According to this model, formal learning methods are not as effective as on-the-job, informal learning methods.

If we think about the last face-to-face workshop we attended we may well not be able to stipulate what difference it has made to our practice, or worse still, struggle to remember any detail. At best we will be able to remember the things that were particularly pertinent and have improved our practice in some way. This is not to suggest that face-to-face training and formal study are not important. However, it raises the question of what the best forms of learning are, how much formal training one should undertake, and how organisations can best support learning and development. Sometimes it seems that the panacea for fixing things in organisations is more training and still some more training! ('But they've been trained, what's wrong with them?' 'We need to get staff trained up!'). This is a deficit-based response. A strengths-based response, however, suggests that we tailor the learning methods and resources to the needs, strengths and aspirations of teams and individuals.

A 'one-size-fits-all' approach to learning cannot be effective in responding to the diverse learning goals and needs of employees in an organisation, given the varying levels of education and experience, the different backgrounds of the people services are provided to, and people's different learning styles and preferences. While training programs are important for skilled employees and quality services, diverse methods of support and learning are necessary. Learning takes place in all sorts of ways in many different contexts. These include:

- workplace or on-the-job learning (for example, being buddied on commencement of employment, shadowing a more experienced worker)
- formal or semi-formal learning opportunities (for example, short courses, face-to-face training)
- community-based activities (for example, visiting agencies to learn about their services)
- professionally-based activity (for example, participating in seminars)
- reflective practice
- integration of learning into practice from formal learning opportunities
- mentoring
- coaching
- peer support
- cultural supervision
- group supervision
- job exchange opportunities.

Establishing learning goals, whether informally or through a more structured professional development plan, is more meaningful, relevant and effective when it is tailored to the needs and aspirations of the individual. Any one or a number of the resources referred to above can be drawn upon to support learning.

Mentoring, coaching, group supervision, reflective forums and reflective practice in groups or between individuals can be viewed as significant contributors to on-the-job and informal learning. These enable a practical and responsive means of tailoring learning to the different practice contexts, experience and prior learning of individuals. It moves away from the one-size-fits-all approach of formal training programs to facilitate the space in which deeper learning can occur. These will be defined and explored further in chapter ten.

A definition of strengths-based supervision

Strengths-based supervision can be defined as a process of shared responsibility for supporting the work of employees in ways that are respectful, inclusive, collaborative, empowering, socially-just and build potential. It is a process in which two or more people work with one another to assist learning, provide support and manage all that is necessary for good practice. It involves parallel practice in order to integrate the principles, processes and skills of the strengths approach.

The principles of the strengths approach can be distilled into four key characteristics of practice: power-with, social justice, self-determination (client-directed practice) and the strengths emphasis. The following table captures the implications of these principles for supervision.

Implications of the Strengths Approach for Supervision

PRINCIPLE	PARALLEL PRACTICE
Power-with: • reducing power imbalances (creating a culture of power-with) • relationships of trust • transparent practice • adding resources in a strengths-based way.	• relationships of trust • open, transparent sharing of practice and other responsibilities • partnership and collaboration • mobilising resources to complement those of employees.
Self-determination: • partnerships that focus on people's goals • people-defined and owned description of issues, strengths, goals and plans • people drive the process of change as much as possible.	• focussing on employee goals (practice, learning, support) • employee defined and owned description of issues, strengths, goals and plans • employees drive the process of change as much as possible.
Social justice: • addressing disadvantage, discrimination, marginalisation • community building.	• social justice and equity issues are addressed within and beyond the workplace.
The strengths emphasis: • identifying, storying and mobilising strengths and skills, and capacities • Exploring and valuing aspirations, hopes and dreams.	• Practice development, learning and support occur through identifying, valuing and mobilising employees' strengths, skills and resources toward their aspirations in the professional context.

Strengths-based supervision uses the stages and skills of the strengths approach to create a process for 'doing' parallel practice. It can be used by anyone skilled in, and committed to, the strengths approach and does not require extensive experience in supervisory or management positions. Ways to apply these stages and skills will be explored in the next chapter.

Some of the advantages of the strengths approach to supervision are:

- It reviews practice in a strengths-based way, therefore providing experience of strengths-based practice for the worker and supervisor.

- It is worker-owned and directed and is therefore meaningful and empowering.

- It enables the worker to take responsibility for practice development and learning.

- Colleagues or supervisors become facilitators rather than 'directors' of the review of practice and at the same time continue to practise strengths-based skills.

- It consolidates and strengthens strengths-based practice increasing the likelihood of client self-determination and empowerment.

- It models strengths-based practices and contributes to a strengths-based culture.

Focussing on the story of practice, not the story of the client

Strengths-based supervision aims to enhance and develop practice through meaningful reflection that focuses on the worker's practice and activity as opposed to the client's issues and stories. It is not uncommon for supervision to get stuck on the client's story, their issues and needs, and the worker's concerns or frustrations and why things aren't working. The greater portion of the supervisory conversation can often tend to focus on clients and their circumstances leaving little time to reflect on what to do next and how. This is no different to expending time and energy analysing problems then jumping to solutions through guesswork.

The primary purpose of supervision is to bring about good processes and outcomes for clients (or any project or activity an employee might be engaged in). However, the client's situation is the context for, not the focus of supervision. For this to happen, the principles, processes and skills of the strengths approach are used to assist reflection, learning and finding ways forward. This naturally includes reflection on, and learning from, successes, achievements and 'what works'. Supervision involves exploring and reviewing the issues, strengths, exceptions, aspirations, goals and plans in the employee's practice, with due regard for the principles of the strengths approach.

Chapter Ten

Strengths-based Supervision Day-to-day

'Reflective practice is aimed at assisting people to learn how to think, or other ways of thinking, as opposed to what to think. It promotes thoughtfulness and critical thinking, improves problem-solving skills and strengthens learning.'

~

'Knowledge is a 'way of knowing' that comes from within and governs our thoughts and actions. Methodologies for learning and improving practice are therefore required that assist people to use information and experience in ways that they can internalise learning. This internalisation allows knowledge to become embedded in a person's mind and heart.'

~

'The strengths-based mind map provides a highly beneficial guide for questions that can be used to assist reflection, clarification, problem-solving, planning, decision-making, action and review in relation to direct service delivery, supervision practice, management practice, group work, community development and all sorts of work activity.'

The strengths approach to supervision creates a culture of respect and empowerment based on relationships of trust and collaboration. It provides a rich means of support and a rewarding learning environment for all.

As discussed in chapter nine, supervision can take many forms, from coaching and mentoring to formal or on-the-run supervision, from group supervision and reflective forums to peer support. These can occur on any given day. Strengths-based, power-with principles, processes and skills can be applied in each of these forms of supervision.

Small portions of material in this chapter derive from training and practice material written by the author for the Department of Children and Families (McCashen 2014).

Building and sustaining autonomy, confidence and learning goes hand-in-hand with strengths-based ways of doing things. Much of this is dependent upon deeper learning that is enabled through meaningful reflection. This reflective learning aims to assist people to learn and think for themselves.

The strengths approach is inherently reflective and, as noted in chapter four, relies on finding the right questions rather than coming up with the answers or assuming to know the solutions to problems or challenges. As discussed on page 105, effective questions are characterised by 'not knowing', curiosity and belief in people's potential and expertise. It models practices of empowerment and valuing, avoiding unnecessary advice giving and jumping in with solutions. This parallels reflective practice in the workplace. It promotes thoughtfulness, problem-solving, critical thinking, learning and autonomy. It sharpens skills and enhances constructive, respectful practice. It is essential to effective supervision. As noted in an interview with Alison Carson, a family services manager (2016):

> It's really easy to jump in and give advice and tell people what to do but I think if you really, you know, genuinely believe that people can find their own kind of solutions and have strengths and capacities, you have a different conversation when they come into your office. You're asking them about what they think. Have they had similar situations to this before and what did they do, and supporting them to do that rather than just giving them...telling them what to do ... I think sometimes we get ... so busy and caught up in our work that we often forget to do that so I think ... we have the responsibility to make sure [we] ask those questions ... and not just you giving advice.

In this chapter we look at how the strengths-based mind map and reflective practice interact to provide support, assist learning and undertake problem-solving across all of the forms of supervision.

Reflective practice

One way in which learning occurs is through reflective practice. The purpose of reflective practice is to critique and to learn from our practice in order to make improvements and develop professionally.

Reflective practice is aimed at assisting people to learn how to think, or other ways of thinking, as opposed to what to think. It promotes thoughtfulness and critical thinking, improves problem-solving skills and strengthens learning. Reflective practice can be understood as an action-learning method where the employee reflects, plans, takes action and reflects again in an ongoing way. It is dependent upon the use of questions to facilitate learning and make sound decisions.

The critical reflection and discussion that are part of supervisory relationships can facilitate the development of practice wisdom and build confidence and autonomy. It can be used in one-to-one and group settings to support individuals and teams, bring rigour to decision-making and mindfulness to supervision processes, and to support professional development strategies. Reflective practice is a key means of assisting deeper learning.

There are important reasons for using reflective practice. Experience and quality information are important for professional development but alone they do not 'equal' knowledge. Knowledge is a 'way of knowing' that comes from within and governs our thoughts and actions. Methodologies for learning and improving practice are therefore required that assist people to use information and experience in ways that they can internalise learning. This internalisation allows knowledge to become embedded in a person's mind and heart.

Used regularly, reflective practice can be continuously transformative and can thus enable continuous improvement in practice. Receiving information, direction and instruction alone does not do this. It is critical and essential for any meaningful learning and effective professional development.

Reflective practice improves decision-making and service delivery processes and outcomes. It supports learning and builds confidence and motivation, contributes to a learning environment and increases skills and knowledge.

A strengths approach to reflective practice

Strengths-based reflective practice is achieved primarily through the use of questions, for example:

- What's happening in your work?

- What are you trying to achieve?

- What are the outcomes? What are you doing that leads to these outcomes?

- What's working?

- How are you going about this?

- Is there anything not going as well as you would like?

- What can you do differently?

Such questions match those that derive from the strengths-based process or mind map described in chapter five.

Reflective practice rests on finding and using the right questions to help learning and find solutions. This promotes mindfulness by avoiding the imposition of answers or assumptions about the problem or the solution to problems or challenges. Examples of the sorts of questions that can assist reflective practice are:

- You've always been good at helping people get in touch with their aspirations and goals. What's different in this situation?

- Thinking about other people you work with, what things are you doing that helps them to engage?

- If we looked at this from a gender perspective, what could be done differently?

- What does the principle of collaboration suggest for your work with this family?

- What did you notice about the group's response when you asked about the things they do well?

- What do you think the team does well despite the challenges?

- What are some of the strengths in the organisation? How might these help overcome some of the challenges we are facing?

- What sorts of things have you tried before that work?

In responding to any reflective questioning, reference should always be made to:

- professional values and goals, practice experience and wisdom
- agency values and goals, standards, policies and procedures
- research, theories and trends in the field and the literature
- models and frameworks relevant to the field in which practice takes place.

This enables a connection to be made with evidence as well as agency and professional standards.

Reflective practice can be used in supervisory and management relationships. It can also be used in a planned way in consultations, goal-setting, work practice reviews, group supervision, reflective forums, mentoring and coaching. It can be used to appraise service delivery, project work, team leader and management practices, and following critical incidents or in response to any issue or challenge that emerges in a work context. It can be utilised peer-to-peer, in formal and on-the-run supervision, in groups, in teams, staff induction, planning days and in larger forums.

Reflective practice then becomes part of the culture of teams and organisations, occurring in fluid and spontaneous ways in meetings, briefing, debriefing, in hallways, across the desk, in staff kitchens and coffee breaks.

A strengths-based mind map for reflective practice
The strengths-based mind map for practice, as discussed in earlier chapters, provides a useful guide for strengths-based supervision:

- Issues are described and clarified.

- A picture of the future is developed and goals are set.

- Strengths and exceptions are identified.

- Additional resources are identified as necessary.

- A plan of action is developed.

- Action is reviewed and evaluated.

As with service provision, these steps are meant to be used flexibly.

The skills of strengths-based supervision are the same as those of other strengths-based work:

- validating and normalising
- strengths-based questioning
- developing concrete description
- identifying and mobilising strengths and exceptions
- identifying resources
- reframing
- developing a picture of the future and establishing goals
- externalising
- identifying steps and strategies
- measuring and noticing change.

The strengths-based mind map provides a highly beneficial guide for questions that can be used to assist reflection, clarification, problem-solving, planning, decision-making and action in relation to direct service delivery, supervision practice, management practice, group work, community development and all sorts of work activity. It provides a structure for strengths-based reflective practice in formal, on-the-run, peer and group supervision, mentoring and coaching, practice reviews and team planning.

The questions in the table on the following page are based on this process.

A Strengths-based Mind Map for Supervision

THE ISSUES AND CHALLENGES	THE PICTURE OF THE FUTURE	STRENGTHS AND EXCEPTIONS	OTHER RESOURCES	PLANS AND STEPS TO TAKE
The context: • Who's involved? • What are the key issues and concerns? • What is your role? • What are the goals of the work? **The issues:** • What are the practice issues or challenges? • What are you and others doing? • When, where, how often? • How long have these issues been around? **Constraints:** • Are there any structural constraints getting in the way? What are they? • Are there any 'unhelpful' ideas or beliefs that are preventing change?	• How would you be feeling if these issues were resolved? • What would you be doing to enable you to feel like this? • What do you want things to be like instead of the way they are now? • How would that make a difference? • What do the principles of respect, empowerment, self-determination, inclusion, consultation, and building on strengths suggest for ways forward? • What do agency values, objectives, policy and standards suggest? • What do current theories, models, research, literature, practice frameworks suggest? • Describe your goals in specific and concrete terms.	• What are the exceptions to the issues? • What's happening when these issues are not present or not as bad? • What is being done differently? • What has been tried that has worked in this situation or others like it? • How have people gone about successfully addressing issues in this situation or others like it before? • What things have people done well? • What skills and strengths have been used?	• What other resources might be helpful? • Who else cares about this too? • Who might be able to help? • What skills, information or knowledge might be helpful? • What does best practice in this field of work/context suggest? • What resources in might be useful? • What resources in the community might be useful?	• Given the picture of the future, strengths, resources and goals, what steps need to be taken? • Who will do what, when, where? • When will these decisions, goals, steps and progress be reviewed and by whom?

The following examples of a supervisory conversation and the group supervision session presented on pages 244–250, demonstrate the use of questions for reflection and problem-solving based on key elements of the process. In any supervisory conversation it is beneficial to start by clarifying desired outcomes. This helps stay focused on the purpose of the interaction. Note that care is taken to avoid jumping to solutions and giving advice.

Worker: Kim contacted me this morning. Jane's been working with her and she's not in today so Kim asked to speak to me. I worked with her a while back and after she talked to me I'm not clear about how to respond.

Supervisor: So what would you like to have achieved by the end of our time together?

Worker: Well, I'd feel better if I had some ideas from this discussion about what to do next ... just a couple of things that might help until Jane's back and follows things up.

Supervisor: Okay. Can you tell me a bit about the background to the situation?

Worker: Well, I've been supervising Jane, who is working with Kim. She's finally been able to leave Adam who's been using violence against her. They've got two kids in care. One is 12 months and the other is two years old. She's been having issues with Child Protection around contact with her children. She wants more contact and also wants her kids back. Child Protection is in the process of applying through the courts for a custody order. I asked what she wanted the agency to do and she said she wants to break the pattern of going back to Adam so that she could get her kids back. She's living with her grandmother at present.

Supervisor: So what's she asking you to do?

Worker: She needed to talk things through. She feels disempowered because she's been able to stay away from Adam for two weeks now and Child Protection are still going to court and she can't see why she can't have her kids back. She needs housing and has applied for priority housing and Jane has supported her in that. I really think she can get on top of things as long as she gets the right support.

Supervisor: What's Child Protection doing?

Worker: Apart from the court order they're providing contacts with the children for Kim and Adam.

Supervisor: And what about Adam?

Worker: Well he's doing drugs still and makes threats to Kim and sees the kids whenever he feels like it which unsettles them and Kim never knows whether he's going to turn up for contact visits or not, which unsettles her too!

Exploring the worker's picture of the future and the practice goals:

Supervisor: So, what do you hope for?

Worker: (Pause) ... There needs to be some conversation and plan that finds a way to support Kim. I feel it requires a real naming of the issues: the domestic violence, Kim's successes in escaping it, the impact of all this on the kids... but I'm not sure how to proceed... I'm not one hundred percent confident in the system's ability to respond to the impact of domestic violence.

Supervisor: So, you'd need to help ensure a good service response to Kim and the children?

Worker: Yes. The bottom line is the kids' safety and Kim's as well. Kim knows what she's got to do but it's so difficult for her with the homelessness, loneliness and poverty issues.

Supervisor: If she was getting a good service what would be happening?

Worker: (Pause) ... There'd be a good understanding of the impact and dynamics of domestic violence. There'd be people who could see and value the strengths Kim has. Kim would be getting help to stay free of the violence and there'd be a plan for reunification of the children with Kim.

Exploring strengths and exceptions:

Supervisor: Okay. Kim has been in this situation before and has been able to achieve some changes. What's been your role in this?

Worker: I've been able to help validate and normalise Kim's experiences especially the domestic violence. I've asked her a lot of questions about what she wants—something I could do more of again. I usually have a picture of what it is she's hoping for.

Supervisor: So if you were supporting Jane to assist Kim to get a good service how would you go about it?

Worker: Gee, that's a good question! I think I know what you're getting at here ... well, I'd need to know how Kim feels about support from others. I'd need to clarify and check with Jane about her understanding of domestic violence, Child Protection's role, her view of Kim.

Supervisor: Okay. So that would help. Is there anything else?

Worker: No, I think that's it. I've spent so much time with Kim and have seen so many strengths and so much courage in the face of all the violence and poverty and homelessness, and come to think of it, so has Jane... I've just realised now that it's a matter of naming all this... with Jane and Kim.

Supervisor: So you're really continuing the work but through your support to Jane instead of directly?

Worker: Exactly! Now I feel really clear about what to do!

Deciding on steps and plans:

Supervisor: So, before we finish, what will you do now?

Worker: Well, I'll phone Kim back and let her know I'll arrange a meeting with Jane so that we can make a plan again. I'll see whether she needs to see me today; it'll depend on how she is when I call back. I'll talk to Jane when she returns to work tomorrow about this discussion and see how she thinks things are going for Kim too.

Goal-setting in supervision

Goal-setting is important and necessary in supervisory processes (formal, informal supervision, peer supervision, group supervision, mentoring, coaching) whether in relation to service delivery or other work practice, learning and professional development activity, or supervision and the supervision relationship itself. Goals describe desired outcomes, and can consist of both aspirations and specific description as discussed in chapter five.

A good starting point for goal-setting in relation to supervision, mentoring and professional development is to ask:

What will I have achieved ...

- by the end of this year?
- by the end of this supervision/mentoring relationship?
- as a result of this coaching?
- when I have finished this project?
- and so on ...

What will I know or be able to do?

This helps to clarify the purpose of the work being undertaken, or of the relationship, as the case may be. It enables the relationship to be tailored to the individual's support and learning needs, and helps keep the relationship focussed on these.

When establishing any learning goal, it can be beneficial to ask:

- What will I have achieved when I have learnt this/these skill/s?
- What will be different?
- What will I know and be able to do?

This helps to:

- describe what will be different to the way things are now
- provide the purposeful context for exploring strengths, exceptions, skills and resources
- identify what other resources are needed that could help
- clarify what steps need to be taken.

The table below uses the column approach to goal-setting for learning or longer term professional development planning. The second column focuses on goals while the other columns provide a meaningful context for the goal-setting.

A Process for Goal-setting

Challenges that come up in my work	What I want to know and be able to do	What I already know and can do well	The resources and supports I can use	The steps I can take
Ask questions that explore challenges, hopes and learning needs.	Ask questions that help describe knowledge and skills that will be present when learning goals are reached.	Ask questions that help describe what skills and knowledge already exist.	Ask questions that identify resources that can be used to achieve learning goals.	Ask questions that identify concrete steps that can be taken to reach the learning goals.

Other factors in making supervision work

There are a number of steps and pre-requisites for responsive and effective supervision practice (see also Gibbs et al. 2014, pp. 51–72). They include the following:

1. Developing a shared understanding of professional supervision including the tasks and functions of supervision.

This assists the supervisor and supervisee to work collaboratively. It gives clarity regarding expectations, boundaries, responsibilities, purposes and benefits of supervision.

2. Understanding and responding to the supervisee's experience of supervision.

Experiences of supervision can vary. Some are fortunate in having positive experiences of supervision; others not so fortunate. Some have good and bad experiences. Whatever the case, a meaningful discussion about the experience of supervision, about what works best for the supervisee, and about what they want from supervision is critically important in helping to make supervision work.

3. Using a supervision agreement (see pages 233–234)

4. Understanding and responding to people's preferred ways of learning.

People learn in all sorts of ways and there can be differences in the way people prefer to learn. A discussion about how the supervisee learns best can be very helpful in informing decisions and strategies for learning and professional development. Learning style inventories can be useful as a tool to help with this as well.

5. Understanding and responding to a supervisee's stage of development.

This can be done in a range of ways. To begin with, where is the employee now in terms of experience, knowledge, skills and the quality of practice? A discussion which involves reflecting on past experience and current practice can be helpful. This establishes a baseline from which learning and development strategies can be developed. Shadowing people and coaching on the job can be directly helpful. Getting this right can avoid setting expectations of the supervisee either too high or too low, and help ensure that learning strategies are realistic, and tailored in response to people's needs, strengths and aspirations.

6. Establishing and maintaining clear standards and expectations of the job.

This normally comes with induction and orientation but may also be supported through face-to-face training, reading and discussing relevant documents.

7. Culturally-competent supervision and practice.

There seems to be limited literature available about appropriate and effective models of cultural supervision and no established approaches for Australian Aboriginal supervision. Research by Natalie Scerra (2012) suggests that a range of approaches could be explored that can assist culturally-safe supervision. Interestingly, some of these coincide with, or are part of, a strengths approach to supervision, which moves away from power-over. These include:

- not using the term 'supervision' because of associations made that imply supervision means compliance

- creating relevant and meaningful reflective space

- using group/peer supervision (because it does not involve a top-down approach)

- using a narrative approach because it enables external perspectives and stories to reflect on situations

- supporting staff to build culturally-inclusive supervision environments and to tailor the content of, and approaches to, supervision sessions to meet different professional and cultural needs

- using Aboriginal practices and stories as a framework for a culturally-relevant model of supervision

- using oral traditions of Aboriginal people to provide a basis for cultural supervision

- aligning Aboriginal cultural practice with individual and peer supervision

- considering supervision by senior Aboriginal staff, internally or externally.

8. Understanding and appropriately exercising authority.

A useful framework for assisting managers to reflect on their feelings about the authority they hold is provided by Gibbs et al. (2014, p. 155) citing Obholzer et al. (1994). They identify three types of authority: authority from above, below and within.

- Authority from above, or role authority, is the authority conferred on the supervisor by the organisation...

- Authority from below, or professional authority, comes from a demonstrated level of competence gained from training, qualifications and experience

- Authority from within relates to how we feel about, experience and express our personal authority.

From the perspective of the strengths approach 'authority from within' is especially important and relevant because this is really about the supervisor or manager's attitude to power; how they use the authority that comes from experience and status. Commitment to parallel practice makes all the difference.

Supervision agreements

Supervision agreements are a 'contract' between a worker and supervisor. They help enable transparency and articulate understandings that can be used as points of reference for reviewing and improving supervision. They can reflect the various standards, policy and functions of supervision, accountabilities, values and principles for supervision, processes that will be used and so on. They can also address needs and expectations, and arrangements for the content, structure and regularity of supervision.

Supervision agreements are important because they help clarify bottom lines and define the principles, processes and content of supervision—helping to make supervision transparent. They can help avoid unnecessary conflicts and misunderstandings about standards and expectations.

So what might an agreement look like? This will be influenced by an organisation's policy regarding supervision as well as experiences, preferences, expectations and needs. There are many considerations for the development of a supervision agreement:

- How often and for how long will formal supervision occur?

- Where and when will supervision take place?

- What arrangements need to be in place for availability beyond regular supervision sessions?

- What additional or alternative arrangements need to be in place?

- What are the bottom line standards, expectations and responsibilities?

- What are the expectations, rules and limitations regarding confidentiality?

- What arrangements need to be in place for addressing 'stuckness', grievances, conflict or disagreements?

- What tools will be used for recording supervision and how will this be done?

- Where will the record be kept and how will it be accessed?

- How will the principles, processes and skills of strengths-based practice be built into supervision content and processes?

- When and how will the agreement be reviewed?

- When will occasional and annual reviews take place and who will be involved?

- How and when will supervision itself be reviewed?

There is reason for concern about the way supervision agreements are developed and used in some organisations. Supervision agreements based on a strengths approach reflect its principles and values including respect, transparency, participation, collaboration, inclusion, consultation, self-determination, empowerment and fairness. This means that agreements will be responsive to people's stage of development, their aspirations and strengths, and their preferences and needs. It means that agreements are understandable and meaningful to the parties involved, that standard requirements and contingencies for things going wrong will be clear and up front, that confidentiality will be respected and the limits to confidentiality made clear, that templates for agreements have built-in flexibility in order to be responsive and avoid unnecessary power-over practices.

Practice issues or practice stories?

An important matter that deserves to be emphasised is that supervision in any of its forms does not need to respond only to practice issues and problem-solving. Supervisory conversations are ones that provide for learning, support and continuous improvement. Many of these naturally involve problem-solving where we start with the 'practice issue' because that's the reason we seek support! But this is not always the case.

The term 'practice story' is more apt in strengths-based supervisory contexts because it does not necessarily suggest that the story shared has to be about issues and problem-solving. Any story can be reflected upon for learning and support, including successes. Using the strengths-based mind map for supervision can be highly beneficial but there are risks! As so eloquently put by Shirres (2016b) the use of the term 'practice issue', as well as structures for group supervision, can have unintended consequences.

> Our eagerness to explore 'practice issues' can have unexpected consequences and the very terminology we use can quickly become a hurdle. Whilst 'issue', in its communal sense, is relatively benign, when equated with an individual, this can feel more like a synonym for 'problem'. We may intend for it to be universal but

the experience of it can be somewhat different. Instead, it may be more useful to consider, and give weight to, the 'burning questions' that need to be asked. Equally, we could apply to peer [group] supervision the lessons learned from practice. That is, the importance of storytelling ...

Similarly, in our urgency to provide the best framework of support and drive its use, we can almost unconsciously remove the personal 'agency' anyone needs to have when they are being supported to make a change. Whether a process is intended to support a client in our work with them, or whether it is intended to support a practice reflection session, heed should be given to the purpose behind its use, endeavouring to make sure it supports, not subverts, that purpose. Just as in our work with clients, we should strive to make available information and support only as it is required and not take 'ownership' of any process that is in place.

These are pertinent and important observations and they highlight the critical part that language plays and the importance of using the strengths-based mind map in flexible and responsive ways, as noted a number of times already in this book.

A structure for formal supervision meetings

Here is a simple but useful process for giving structure to a formal supervision meeting:

1. How are you going in the job? Is there anything we need to discuss or resolve before we proceed? Either or both parties may need to discuss and resolve concerns, anxieties, or pressing matters that may get in the way of an effective and productive supervision session.

2. Setting the agenda: What do we need/want to talk about today? What are the most pressing topics or issues? What good things have been happening? Let's prioritise. What do we hope to have achieved by the end of this session?

3. List topics for discussion and reflection.

4. Work your way through each of the agenda items. Record the topic, related decision and any action to be taken.

5. List any follow up actions.

The remainder of this chapter defines other forms of supervision and provides suggested guides and structures for undertaking each of them.

On-the-run supervision

The role and responsibilities of supervisors are not confined to formal supervision meetings. Supervisors must be accessible, responsive and approachable. 'On-the-run supervision' is the term often used to describe this. It involves interactions between a supervisor and the supervisee (or mentor, coach or peer) for the purposes of learning, support or administration. These interactions may involve briefing, de-briefing, guidance, reflection or support. If allocated supervisors are unavailable, peers, mentors or other senior staff can undertake on-the-run supervision.

Here is a simple framework of steps using the strengths-based mind map for on-the-run supervisory interactions that require problem-solving:

1. Identify the issues.

2. Identify what the worker hopes to achieve by the end of the discussion.

3. Explore what's happening.

4. Identify the desired outcome relevant to the immediate issues: what are you hoping to achieve?

5. Identify what has been done well and explore exceptions to the problem: what's been tried before in this situation or others like it, that has worked?

6. Decide on some steps that need to be taken, at least for the time being

7. Arrange a time for follow up.

Peer supervision

Peer supervision involves staff of the same or similar status or experience coming together to review their work and develop plans in the professional context. This can involve a group but more commonly involves two employees. Mentoring and coaching can be undertaken through a peer relationship but peers may also engage in more structured supervisory interactions such as problem-solving.

Peer supervision has numerous advantages. It can be a part of an employee's professional development, a means of valuing staff and their contributions, and sharing the load of support and learning responsibilities in teams. Peers share common experiences, concerns, strategies and solutions and are familiar with the complexities of the work.

At the same time there are cautions regarding peer supervision. Peers may feel too overwhelmed by the same problems and challenges to be helpful. Peer conversations need sufficient structure to avoid getting stuck. If there are complex or particularly difficult issues to be dealt with in the absence of more experienced employees, senior staff need to be consulted.

The following framework of steps appropriate for problem-solving is like that presented for on-the-run supervision. It uses the strengths-based mind map but is adapted to the peer supervision context (McCashen 2014).

1. Identify the issue that needs to be discussed.

2. Specify the desired outcome of the discussion.

3. Clarify the issue further.

4. Check: Am I the right person to provide support on this? If not, decide who is and what needs to be done. If so ...

5. Identify the desired outcome relevant to the issues.

6. Explore what's been tried to resolve the issue, what's worked and what hasn't.

7. Explore what's been tried that's been successful/more successful in other situations like this one.

8. Identify what other resources might be needed.

9. Decide on a plan and run it past a more experienced or senior worker.

Coaching
Coaching is a valid and important form of supervision. There are sometimes misunderstandings of what coaching is and the differences between it and mentoring. Mentoring is explored in the following pages and the differences will be evident.

Here I describe coaching as a learning activity that provides a first-hand demonstration of how to undertake a skill or task (or set of skills or tasks) and enables and supports people to practice the skill until they are confident to do it. Preparation tasks are specified in each step. Anyone can provide coaching if the following four conditions are met:

1. The coach is experienced in the skills involved.

2. The coach has the necessary communication skills.

3. The coach is confident to explain and demonstrate the particular skill or task.

4. The coach is able to assist reflection.

A useful structure for coaching is described here.

Key steps in coaching:

1. The first step involves explanation of how a task is done. The coach defines the task, its purpose and aims, and the steps involved. Because of the way adults learn it's important to check what the employee knows already and then fill in any gaps. Remember, it's important that the employee understands why the task is important, how it is relevant as well as what's involved in doing it.

    Preparation: What do you need to explain? What information do you need to provide?

2. The second step involves demonstrating how to undertake the given task. It's critical that the coach explains this clearly so that the person knows what to look for when they observe the demonstration of how to undertake the task.

    Preparation: What needs to be demonstrated? What will the employee be looking for/observing?

3. The third step involves preparing the employee to do it themselves. Check their understanding by asking them to explain what to do and how.

    Preparation: What do you need to do to prepare the employee to practise?

4. The fourth step involves the employee practising the task.

    Preparation: What does the employee need to practise?

5. The fifth step involves reflection on what they did and how well they did it. This is assisted by asking: How do you think you went? What did you do well? Was there anything you think you could have done better? The coach can then provide feedback.

    Preparation: What do you need to do to help the employee reflect on what they did? What sorts of questions do you need to ask? What sort of feedback do you need to give?

6. Seek feedback from the employee on what they found helpful and what you might have been done differently as the coach.

    Preparation: How will you seek feedback for yourself? What sort of question/s will you ask the employee?

7. Repeat the process or any relevant part of it until the employee is confident and competent.

Strengths-based mentoring

Mentoring can be described as a two-way relationship between two people—mentor and mentoree (sometimes referred to as 'mentee'). The purpose of mentoring is to respond to the learning and support needs and goals of the mentoree. Mentoring can involve conversation, reflection, support, feedback, modelling by the mentor, coaching, planning, advising, and sharing ideas, skills and knowledge—supervision without the management function!

Strengths-based mentoring does not involve planning and monitoring by the mentor, instructing, telling, controlling or directing. It is not a top-down relationship. It values the knowledge and experience of the mentoree and uses these as building blocks for learning. The mentoree has a high level of ownership and control of the learning process, and learning is relevant to their needs and goals.

The mentoree is assisted to plan, review and reflect. The mentor's role is that of enabler, but good mentoring means that mentors can learn as much as mentorees. Again, the strengths-based practice mind map is useful for reflective processes that are central to mentoring. It can also be highly useful in reviewing the mentoree's progress and for reviewing the mentoring relationship itself (see the guides below).

Mentoring can contribute to a culture of learning and support and provide opportunities for employees, as mentors, to share and develop their knowledge and experience, and feel valued. It supports staff retention and can complement other learning. It enables the mentoree's learning to be individually-tailored, self-paced and flexible in terms of time-frames. It can spread workloads and share the responsibilities of supervising and managing.

Establishing the mentoring relationship

As a general rule establishing the mentoring relationship involves certain parameters and steps. These include:

1. Establish the desired outcomes of a mentoring relationship. Discuss this with your supervisor and who might be an appropriate mentor.

2. Check: Have I got the right mentor for what I want/need to learn?

3. If so, establish the desired outcomes, mentoring plan and a rough timeframe for the relationship. This will depend on the desired outcomes, goals and methods of learning agreed to, and whether or not the relationship is open-ended.

4. Decide how often, when and where you will meet.

5. Establish rules of confidentiality and mutual responsibility and an agreement for how you will work together.

6. Keep a record of sessions.

7. Review the relationship at regular intervals.

New learning goals and support needs can emerge during the life of the mentoring relationship, which can be open-ended. Mentors and mentorees need to be mindful of codes of behaviour, policies and procedures relevant to both the profession and the organisation.

The following sets of questions can be useful in giving structure to mentoring conversations. They can be equally useful for supervisory interactions.

A guide for planning the learning
What do you already know?
What skills and strengths do you already have? What are you good at?
What do you want to learn?
What will you know and be able to do when you have learnt this?
What resources can you use/do you need?
What could you try?
What will you do?

Reviewing progress towards goals
My goals were ...
What steps were taken to achieve the goal/s?
What were the outcomes?
How was this achieved?
What strengths, skills and resources were used?
What was done well?
What worked?
What, if anything could have been done differently?
What did you learn?
What else can you try?
Are there other goals that have arisen from this review?

Reviewing the relationship (with a mentor, peer or supervisor)
What has been useful?
What has been achieved?
What worked well?
What were the challenges?
What might have been done differently?
What can we learn from this?
What can we change for the future, if anything?

Group supervision

In some organisations workers and/or managers come together from time to time for supervision as a group. The term 'peer supervision' is often used but is problematic in this context because it implies that the people coming together are peers in the usual sense of the word; that is, they share similar status and experiences. On the other hand, within the context of the strengths philosophy we are all peers—workers, clients, directors, managers, volunteers and supervisors. This view is consistent with the notions of power-with and parallel practice. The very nature of the strengths approach to supervision enables anyone with a commitment to it, regardless of status and experience, to participate as peers.

This approach to strengths-based group supervision is a process that applies the principles, processes and skills of the strengths approach to learning and practice development in a group setting. The focus is on the review of practice. The group facilitates the session with the guidance of a key facilitator. The role of the key facilitator is to help keep the group focused on the process and its underlying purpose, to enable reflection on the practice of one worker at a time.

In parallel with strengths-based practice, during group supervision:

- issues are identified by the worker/supervisor/manager (whoever is bringing something to review)

- the picture of the future is considered and the goals of practice are defined

- the strengths, exceptions and resources are identified and described

- the worker/supervisor/manager decides what to try

- the session is 'worker-owned'

- strengths-based practice principles, processes and skills are the point of reference for reflection.

As with one-to-one supervision, minimal attention is given to the client's story; only the context is needed. In a group environment it is particularly important that participants do not jump to solutions or give advice. This group approach to supervision has many advantages:

- It provides opportunities for reflection and learning not otherwise available to employees.

- It provides opportunities to develop strengths-based skills.

- It provides opportunities to practice facilitation skills that are parallel to practice.

- It enables a normalising experience for participants.

- It enables a greater understanding of practice issues and what can be done to address them.

- It enables greater access to support and challenge.

- It enables team building.

Group rules

Group rules are important in groups and no less in group supervision. Individual groups may want to develop their own rules and these may change according to group composition. A useful basis for group rules is as follows:

- Everyone has the right to be heard.
- Everyone has the right to contribute.
- Everyone deserves to be treated with respect.

Principles of the strengths approach and other anti-oppressive practices strongly emphasise avoidance of giving unsolicited advice, jumping to solutions and blaming:

- Participants do not jump to solutions.
- The focus of sessions is on worker practice, not clients.

The following process of strengths-based group supervision was developed in Bendigo, Australia, at St Luke's (now merged with Anglicare Victoria) many years ago and consists of a set of key steps. It has been adopted by numerous human service organisations over the years. Of course, it is not the only way to do group supervision, but it illustrates the usefulness of the strengths-based process for group supervision and is used widely in the field. The process is meant as a guide to be used flexibly. The definition, importance and purposes of group supervision and the use of the process should be explored and clearly understood by participants before practising group supervision. Using the framework flexibly is of great importance.

In starting out, the facilitator focuses the group by reminding them of group rules, the process, spirit and intentions of the framework.

1. The worker is asked to describe the context in which the practice is taking place: a brief description of the key issues in the client's life, the client's goals, any other goals (e.g. statutory authority) and an outline of the worker's role and involvement. (In the case of issues not connected with direct service delivery, key issues, goals and roles are identified.)

2. The group supports the worker to identify and describe the practice issues in specific and concrete terms. This involves a process of clarifying the challenges and concerns before the worker. Care is taken to validate and normalise as necessary, and to avoid coming up with solutions or giving advice. Once the worker feels clear about the issues the facilitator prompts the group to move on the next step.

3. The worker is assisted to develop a picture of the future: what their practice will look like if the issues were resolved. These are the same sorts of questions that help anyone develop a picture of the future. So the group asks questions such as: If things were going well what would be different? What are you hoping for? How would you be feeling? What would you be doing differently?

4. The worker is assisted to identify exceptions, strengths and resources. These are the same sorts of questions that are used to help anyone find strengths and exceptions. So the group asks questions such as: What are you already doing that is working in this situation? What are things that are going well? What are some of the good things? What have you done in other situations like this that have been helpful? With regard to resources, what supports, information or knowledge might be helpful to draw on?

5. The group assists the worker to explore and identify any constraints (beliefs) or structural issues that might be getting in the way, if not already covered earlier. So the group asks questions such as: Is there anything that's getting in the way of achieving the things that you want to? If so, what are they? Are these things that you can influence? Are these things structural or resource issues? Are these to do with our culture in the organisation or things people believe?

6. Group participants give constructive feedback to the worker. This includes affirmation and acknowledgement as well as the sharing of personal reflections and ideas on the situation. In this part of the process participants give recognition to the worker about the challenges, successes, strengths, and good things that they have heard about. They also share ideas, suggestions and thoughts about what they think might be helpful. It's important that any suggestions or ideas are contributed in a tentative way for the worker's consideration.

7. The worker is invited to specify and define the steps he or she will take in light of the constraints, practice goals, strengths, exceptions and resources.

8. Each group participant briefly shares personal learning from the session about:
- the worker's experience
- strengths and decisions
- the relevance to their own practice
- the session generally.

This part of the session is most important because it honours and cherishes all that has been shared by the worker. It recognises and values the worker and their work. Sometimes there may be participants who do not contribute or ask questions because others have said or asked what they intended to. In these circumstances it can be reassuring to the worker to hear those people's responses and what they have learnt. This is particularly important when sharing comes from the heart and soul.

Using the strengths-based group supervision process

The following example involving four workers illustrates the use of the process. It reflects parallel practice in supervision. In this example, the process unfolds relatively neatly following the process as outlined above. Members of the group simply use questions based on the strengths-based process to help a worker, Anna, find her own way forward. Note the use of reflective practice. The worker is asked to give a brief description of the context in which the practice is taking place, the key issues in the client's life, the client's goals, any other goals (for example, those of the statutory authority) and to give an outline of their role.

Facilitator: Anna, can you give us a picture of what's happening?

Anna: Well, it's something that's been bothering me for a while. I've been stuck really.

I've been working with Donna for about six weeks now following a request from a family friend on Donna's behalf. It turned out she'd been struggling with depression for years and there'd been a general sense of hopelessness that pervaded her. I felt like we'd built a good relationship. I'd validated her experience and helped her talk about what things were like in her life. Then on the fourth visit she disclosed sexual abuse in her childhood by her husband's father. I was stunned by this disclosure and even more so when Donna told me she'd never told anyone before, not even her husband. I was touched deeply on a number of levels that she'd shared this with me. Currently, I'm visiting once a week and we've spent a lot of time discussing the hopelessness and despair she's experiencing.

Worker 1: Anna, this is a very sad situation. I get such a sense of sadness and hopelessness. Are you okay?

Anna: Sure, I've gotten over the initial shock of the reality and have had plenty of support.

Facilitator: Can I just check—have you been able to establish any goals?

Anna: Well, I've tried but all my visits have been given to listening. When I've tried to talk to Donna about what she really wants for her life and her family she breaks into tears. It just reminds her how bad things are. It seems to make things worse. I guess the challenge is how to ask the right questions but at the moment I visit to provide support.

The group assists the worker to identify and define the issues in specific and concrete terms. Group members reflect back what they have heard as the issues.

Worker 1: So, at this stage the expectation from Donna is that you provide support, visit and talk about things?

Anna: Yeah. I try to give feedback about her strengths and she really responds to this.

Facilitator: So, let's check with you—if I've heard you correctly—one of the strongest issues for you is the impact of the disclosure?

Anna: Yeah. I have a huge sense of responsibility because I'm the only person she's told.

Worker 2: But is the issue the impact of the disclosure or that you are stuck because of it and don't know where to go from the stuckness?

Anna: It's more the stuckness ... maybe my stuckness is caught up in Donna's...

Facilitator: So other than the weight you're carrying because of the disclosure and the stuckness, is there anything else in the work that's affecting you or getting in the way?

Anna: Well, I just don't have any real direction.

Worker 2: Linked with the fact that you don't have any clear goals?

Anna: ...Mmm...

Worker 1: Is that the crux of it?

Anna: I think it is. The questions you've asked me lead me to think it is. My response to the disclosure is big but having no goals makes me stuck.

Worker 2: I'm wondering whether the bigness makes it hard to press for goals.

Anna: Yes, and I have such big sense of responsibility in this.

Worker 1: So, for you the practice issue is that the stuckness comes out of not being clear about your role because of the lack of goals. It's hard for you to get a practice goal because you don't know what Donna's goal is?

Anna: Yes.

Facilitator: I feel like I have an understanding about the issue now but I'm wondering what it looks like day-to-day in your contacts with Donna. What are you actually doing when you visit?

Anna: Well, I try to focus before I visit and identify the questions. I also try to externalise the shame and guilt that Donna feels and normalise things. I asked her what things might be like when the shame doesn't have as much of a stranglehold. I ask her about her family's strengths. She responds really well to this but we get a bit down the path of exploring her future and she bursts into tears. I check whether or not it's okay to keep going and mostly it's too hard for her.

Worker 1: So, you see the challenge as being able to get beyond the stuckness so that Donna can make a shift?

Anna: Yes. Yes, that's exactly what I think I need to do.

The worker is assisted to develop a picture of the future: what their practice will look like when the issues are resolved. How will they be feeling? What will they be doing? (Concrete description is developed.)

Worker 1: So, if you were doing that what would you be doing?

Anna: Umm... I probably wouldn't be doing stuff that's not worked so far... (Laughter)

Worker 1: Which is? (Laughter)

Anna: I suppose ... one of the things I wouldn't be doing is focussing on trying to get goals so much. Like, I'm really focussed on getting some goals... giving too much thought to this. I've done this a lot—every time—and it doesn't work ... and I keep doing what doesn't work! (Laughter)

Worker 1: And doing it again! (Laughter)

Anna: But that doesn't answer your previous question about what I'd be doing instead. I think I need to start more where she's at.

Worker 2: Do you have an idea of what that might look like?

Anna: Um... I feel like I do. I've spent so much time over the six weeks... but it's just struck me that this has been ten years' worth of the effects of guilt and depression... I'd be listening more closely for the strengths and exceptions around the things that have gone well for her... especially when she's confronted difficult issues in her life. Then I'd have more of an idea of what might be useful.

Facilitator: We've asked before what you might be doing differently if things were to be different in your work with Donna. I wonder how you'd be feeling?

Anna: ... Confident. I'd be less stressed. I'd be feeling clear.

The worker is assisted to identify exceptions, strengths and resources (concrete description is developed). The group assists the worker to explore and identify any constraints (beliefs) or structural issues that might be getting in the way, if not already covered.

Facilitator: One of the things I know about your work is that you are good at asking questions. You also said Donna responds well to feedback about her strengths and those of her family. Is there something you haven't asked that might help?

Anna: Well, I haven't asked her what her experience has been of our time together. I haven't asked what she thinks I might do. And I haven't asked her about how all their strengths might figure in their future. One of the things I've been doing is keeping it all up here in the head instead of putting it out there and talking about it—sort of externalising it all. Maybe I need to ask, as a team, I mean me and Donna, what we might do.

Worker 1: Have you done that before in other work?

Anna: Yeah. I have... Lots! (Laughter)

Worker 1: And what happens?

Anna: It stops being my problem and anxiety! We have shared responsibility and I don't feel responsible. It's an opportunity to hear whether I'm on track or not. It's a very powerful thing. Yeah, she's always responded well to externalising; grasped it very well. I think I've been running in too quickly to get goals and it's been counter-productive.

Worker 2: So, coming back to what you'll be doing when things are working out: How does what you've just told us inform what you'll be doing differently?

Anna: Well, I can talk to her about how I've been stuck and externalise our stuckness together. Ask her about what's helpful and get some feedback about what's working to change things. I know she wants to change things. We could talk about a picture of things without stuckness; how we'd be working together. Yeah, I think that's the next step.

Worker 1: You said before that bringing a focus on exceptions can be useful.

Anna: Yeah. Yes, I think I need to do that more, too.

Group participants give constructive feedback to the worker. This includes affirmation and acknowledgement as well as sharing of personal reflections on the situation.

Facilitator: Anna, I wonder if it's appropriate at this point for the group to give some feedback. It seems like we've got to the point where you have a picture of where you might go from here. What do you think?

Workers: Sure.

Anna: I feel a lot clearer. That would be good.

Worker 2: This is such a huge challenge. I've been identifying with your stuckness because I've been in situations like this, too. One of the things I've tried to do that seems to be helpful is to ask whether there are other resources that might be helpful. Is that something you've discussed?

Anna: No, not really. I'm scared Donna might think I'm giving up on her. But I guess that it could be something I ask her about in the context of a picture without the stuckness. Yeah, that's a good idea.

Facilitator: Anyone else have any thoughts at this stage?

Worker 1: I've been wondering about Donna's husband in all of this. How do you see his role in this or is it too soon to be thinking about that?

Anna: Phew! It's something I've been aware of but somehow it all depends on Donna and how she proceeds from here.

Worker 1: Maybe there are strengths and exceptions in the relationship that could shed some light on the situation.

Anna: That's true and there are a few examples of that. Yeah, there are possibilities there too. That's something I could pursue.

The worker is invited to specify and define the steps they will take in light of the practice goals, strengths, exceptions, resources and feedback.

Facilitator: Okay. I wonder if we could move on. Anna, do you feel okay about sharing some of the steps you might take now?

Anna: Sure. This has been really helpful. As I said before, I can name my stuckness to Donna and see if we can externalise and start to tackle things that way. Build a picture of how we'd be working without the stuckness. That's the main thing. I'll ask her for feedback and also I like the idea of looking at other resources in that picture. The stuckness has led me to overlook the positive outcomes of focussing on strengths. It might be possible to see whether the strengths in Donna's and her husband's relationship can play a bigger part in her future picture, if we get that far.

Each group participant briefly shares their personal learning from the session about the practice issues and the worker's experience, strengths and decisions; about the relevance to them for their practice; and about the process of the session generally.

Facilitator: I'm not sure about others but it seems as though this has been useful.

Anna and others: Yes. For sure!

Facilitator: So what about some final reflections. What have been the main learnings here?

Worker 2: Well, for me the process has been really enlightening because I've been a bit stuck lately with a couple of people I'm working with and I realise how important it can be to name what's happening; I've forgotten about the importance of transparency. I mean in being up front even about stuckness. I mean, it's so easy to fall into the trap of taking all the responsibility as if we have the all the answers. And the other thing I've got from this is not to forget the strengths inherent in people's experience no matter how rotten things are. So thanks, Anna.

Worker 1: Yeah, I agree with that. I'm also struck by the intensity of the situation. Anna, I really admire the way you have been able to hang in there with Donna in such a difficult situation; the emotional issues seem so overwhelming and I think I'd find it extremely difficult working out where to go with this situation. I've found this supervision session really helpful.

Anna: Yeah, it's been hard but I feel like a big weight has been lifted off me now.

Facilitator: Anna, I can only reiterate what's been said. I couldn't agree more! And thanks for sharing the experience with us.

Others: Yeah, thanks.

Anna: Thanks, everyone.

This example of a strengths approach to group supervision illustrates the way in which questions are important in enabling a worker-owned process. Anna is the one who defines the issues, strengths, exceptions, goals and steps. Workers' offerings are made in a respectful and tentative way and only after Anna has been assisted to explore her own strengths and ideas. It illustrates parallel practice as a way of supporting workers to develop and improve their own practice and thus create the conditions necessary for people's empowerment.

This process need not be used only for shared problem-solving. It can be used retrospectively as a valuable learning process in groups where people are invited to share the positive stories about their work, even small achievements.

Reflective forums

Another form of group supervision found to be effective and practical is the strengths-based reflective practice forum. In these forums, people meet to consider achievements, successes, issues or challenges of common interest or concern and critically review and reflect using the strengths-based mind map.

They are facilitated gatherings. The difference between these forums and the group supervision structure explored on previous pages, is that while group supervision is aimed at the support for, and learning of, an individual, these forums are used to address matters that are common to all or most of the participants.

Anyone with a common interest or concern can participate in these forums including service delivery staff, team leaders, managers, or stakeholders from other agencies or the general community. Forums can be team-based, office-based, agency-based, locality-based, or region wide.

A process for reflective forums

The following process is recommended for reflective forums. Questions used by the facilitator and participants generally are derived from the steps outlined.

1. The context in which practice is taking place is established: a brief description of the key issues, the goals involved and an outline of roles.

2. Issues are explored and defined in specific and concrete terms.

3. The facilitator summarises the key issues.

4. The group develops a picture of what things will look like when the issues are resolved

5. The group explores and identifies exceptions and strengths.

6. Any necessary additional resources are identified.

7. The group specifies the steps they will take in light of the goals, strengths, exceptions and resources.

8. Decisions are made regarding follow-up: When will decisions, goals and progress be reviewed?

Strengths-based straight talk

Autonomy for workers and supervisors is an important characteristic of good supervision because it allows for ownership of learning and self-determination. The challenge is to achieve a balance between accountability and autonomy that enables self-determination and empowerment in the professional context.

Supervision is inherently hierarchical just as the worker/client relationship is, even in organisations or teams with non-hierarchical structures. The strengths approach to supervision recognises the responsibility of supervisors to raise issues of concern about practice and accountability, and aims to address these using the same frameworks and processes used to address those of clients. This involves what has been dubbed 'strengths-based straight talk' (Parker 2000):

Strengths-based straight talk involves:

- being honest and up-front while validating feelings
- naming anything that might be getting in the way of addressing issues of concern
- being clear about bottom lines, rights, responsibilities, roles, boundaries or limitations
- balancing accountability and self-determination.

It is respectful and sensitive (validates the impact of the straight talk), non-blaming, based on evidence that is concrete and specific and mindful of strengths, exceptions and good intentions.

It is important because it can help address safety issues, meet agency obligations and address bottom lines. It can provide opportunities for people to take responsibility for issues of concern.

It should be specific and based on evidence (avoid assumptions) and requires sensitivity (putting ourselves in people's shoes). It should be considerate of and honour strengths and exceptions, and acknowledge constraints that people have little or no control over. It needs to be responsive rather than reactive—good listening is always important.

Strengths-based straight talk typically involves the following steps, which can be used flexibly:

- Providing a context; the reason for the discussion/naming the issues
- Validating the impact of the naming of the issues
- Describing the issues and concerns in specific and concrete terms
- Enquiring about and acknowledging people's efforts and intentions
- Acknowledging strengths and exceptions
- Checking for constraints (are there other things getting in the way?)
- Specifying what needs to be different
- Deciding steps: what needs to be done?

Feedback

One supervisor describes her experience of giving and seeking feedback:

Feedback's a really essential part of supervision that goes both ways so it's about being able to provide feedback about the things you've noticed, about the things that people bring to the role, their talents, their skills, their strengths, what you appreciated about them and being really concrete about that. But equally being able to have conversations about things that you've noticed that you're not sure about and ask them some more questions about that. When I'm providing supervision, I always seek feedback at the end, you know, using a scaling tool as a way of getting some direct feedback so that I can change things ... for the next supervision session. I think being able to model some of those things in supervision is really helpful because that's kind of what we're asking workers to do with families.

Carson 2016

Feedback is integral to learning and support. It involves sharing observations and thoughts about another person's work with the view to ongoing encouragement of good work and continuous improvement. Feedback is meant to help learning, support and encourage, reinforce skills and strengths and address areas that need improvement.

Feedback can sometimes be associated with criticism rather than a way of learning. This depends on people's prior experience of feedback, their relationships, and how well the feedback is given. Gibbs et al. (2009, pp. 108–110) emphasise the importance of discussing feedback, its purposes and how it will be given. They underline the value of providing regular feedback as a means of building a culture of critical thinking and practice that staff become accustomed to. They emphasise good preparation for effective feedback and underline the importance of 'ownership' of the feedback by the giver of feedback; that is, it reflects their perspective.

Inviting feedback and modelling the receiving of feedback is also important in creating a culture of feedback. While feedback can be of value in helping people get a sense of how they are going on the job, it can sometimes be off the mark or poorly delivered.

Strengths-based feedback always occurs with an emphasis on people's strengths, the exceptions or unique outcomes, their aspirations and values, and their hopes and intentions. It is mindful of structural and cultural/personal constraints, and the part that dominant discourse plays in people's personal and professional lives. It is a meaningful and respectful critique of practice.

An effective and positive approach to meeting the objectives of feedback (encouraging, supporting and improving people's work) is to seek the person's own story, reflections and perspective. Four key questions make this possible:

1. How do you think you did?

2. What do you think you did well?

3. Was there anything you think you could have done better?

4. What could you do differently next time?

These reflective questions and others like them invite sharing and reflection that is strengths-based. They enable the person to provide a self-critique of their work. Then it allows the supervisor, mentor or peer a space for sharing their view, observations and perspective in a complementary and meaningful way, including areas that may need improvement.

Chapter Eleven

The Strengths Approach to Community Connectedness

'What if workers saw the people in front of them as advisors, experts, community builders, entrepreneurs, and holders of wisdom? How might this paradigm shift fundamentally change practice?'

~

'One thing's for sure, you've got to have an agency or leadership that promotes the culture of social inclusion. If the organisation doesn't have that culture, the workers won't either.'

~

'The principles of respect, power-with, self-determination, social justice, transparency, collaboration, consultation and inclusion are not only principles of action in the present but drive our way forward. These principles are also aspirations for a better world. They are vital for the development of a just society and secure, peaceful, vibrant communities. '

~

There are fundamental conditions and resources that are necessary for healthy human development: food, clothing, shelter, income, safety and peace, sustainable resources, social justice and equity (WHO 1986). Community has a crucial role to play in providing for these resources.

Community and its importance

Community can consist of a group or groups of individuals based in any given locality, or groups of individuals with a common interest (communities of interest). For example, a group of people may come together from a neighbourhood to address some local concerns (locality-based), or a group of Indigenous people from across a region may come together to address common concerns (a community of interest).

Sometimes people may belong to both sorts of groups; for example, a group of parents from the same locality may come together to address concerns about teenage behaviour in their streets. Both locality-based communities and communities of interest can be the focus of community building, and activities often include a mix of locality development, social action and planning. People may connect in a multitude of ways and when they do we have the makings of community. The advent of on-line communities is an example.

Community is for and about people. It is the life-blood of society and the landscape for human interaction and nurturance. It provides stability, safety and security. Community is characterised by connectedness, interdependence, belonging, mutual support, respect, sharing, acceptance of others and a sense of pride and identity. It involves cooperation, collaboration, shared responsibility and common purpose. These characteristics are commonly identified by communities themselves and by researchers as essential to healthy communities.

Individualised service delivery (designed to respond to individual needs) can enable independence from specialist services, provide for advocacy and support, and enable change to individual and family circumstances. It is limited by boundaries placed on it by funding arrangements. It does not aim to develop collective action to address wider social, structural, economic or political issues that affect people's lives. But as put by Jim Ife (2016, p. 20) in a discussion on human rights:

> ...we can only achieve our human rights in social interaction with others — in community — rather than in splendid isolation. In the future, as many writers have pointed out, our humanity and indeed our survival will be dependent

on the ideology of interdependence, not independence, and on strong vibrant and inclusive communities. For this reason, social workers, with a community development perspective, become absolutely central.

Individually-tailored service delivery can, however, be a springboard for building connectedness and addressing social issues in a collective way. Individualised services can also be the starting point for community building activity.

The potential of individualised service delivery to be a starting point for community building is evident in the story told of the women's group in chapter four. This is not only a story of growth and positive change for a group of individuals. It illustrates the way in which a support service can move beyond a focus on individualised service delivery to contribute to the building of 'community connectedness'. The women who made up this group created their own community and affected the lives of family and loved ones in ways that would not otherwise have been possible.

Social inclusion
Social inclusion strategies are another important means of building community connectedness. Social inclusion means people are engaged in:

- Employment and other productive or creative activity that is both meaningful and rewarding

- Education, training and other activities which help people to build their qualifications, life skills, social and cultural literacy and which provide a positive experience of education overall

- Community connection through meaningful, rewarding, self-directed and sustainable community engagement, civic participation and social action

- Financial security where people can gain control of their financial situation and to be able to plan and make decisions about their future

- Health where people can gain appropriate access to the health services system so that their physical and mental health does not unnecessarily constrain their capacity to participate in the other four domains of social inclusion.

St Luke's Anglicare 2013

The strengths approach is fundamentally connected to these means of social inclusion in that it provides a philosophical and practical base for addressing social justice. The principle of inclusion in the strengths approach relates to people's right to participate in, and control, change processes in matters that affect their lives. Inclusion involves practices that actively engage people in change processes by being consultative, collaborative and transparent for the purposes of self-determination and empowerment. It also responds to people through a deep respect for their human dignity regardless of their status, culture and identity.

People can be excluded according to their social or income status, race or ethnicity, sexuality, age, gender or ability. Exclusion can occur through language, stereotyping, labelling, assumptions about capabilites, and economic barriers among others. All of these concern anyone committed to a strengths approach.

Socially-inclusive practices as defined by the Australian Social Inclusion Board (2012) are strengths-based in that they view people as having the resources, opportunities and capability to:

- Learn by having opportunities to participate in education and training

- Work by participating in paid employment or voluntary work which contributes to their community and in family and caring

- Engage by connecting with other people in their community and have access to community resources and

- Have their voice heard so they can influence decisions and services that directly affect them and, more broadly, the community they work in.

Strengths-based practice mentor, trainer and champion of social inclusion, John Bonnice, captures the four pillars of socially-inclusive practice:

1. Belief in the capacity and skills of the people we work with.

2. Supporting people's aspirations and demonstrating a high level of expectation.

3. Our view of the people we work with: seeing people as partners and contributors not consumers and beneficiaries.

4. Practice skills: our practice skills and social inclusion frameworks (social justice, rights-based, community development and the strengths approach). Our ability to explore social inclusion dimensions with people and support steps towards social inclusion.

Bonnice 2015a

This requires reflection by workers and their organisations on their beliefs and assumptions about people they provide services to. Honoring people's aspirations means that workers will often need to move beyond the parameters of the service that they are engaged in.

Building social inclusion into everyday practice

Helen, a family service worker, had attended a practice reflection session on social inclusion. In her conversations with families she began to incorporate a greater range of questions with a focus on exploring the social inclusion opportunities for parents. On a home visit to a family, Helen started asking a mum, Cath, about her history of working, what her hopes and aspirations had been in the past and what they were now. Cath was currently unemployed and had been for some time.

She described how she used to work as a florist when she was young and what this was like for her and what it meant to her. The conversation finished at that point but a few weeks later Cath raised with the Helen their previous conversation about her work history and her hopes. Cath told Helen that she had been reflecting on their conversation and that it got her thinking about what she would like to do in the future. She said she wanted to get back into work and that she wanted to be more connected to the community. From this conversation and with encouragement from Helen, Cath enrolled in a vocational training course to better her chances of getting back into the workforce.

For Helen the conversation with Cath highlighted the importance of exploring people's hopes and dreams, outside the immediate issues that a service is designed to address, and looking for what people have done in their lives and the skills they have. This type of conversation opens up social inclusion possibilities and expresses belief in people's skills and capacities.

Social inclusion: is this the key to a paradigm shift?

Bonnice (2015b) raises these pertinent and challenging questions:

- Is the way we think about the people we work with actually preventing change?

- What if we thought of the people we work with as contributors not clients? People not cases?

- What if workers saw the people in front of them as advisors, experts, community builders, entrepreneurs, and holders of wisdom?

- How might this paradigm shift fundamentally change practice?

Here is an interview with John about social inclusion by Karen Bedford, managing editor at Innovative Resources (2016).

Karen: What is social inclusion?

John: Social inclusion includes a range of dimensions. It is about economic participation. This can be paid work, unpaid work or volunteering. It is about being a learner and being involved in education. It is about being a contributor to the community, not just a participant. It is about seeing your skills recognised. Social inclusion is also about financial inclusion and health inclusion. So it's a range of dimensions and you've got to work across all of them.

Karen: Why is social inclusion important?

John: What has enabled you to be the person you are? What do you get out of your social inclusion? We see how our work and social participation help build our confidence, self-esteem and sense of purpose. And we often see the people we work with experiencing a sense of exclusion and isolation; of not being a contributor within society. Asking a different set of questions and exploring the things that would help address this sense of exclusion in the community, and focussing on what people can (and do) contribute in their everyday lives—that's the mind shift. In my experience, this approach has helped address a range of things that hold people back, such as our low expectations of them.

I think social inclusion is one of the real game changers.

Karen: Is social inclusion relevant to all services?

John: It's applicable across the board whether you're working in youth services, family services, mental health services, or disability services. It's more than, 'I'm just going to link someone to a sporting club and they're going to be a participant.' It's about someone being involved in creating that sporting opportunity or contributing to the way a particular event or team is being run. Meaning comes out of being an active participant in that process, rather than just being a consumer of something. It's the act of being a creator.

Karen: Do you see a need for worker reflection and training on social inclusion?

John: Yes, to encourage workers to explore how they can think differently about those they're working with. Generally, our system encourages a particular mind set. Workers often don't think about the person they're working with as having creativity, skills, and resources. We are very deficit-focussed. We may say, 'The client is an expert', but often we're still putting people in a box. Reflection and training on social inclusion is about getting people to ask questions like, 'How is the person I'm working with a teacher, a leader, an expert, a person with skills?' We need to shift the paradigm from seeing the client as the consumer receiving services from us, to seeing a person who can change not just their own circumstances, but those of others as well.

Karen: How does social inclusion work change the role of workers, organisations and services?

John: The worker's role changes from being the expert to being the facilitator. One way that clients can be contributors is in the design, delivery and governance of services. But the people we work with have not traditionally been active in the design of the services we deliver for them. So we, as workers, agencies and as a system, have to ask ourselves: 'Do we need to make a shift in our approach?' Because what we are designing is not necessarily delivering the outcomes we hoped for.

One thing's for sure, you've got to have an agency or leadership that promotes the culture of social inclusion. If the organisation doesn't have that culture, the workers won't either. Organisations must be willing to ask these questions about social inclusion. This can't be done by one organisation in isolation; it needs to be done across the wider service sector. It's about building a practice, which sits across a range of organisations and engages with the wider community differently. Our organisation becomes a resource to the community, a contributor to the community, bringing a set of skills and resources to a community.

The way workers view the person sitting in front of them is absolutely critical.

Strengths-based community building

When workers respond to the interests of individuals or families and invite them to come together for projects where those interests can be given expression, they not only engage in a process of meeting individual needs, but they also help build connectedness with others.

Community-building activity is another way in which community connectedness can be developed. Building community is an essential component of lasting change and therefore should not be seen only as an additional activity to individualised service delivery. It needs to have a place in the vision of every human service organisation. In strengths-based work community building can begin with the individuals, families and groups that workers engage with.

The practical implications of the strengths approach for community building mean that the structures and processes of community activity need to be built on people's unique experiences, strengths and resources, common aspirations and goals with the community driving the process. Activities are tailored in ways that enable communities to become their own 'managers'. Projects and activities start with the community's strengths, interests and aspirations as opposed to 'needs assessments'. Workers engage with communities in ways that enable community ownership of change processes, and that build the capacities of communities as opposed to rescuing or doing things for them.

The principles of respect, power-with, self-determination, social justice, transparency, collaboration, consultation and inclusion are not only principles of action in the present but drive our way forward. These principles are also aspirations for a better world. They are vital for the development of a just society and secure, peaceful, vibrant communities.

If we are to build community we need to be concerned with interdependence rather than independence. People are social beings and rely on each other for sustenance. The principle of independence has its basis in the belief that people should be able to manage on their own. This is seen as desirable because they are less likely to place demands on others.

In economic rationalist thinking this means that people should also be economically independent and responsible for themselves, placing less responsibility on governments or other social institutions for people's welfare. Individualism and individual responsibility are highly valued while globalisation and corporatisation devalue or minimise the importance of social life and community, so necessary for safe, secure, respectful and peaceful societies. Any change, learning or growth depends upon ongoing interaction with others and is more likely to be sustained or enriched with the support of communities.

As noted by Beilharz (2002, pp. 10–19) safe, healthy communities have a high level of trust, multiple networks or opportunities for interaction, and are tolerant of diversity. They are supportive, have non-hierarchical relationships, meet personal needs and have creative responses to problems. People who feel safe, secure and supported are more likely to be reliable, respectful, confident, assertive and comfortable with difference, aware of feelings, capable of appropriate expression and have empathy for others. Social support and interpersonal connectedness, social status and sufficient wealth, control and self-determination are crucial to the health and wellbeing of individuals and communities.

When workers engage with people as members of a community, they need to respond in ways that lead to interdependence within and sometimes beyond their communities. The creation of interdependence requires the development, recognition and appreciation of common aspirations and the establishment of a shared vision. In interactions with individuals we look for commonalities in people's experiences, concerns, interests, strengths and their aspirations, on which community-building activity can be based.

Connectedness, access to resources, influence on the wider world and the relationship between individuals and their environment are crucial to community. At the same time these characteristics can belong to any social group that is 'colonising' and abuses power. Respect for diversity and difference is therefore a crucial characteristic of any healthy and socially-just community.

Strengths-based community capacity building involves:

- sharing power by creating cultures of respect, justice, participation, inclusion and self-determination

- building capacities through the identification and mobilisation of the community's expertise, strengths and resources

- building connectedness and cooperation through the development of a community-owned, community defined vision of what people want for their communities

- establishing avenues and structures for inclusion, participation and action

- contributing to social change

- building networks and partnerships within and beyond the community

- addressing the social, cultural, economic and structural constraints to growth, learning, and change

- building on commonalities and creating interdependence and connectedness between people in ways that respect diversity, choices and individuality.

Working with, not for, people

In a strengths approach workers are concerned with the building of people's capacities and potential as opposed to rescuing or doing things for people. Sometimes community development work does not sufficiently address people's aspirations and strengths, or the ownership of change processes, and the importance of these things in building community. In many circumstances expertise is considered to lie with specialists or institutions such as government. 'Experts' carry out visioning and planning, sometimes in consultation with communities (often tokenistic or inadequate), but the primary aim is to get the job done! Beilharz (2000) illustrates this point well by comparing elements of community planning with elements of community capacity building:

COMMUNITY PLANNING	COMMUNITY CAPACITY BUILDING
• Expertise lies with specialists.	• Expertise lies with the community.
• Expertise is about issues and solutions.	• Expertise is about the community.
• Planning involves a small team who make decisions about the community on the basis of research and practice traditions.	• Planning involves discussion between many people and includes identification of what would work in that community.
• Planning includes consultation with community members.	• Planning includes consultation with specialists.
• Goals are developed and known by only a few.	• Many people contribute to a shared vision of a preferred future for their community.
• The planning group retains and builds on planning information and skills.	• Skills and specialist information is transferred to community members.
• The primary goal is physical development.	• The primary goal is social development.
• The process is fairly quick.	• The process takes a long time.

The following example highlights the importance of working *with*, not *for* people.

A local community had engaged in a process of establishing a recreation park in their neighbourhood. The project was part of a wider vision for greater community pride; a community without stigma, a community that is a source of pleasure and where people can be together. The park had been part of the community's vision for a long time and once planning and activity got underway a great many people became involved, including many young people.

The community involved many people in numerous activities but needed additional resources because of the costs involved. The local government authority was approached to provide funding and a consultant. In a short space of time and despite good intentions, the local government department almost took over the project! After all the painstaking planning to involve people in activities within and beyond the community, and given the importance and meaning of the project for developing pride and connectedness, it felt like the park project was no longer theirs. It looked as if the involvement of so many would come to a halt.

Community members, with support from workers, asserted the right to continued involvement. They underlined the importance of people's contribution prior to council involvement and their continuing contribution to the park's development and the part it played in strengthening the community. In response, the council slowed the pace of their work to fit the community's other activities and contributions. In this way the community maintained its pride and confidence, and the connections it had developed with so many people from outside the community.

All effective, empowering work with communities focuses on social development and the building of community by the community. The goal is to mobilise collaborative community action. The expertise lies with the people, and planning and decision-making are 'owned' by them in consultation, when necessary, with specialists. Additional expertise, information, knowledge and other resources are accessed and mobilised by the community to complement its vision and its strengths and resources. This is community capacity building.

Stages and processes for community building

Building community involves essential processes and stages. These are characterised by the principles of respect, social justice, self-determination and the sharing of power. Positive relationships and good listening are crucial throughout the stages and processes of community building. The first step in building community is to get to know people and consolidate existing relationships.

Getting to know people and building trusting and respectful relationships, therefore, become purposeful. They are not simply social niceties but are integral to the process of community capacity building. In this process workers become aware of people's concerns, aspirations, dreams, interests, strengths and capacities. They then consider what people have in common and invite them to come together to share their common interests, concerns, aspirations, and so on. Noticing and appreciating the aspirations that people have in common is significant to the development of a new sense of identity, new possibilities and the development of collaborative action. In community capacity building it is essential that the community vision is a shared one.

This process involves the same strengths-based stages of practice described in chapter five. These stages provide a framework for strengths-based conversations and planning. However, there are additional steps to incorporate in the process of community building. Once people do meet and share a 'picture of the future' workers may need to help establish a structure and infrastructure that can support the group and their action. As action develops workers need to help ensure that people's efforts and changes can be sustained. The stages of community building can unfold as follows (with an example to illustrate what the process can look like).

1. Building relationships and exploring individual and common concerns, interests, and aspirations.

    Workers meet residents at the local community house and join them for social activities over many weeks. They talk with residents about their children and what it's like for them living in the neighbourhood, at home and at school. Parents share their concerns about their children's future, about difficulties some children are having at school, not feeling confident about talking to the teachers, and the absence of community interaction in the neighbourhood.

2. Bringing people together, sharing stories and experiences and 'naming' the common interests.

    The workers and parents begin to meet, having discovered a number of common issues and a desire to do something. They identify safety and confidence, respectful relationships, children's learning and the community environment as being central to their concerns.

3. Establishing a common vision or 'picture of the future' and developing concrete and specific descriptions of the vision.

The group develops a picture of what they want things to be like instead of the way they are now.

- *Parents know that the school is teaching children about how to keep themselves safe. Parents are helping to design the program and reinforce it at home.*

- *Parents support each other in the job of parenting and offer each other help. They talk to each other about issues that concern their children.*

- *Children and adults do things for each other. Children comfort each other when a child is feeling sad or hurt. Neighbours look out for each other's welfare and help when able, if asked. People offer to help each other.*

- *People who live outside the area visit and join in activities there. The parks and open spaces are used to hold events for the whole Bendigo population. The community is organising events such as concerts.*

- *The park contains an open space with shelters nearby where the community has barbecues and parties together. There are play stations for children. There are seats for parents so they can watch their children play while they talk to each other. Even the teenagers are interested in the area because it has facilities for things they do.*

- *There is a Long Gully sports club. Adults and children are in a variety of teams in different sports. Other people help out with organising, training, coaching and umpiring. A fundraising group helps to cover the costs of uniforms and fees.*

Beilharz 1998

4. Exploring strengths and exceptions in the past and the present.

The group shares its experience of the good things in the neighbourhood and stories of people helping each other. They identify times when the school and teachers are helpful and respectful and share examples of what parents do that makes a difference to their children's learning. They describe some of the activities that the community house has organised in the community that went well and what was done to achieve this. They identify the local pub, the community house and a local business as resources the community can use to achieve its vision. They know many people with skills who can help.

5. Establishing a structure to support the process.

   The group decides to keep meeting. They talk with other community members about their ideas and learn that there is a lot of interest. Committees are formed to organise community events and a group of teachers and parents meet where their vision and ideas are shared and a decision is made to meet regularly.

6. Identifying and exploring additional resources that can help. Developing plans and strategies based on people's vision, strengths and resources (adding resources in ways that complement people's strengths, resources and vision).

   Other plans are made: organising a concert and other activities in the local park, discussions and consultations in the community and with local government, more meetings between the community and schools. They identify the things that they need, but don't have as a community.

7. Mobilising strengths and resources to begin living the vision.

   Plans are put into action: a highly successful concert is organised, teachers start visiting in the community with parents and children after school, the foundations are laid for the establishment of a sport and recreation club, organisations from outside the community become involved.

8. Developing networks, sustainability and infrastructure.

   All activity is reviewed and evaluated. Contacts and networks are strengthened, infrastructure developed and new activities started to meet the growing involvement and interest of people. Change and learning are reflected on in light of the community's vision. Strengths are affirmed and new ones identified.

Each of these stages and processes is characterised by community ownership. It is a community-focussed approach as opposed to an individual-, family- or group-focussed approach.

A community-focused approach facilitates community members to drive the processes of action and change and assists people to recognise and mobilise their strengths and resources toward their vision. A community-focused approach advocates with the community rather than for it and treats community members as the experts. It provides opportunities for people to make decisions about their lives. This includes the right to participate according to their level of interest and the right to 'come and go'. It includes the right to determine the rules of participation, the use of the community vision as a framework for planning, action and evaluation, and to decide the indicators of success.

Developing a community vision and goal-setting

To reiterate the discussion of future picture development in chapter five, in a strengths approach to goal-setting people are invited and assisted to consider a vision of what they want for their lives. The vision or picture of the future consists of a description or set of stories and ideas about what they prefer for their community. It involves a shared vision; it describes common preferences and ideas that have been developed by a group of people. This vision includes both the aspirations (what people value and see as the desired qualities of their community), and specific or concrete descriptions that capture the goals of community action.

The following example outlines the vision of a group of people who came together to discuss what they wanted for their community. It describes the sort of community they wanted and at the same time is an expression of what they value:

- *People feel safe and supported.*

- *People are learning together and doing things together.*

- *There are respectful relationships.*

- *There is a sense of belonging and celebration, pride, confidence and trust.*

- *There is a sense of wellbeing.*

- *People know their rights and have resources to make choices.*

- *People have confidence to ask for help and can get it when they need it.*

- *People are participating, working together, encouraging and supporting each other and acknowledging other people's strengths.*

- *People are offering something to the wider community and the wider community is offering what people need.*

As discussed in chapter five, specific and concrete description is important. When people's aspirations are described in concrete ways they are more likely to achieve them. For example, in the vision outlined above, one of the statements is, 'There are respectful relationships'. In concrete and specific terms this means such things as, 'My child is playing on the road and neighbours don't ignore him; they remind him it's unsafe or even come and tell me so I can do something about it' or 'I am offering to watch someone's kids at the playground while they take a break' or 'The police let you know straight away if your teenager's in trouble and let you know what you can do.' All good community building practice involves clearly articulated goals that are meaningful to, and owned by, the community.

Consultation as a process for community building

Initiating and developing community building involves a process of consultation. When we have concerns about issues in a community we start with a general idea about what needs to change and why, but we don't assume to know whether we are right, what can be done or how. The example included with each step illustrates how these steps can unfold:

1. The aims and purposes of the consultative process and its stages (including your ideas or vision) are articulated and key questions are identified.

Some workers wanted to open up the possibility of establishing collaboration between a disadvantaged community and human service organisations. The purpose was to find ways to support and promote community-strengthening activity. The aims were to:

- *learn about their experiences of intervention by human services*

- *identify ways human service organisations could contribute to the building of their community*

- *identify ways in which the human service organisations most significant to them could contribute support and help make the community safe.*

The services nominated by the community as significant to them were also consulted about their experiences and views. The key questions identified were:

- *How do human services contribute to support and safety in the community?*

- *How do human services contribute to the development of community?*

- *What can they do differently?*

Starting with a broad idea is more likely to allow for change in the purposes of the consultation if it is not as relevant as first thought. Using open questions invites people to reflect on their experience and is less likely to influence their ideas.

2. The worker meets people and outlines the purposes of the consultation, consulting them about their concerns, aspirations and interests, strengths and resources.

Workers met with individuals and discussed the proposed consultation. The key questions were the focus of many of these discussions right from the start and there was a passion among community members about the issues, which led them to share their experience and opinions. Arrangements were agreed on for the first 'formal' consultation. Established relationships with the services nominated, and an interest in the issues, enabled engagement in sharing their experience and ideas.

A series of consultations using the key questions followed over a period of a year.
The focus was on identification of the issues and concerns, the strengths and resources,
and goals of the community and the services involved.

Focussing on what people already do well and honouring their aspirations is respectful. It makes the hard issues less threatening and enables people to keep a strengths perspective on what they could do better.

3. Key issues and interests, and the strengths, resources and aspirations of community members are summarised. This information is shared with those who have been consulted.

As the consultative process proceeded, common themes emerged within the community
and within the individual services. After each consultation this information was
recorded, circulated and checked for accuracy. Common themes and ideas for improving
service delivery were identified and a proposal accepted to bring together community
members and workers from the various services involved.

Consistently looking for common themes helps link the many issues, strengths, and aspirations, and develop a bigger picture of what's happening. It helps connect people to a common vision. Recording and making the record available strengthens the sense of ownership and makes workers accountable to participants in the consultation.

4. People are invited to come together to discuss the information as a group. If there is enough interest in meeting again, attention is given to establishing agreements, goals and purposes, and deciding on an infrastructure to support ongoing action.

Meetings between the community and workers from individual services were arranged
to share learning. Ways of improving services and their contribution to community
building were discussed and recommendations were made. Later, at a meeting of all
the services and the community, the conclusions of the consultations were reviewed.
A decision was made to pursue the recommendations. These included commitments
by services to address the service delivery issues raised by the community, undertake
action to enable participation in community-building activity, and form a focus group to
assist coordination and follow-up.

Bringing people together and sharing ideas and learning helps develop understanding, build the vision, and build connectedness and cooperation.

The following outline provides more detail of the steps involved in a community consultation:

1. Describe the general purpose of the project you want to undertake, based on a general vision for your project.

2. Describe desired outcomes (the picture of the future).

3. Make contacts, arrange to meet people and discuss your ideas.

4. Consult with the people you meet about their experiences and about the project or activity you have in mind.

5. Invite interested people to participate in revising and expanding the project's purposes according to the outcome of consultations with individuals. This will include people's vision, strengths and resources.

6. Plan the first group meeting based on your consultations with individuals. Formalise invitations and follow up with each individual.

7. Bring people together and establish some group rules and purposes.

8. Keep a record of each meeting.

9. Review each meeting and plan the next.

10. Follow up individual needs or issues as relevant from each meeting.

11. Circulate the record of the meeting.

12. Start each meeting with a summary of the previous session.

Skills for strengths-based community building

The skills used in community building are the same as those for working with individuals and families. The difference is that in the community building context workers are involved with many individuals and groups at once.

Skills that encourage and sustain participation are crucial for community building, as are skills of group and meeting facilitation. Workers also often need to be the people who help keep the focus on the vision. They need to be patient and able to adapt as people come and go, and support and encourage people when things are not going so well.

In the initial stages of community capacity building the worker will usually be the person who facilitates meetings and groups. This is an important role and an opportunity to model respectful listening, facilitation and strengths-based principles generally. As time goes by and community action develops community members will more commonly take a role in facilitating meetings. The worker's role is to enable the building of these skills.

Good group facilitation:

- keeps sufficient focus on the task at hand and the purposes of the meeting
- is flexible and responsive to people's participation
- keeps the group's vision and the wider community's vision in mind
- is consultative and collaborative
- validates and appreciates people's input, experience, views and feelings.

Group or project rules are essential because they provide points of reference for respectful interaction and communication (these are the same as those discussed for group supervision in chapter ten). They are not likely to work though if the group does not agree on them. The purposes of the group provide points of reference for group rules, but the underlying principles for the formation of group rules are:

- Everyone has the right to be heard.
- Everyone has the right to contribute.
- Everyone deserves to be treated with respect.

There are other useful reminders that are relevant in considering rules and codes of behaviour. Of course, these are just as relevant for workers as they are for communities:

- All people are important.
- There are more similarities between people than there are differences.
- People have strengths and resources, both known and unknown to them.
- People need resources to reach their potential.
- We can all get trapped by thinking and behaviour that prevents change.
- We can all do things that aren't good for us.
- We can all have difficulties changing habits.
- Our picture of ourselves influences what we do.
- Our beliefs influence what we do.
- Blaming makes things worse.
- Each individual is unique.
- Respect is contagious.

(McCashen 1996)

In any meeting or interaction it's important that people's experience and ideas are validated and acknowledged. It's not uncommon for people to come along to a meeting or activity with a need to off-load negative experiences or feelings, or for disagreements—even serious ones—to arise. It's important, as in all practice, to use strengths-based listening and to ensure that any sharing about negative feelings or experiences is acknowledged and validated before attempting to reframe it or move on.

The principle of transparency is essential in community meetings and action. In any meeting or interaction the purposes and processes should be clear and open. There should be no hidden agendas and any recording should be shared openly. Records should only be used with the informed consent of participants. This helps build and sustain trust.

Community building can start with any concern or interest, in any context or in relation to any issue encountered through the delivery of human services. Structural constraints, including the political and economic constraints that marginalise or oppress people, can only be addressed effectively in the long term through collective action.

It is therefore essential that human service workers and organisations join geographic communities and communities of interest to share their knowledge, strengths, resources and skills. But it is essential that this be done in ways that involve power-with and self-determination.

When structures and processes for community building are built on people's concerns, interests, strengths, resources, aspirations and goals; when communities drive the processes of change; when uniqueness, commonality and diversity is respected; when resources are mobilised to complement those of the community; when power is shared; a microcosm of a just, respectful society is in the making.

The strengths approach encapsulates the values, the skills, the knowledge, the frameworks, processes, vision and ethics that can always build connectedness, interdependence and autonomy. These are all transferable from one context to another, and can be tailored to different people in different places in response to different concerns or aspirations. They are always just and respectful. The strengths approach gives ways to build community that complement, coincide with and even enhance community capacity building and community development frameworks.

It is important, indeed critical, that we get beyond the confines of the service delivery structures imposed on us to engage whole communities to address people's concerns and aspirations.

 EXERCISE – *Planning for community building*

1. Explore and identify the issues.

What are the current issues of concern about your community? How do members of your community feel and what do they think? Which are the most important? What are the challenges? What are you doing now that you don't want to be doing? What is happening now that you don't want to be happening? What is happening that you want to be happening differently? Specify these issues and challenges in concrete and specific terms.

2. Develop a picture of the future.

What will be happening in your community when these issues and challenges are resolved? What will others be doing? What will things look like? What qualities will be present in community relationships? What will you be doing that will be contributing? Describe this as concretely as possible.

3. Explore the strengths and exceptions.

What are the strengths of your community? Who are your community's appreciative audiences and what do they have to say about it? What already works well in your community? What are the exceptions to the problems? What do other people say about you that you do well? What do you think you do well? What have you already done that demonstrates your ability to reach your picture of the future? What works well? What are some examples?

4. Explore other resources.

What other resources are available that could help reach your picture of the future? Who are the other people who are concerned? Who else could help? What organisations might be able to help? What other resources might be available beyond your community?

5. Plans and steps.

Given your community's strengths, resources and your picture of the future, what steps will you now take? What will you do first? What will you do next? Who will you talk to? When will you do it? How will you know when you have achieved your goals?

CLOSING REMARKS

At the close to this book, it is worth reflecting on the core principles of the strengths approach; the glue that holds it together.

The strengths approach is founded on just practice and an emphasis on people's strengths and potential. Its values and ethics give strong expression to the values of social work through its emphasis on self-determination and empowerment, collaboration, inclusion and social justice.

People's strengths and the stories behind those strengths, as well as their aspirations and resources, are the building blocks for change and the ingredients for hope.

Seeing the problem as the problem, not the person as the problem, not only avoids paternalistic, judgemental, labelling, deficit-based ways of working, but can also profoundly enhance people's power to change their circumstances and their lives.

Treating people as their own experts is deeply respectful. It also helps avoid power-over practices.

Power-over ways of working with people, whether deliberate or inadvertent, prevent empowerment and self-determination. Power-over ways of working with people can be destructive.

Power-with ways of working with people enable empowerment and self-determination. Power-with ways of working with people can liberate people from oppressive realities.

Strengths-based, power-with ways of working with people always involve conversation, reflection, planning and action that centre on their experiences, perspectives, strengths, aspirations, values and resources. It involves finding positive stories, exceptions and unique outcomes that have within them the potential to free people from problem-saturated, self-blaming and constraining ways of seeing themselves, others and the world.

Strengths-based, power-with ways of working with people can build connectedness with others and support people's engagement in their communities.

Working in power-with, strengths-based ways rests primarily on attitudes and values.

It comes from the heart. So must management and organisational practices. Best practice is made even more possible in environments, cultures and structures that reflect and support the strengths approach.

The strengths approach:

- avoids the reinforcement of hopelessness that results from stigmatisation, stereotyping, labelling and classification

- counters oppressive and debilitating ideas and practices that keep people stuck or lead them to spiral down into worse circumstances

- leads to increased motivation and feelings of respect and worth by honouring people's rights, knowledge, skills and aspirations

- reduces power imbalances between human service workers and those they provide services to by enabling a high degree of transparency and ownership of change processes

- finds foundations for change that already exist in people's lives and environments

- generates hope by eliciting positive stories of strengths

- builds confidence and autonomy by focussing on people's expertness regarding their strengths, aspirations and knowledge about what does and doesn't work in their lives and circumstances.

As Latino-American civil rights activist, Cesar Chavez said:

From the depths of need and despair, people can work together, can organize themselves to solve their own problems and fill their own needs with dignity and strength.

The strengths approach might be called something else. If it hadn't emerged in the human services it *would* have been called something else. I'm not sure what it would have been called but it is not at all unlike practices and forms of social action that have emerged in other places and times.

The strengths approach is a positive, powerful and profound philosophy for practice that has the power to transform and build interdependence and community. For many it is not only a philosophy for practice but also a philosophy for life, because it is built on attitudes and values so deeply respectful of people's intrinsic worth, their potential and their human rights.

As a philosophy, the underlying values and beliefs of the strengths approach are not really new. But the strengths approach brings new language and new frameworks to capture timeless and universal ideas that emerge in every age about the essence of justice and the essence of people and their possibilities.

I commend the strengths approach to all and hope it can continue to inspire those who embrace it, for the sake of all of those who engage human services and people everywhere.

REFERENCES

Aotearoa New Zealand Association of Social Workers 2007, *Code of ethics*, Christchurch, New Zealand.

Australian Association of Social Workers 2010, *Code of ethics*, Canberra, Australia.

Australian Social Inclusion Board 2012, *Social inclusion in australia: how is australia faring?*, Commonwealth of Australia, Canberra, Australia.

Asquith, S, Clark, C & Waterhouse, L 2005, in Trevithick, P 2014, 'Humanising managerialism: reclaiming emotional reasoning, intuition, the relationship, and knowledge and skills in social work', *Journal of Social Work Practice*, vol. 28:3, pp. 287—311.

Beddoe, L 2010, 'Surveillance or reflection: Professional supervision in "the risk" society', *British Journal of Social Work*, 40:4, pp. 1279—96.

Beilharz, L 2002, *Building community: the shared action experience*, St Luke's Innovative Resources, Bendigo, Australia.

Beilharz, L 2000, *Community building training handouts*, St Luke's Anglicare, Bendigo, Australia.

Beilharz, L 1998, *Shared action mid-term review*, St Luke's Anglicare, Bendigo, Australia.

Berg, IK 1994, *Family based services: a solution-focused approach*, WW Norton, New York, USA.

Bonnice, J 2015a, *Social inclusion workshop notes*, St Luke's Innovative Resources, Bendigo, Australia.

Bonnice, J 2015b, 'Social inclusion: is this the key to a paradigm shift?' *SOON*, online newsletter of St Luke's Innovative Resources, Bendigo, Australia, vol. 90, p. 2.

Bradley, G & Hojer, S 2009 'Supervision reviewed: reflections on two different social work models in England and Sweden', *European Journal of Social Work*, 12:1, pp. 71—85.

British Association of Social Workers 2012, *The code of ethics for social work, statement of principles*, Birmingham, UK.

Bushe, G 1998, 'Five theories of change embedded in appreciative inquiry', in Cooperrider, L, Sorensen, F, Yeager, T & Whitney, D (eds) 2005, *Appreciative inquiry: foundations in positive organization development*, pp. 121—132, Champaign IL, Stipes Publishing LLC, USA.

Carrie, M and Russell, S 2002, 'Externalising: commonly asked questions', *International Journal of Narrative Therapy and Community Work*, no. 2, Dulwich Centre Publications, Adelaide, Australia.

Carson, A 2016, *What does great supervision mean to you?* Video interview with Andrew Shirres, St Luke's Innovative Resources, Bendigo, Australia.

Chang, J & Nyland, D 2013, 'Narrative and solution-focused therapies: a twenty-five year retrospective', *Journal of Systemic Therapies*, Vol. 32:2, pp. 72—88.

Cooper, V 1999, in Brooks, M (ed.) *Sharing the journey: psychosocial rehabilitation – working with people with a disability*, New Paradigm Press, VICSERV Victoria, Australia.

Cooperrider, D & Whitney, D 2001, *A positive revolution in change*, in Cooperrider, D, Sorensen, P, Whitney, D & Yeager, T (eds) 2001, *Appreciative inquiry: an emerging direction for organization development*, pp. 9—29, Champaign IL, Stipes Publishing LLC, USA.

Deal, R & McCashen, W 2001, *Name the frame* (card pack), St Luke's Innovative Resources, Bendigo, Australia.

Deal, R & McCashen, W 1998, *Reminders for doing respect and justice* (poster), St Luke's Innovative Resources, Bendigo, Australia.

Department of Human Services 2011, 'Child protection workforce: The case for change', Victorian Government, Melbourne, Australia.

De Shazer, S 1985, *Keys to solutions in brief therapy*, WW Norton, New York, USA.

De Shazer, S 1988, *Clues: investigating solutions in brief therapy*, WW Norton, New York, USA.

De Shazer, S 1991, *Putting difference to work*, WW Norton, New York, USA.

Egan, R 2012, 'Australian social work supervision practice in 2007', *Australian Social Work*, 65:2, pp. 171—84.

Elliott, B 2000, in Elliott B, Mulroney, L & O'Neil, D 2000, *Promoting family change: the optimism factor*, Allen and Unwin, Sydney, Australia.

Epston, D 2005, in McCashen, W 2005, *The Strengths Approach: A strengths-based resource for sharing power and creating change*, St Luke's Innovative Resources, Bendigo, Australia.

Epston, D 1994, 'Extending the conversation', *Family Therapy Networker*, vol. 18:6, pp. 30—7.

Ferguson, I 2008, *Reclaiming social work: challenging neo-liberalism and promoting social justice*, Sage Publications, London, UK.

Freedman, J & Combs, G 1996, *Narrative therapy: the social construction of preferred realities*, WW Norton, New York, USA.

Galeano, E 1992, *The book of embraces*, WW Norton, New York, USA.

Gibbs, J, Dwyer, J & Vivekananda, K 2014, *Leading practice: a resource guide for child protection leaders*, Second Edition, Child Protection, Victorian Government Department of Human Services, Melbourne, Australia.

Gibbs, J, Dwyer J & Vivekananda, K 2009, *Leading Practice: A resource guide for child protection frontline and middle managers*, Child Protection, Victorian Government Department of Human Services, Melbourne, Australia.

Government of Western Australia Department for Child Protection 2011, *The signs of safety child protection practice framework*, second edition, Perth, Western Australia.

Hart, B 1995, 'Re-authoring the stories we live by: situating the narrative approach in the presence of the family of therapists', *The Australian and New Zealand Journal of Family Therapy*, vol. 16:4, pp. 181—9.

Ife, J 2016, 'Rethinking human rights in the 21st century', *Sir John Quick Lecture* held on 27 October for La Trobe University, Bendigo, Australia.

International Federation of Social Workers 2012, *Statement of ethical principles*, Berne, Switzerland.

Kadushin, A 1976, *Supervision in social work*, Columbia University Press, New York, USA.

Kajewski, K & Madsen, V 2012, *Demystifying* 70:20:10 white paper, DeakinPrime, Deakin University, Melbourne, Australia.

Kelly, C 1997, 'A Success Story', *Family Agenda*, newsletter of St Luke's Anglicare, Bendigo, Australia, vol. 11:3.

Kowalski, K & Kral, R 1989, 'The geometry of solution: using the scaling technique', *Family Therapy Case Studies*, vol. 4:1, pp. 5—66.

Laussel, A 2001, *Strengths-based practice training material*, St Luke's Anglicare, Bendigo, Australia.

Ludema, J 2001, 'From deficit discourse to vocabularies of hope: the power of appreciation', in Cooperrider, L, Sorensen F, Yeager, T & Whitney D (eds), *Appreciative inquiry: an emerging direction for organization development*, Champaign IL, Stipes Publishing.

McCashen, W 2014, Department of children and families learning and development unit training materials, Northern Territory Government, Darwin, Australia.

McCashen, W 2013, Department of children and families draft mentoring framework, Northern Territory Government, Darwin, Australia.

McCashen, W 2005, *The strengths approach: a strengths-based resource for sharing power and creating change*, St Luke's Innovative Resources, Bendigo, Australia.

McCashen, W 2004, *Communities of hope: a strengths-based resource for building community*, St Luke's Innovative Resources, Bendigo, Australia.

McCashen, W 1999, *Shared action: a report on community consultations on the contribution of services to community life in Long Gully*, St Luke's, Bendigo, Australia.

McCashen, W 1996, *From strength to strength: a framework for competency based practice in the human services*, St Luke's Innovative Resources, Bendigo, Australia.

Madsen, WC 1999, *Collaborative therapy with multi-stressed families: from old problems to new futures*, Guilford Press, New York, USA.

Mallucio, A 1981, 'Promoting client competence and worker competence in child welfare', *The Social Work Forum*, pp. 136–153, Columbia University Press, USA.

Morgan, A 2000, *What is narrative therapy?* Dulwich Centre Publications, Adelaide, Australia.

Morrison, T 1993, *Staff supervision in social care: an action learning approach*, Longman, Essex, UK.

National Association of Social Workers 2008, *Code of ethics of the national association of social workers*, USA.

Noble, C, & Irwin, J 2009, 'Social work supervision: An exploration of the current challenges in a rapidly changing social, economic and political environment', *Journal of Social Work*, 9:3, pp. 345—358.

Obholzer, A & Roberts, VZ (eds) 1994, *The unconscious at work: individual and organisational stress in the human services*, Routledge, UK.

O'Hanlon, B 1994 'The third wave', *Networker*, November/December, pp. 19—29.

O'Neil, D, Deal, R & McCashen, W 1998, *Service folders: a worker's guide*, St Luke's Anglicare, Bendigo, Australia.

O'Neil, D & McCashen, W 1991, 'Competency-based family support: brief therapy as a tool in goal setting and family valuing in child protection work', *Family Therapy Case Studies: A Journal for Practicing Therapists*, vol. 6:2, pp. 3—12.

Parker, D 2000, *Strengths-based practice training material*, St Luke's Anglicare, Bendigo, Australia.

Pugh, D & McCashen, W 1999, in Brooks M, (ed.) 1999 *Sharing the journey: psychosocial rehabilitation – working with people with a disability*, New Paradigm Press, VICSERV, Victoria, Australia.

Rogers, C 1951, *Client-centred therapy: its current practice, theory and implications*, Houghton-Mifflin, Chicago, USA.

Rogowski, S 2012, 'Social work with children and families: challenges and possibilities in the neo-liberal world', *British Journal of Social Work*, vol. 42:5, pp. 921—40.

Saleebey, D 2010, *The strengths perspective*, Strengths Institute, University of Kansas School of Social Welfare, USA.

Scerra, N 2012, 'Models of supervision: providing effective support to aboriginal staff'. *Australian Aboriginal Studies*, 1, pp. 77—85.

Searles, H 1955, 'The informational value of the supervisor's emotional experience', *Psychiatry*, 18, pp. 135—146.

Shirres A, 2016a, 'People not cases: who are the people we work with?—a practice paper', St Luke's Innovative Resources, Bendigo, Australia.

Shirres A, 2016b, 'Rethinking strengths-based peer supervision in human services: practice issue or practice story?—a practice paper', St Luke's Innovative Resources, Bendigo, Australia.

Smith, E 2006, 'The strengths-based counseling model', *The Counselling Psychologist*, vol. 34:1, pp. 13—79.

Sumerel, M 1994, 'Parallel process in supervision', *Clearing House on Counseling and Student Services*, ERIC Digest, Greensboro, North Carolina, USA.

Trevithick, P 2014, 'Humanising managerialism: reclaiming emotional reasoning, intuition, the relationship, and knowledge and skills in social work', *Journal of Social Work Practice* vol. 28:3, 2014.

St Luke's Anglicare 2013, *Social inclusion strategy*, Bendigo, Australia.

Turnell, A 2012, *The signs of safety workbook*, Resolutions Consultancy, Perth, Australia.

Walter, W & Peller, J 1992, *Becoming solution-focused with brief therapy*, Brunner/ Mazel, New York, USA.

Watson, P 2016, *Strengths in action*, video interview with Andrew Shirres, St Luke's Innovative Resources, Bendigo, Australia.

Watzlawick, P, Weakland, J & Fisch, R 1974, *Change: principles of problem formulation and problem resolution*, WW Norton, New York, USA.

White, M 1994, *The politics of therapy: putting to rest the illusion of neutrality*, Dulwich Centre Publications, Adelaide, Australia.

Wonnacott, J 2003, *The impact of supervision on child protection practice – a study of process and outcome*, University of Sussex, unpublished Master of Philosophy thesis.

White, M & Epston, D 1990, *Narrative means to therapeutic ends*, WW Norton, New York, USA.

White, M 1995, *Re-authoring lives: interviews and essays*, Dulwich Centre Publications, Adelaide, Australia.

World Health Organisation 1986, *The ottawa charter for health promotion*, WHO, Geneva.